YOU CAN BE A BETTER COOK
THAN MAMA EVER WAS

Also by Elise Landauer Meyer

THE ART OF COOKING WITH SPIRITS

You Can Be A Better Cook Than Mama Ever Was

A Liberal Education for Those Who Would Cook Well with Ease

ELISE LANDAUER MEYER

Garden City, New York
DOUBLEDAY & COMPANY, INC.

". . . it is much better to want a teacher than to want the desire to learn."

THOMAS H. HUXLEY

"A Liberal Education: and Where to Find It."
(An Address to the South London Working Men's College—1868)

Foreword

You can be a better cook than mama ever was. In fact, you can be a better cook than Escoffier, Carême and Brillat-Savarin. I would not minimize in the least mama's talent nor Escoffier's, Carême's, and Brillat-Savarin's genius, but what they never had, you have.

Modern technology has put a jinni in your kitchen far more powerful than the jinni Aladdin's lamp could summon. Today, with practically no effort on your part, you can be the master not only of your soul, but also of your stove, frying pan, or griddle; you have refrigerating and freezing equipment to keep food in prime condition indefinitely and to permit you to prepare frozen and congealed foods that a few years ago only a great chef or caterer with the best of commercial equipment would have dared to try; you have a food mixer and a grater and grinder that do the hard labor in the kitchen while you look on; you have measuring spoons and cups that eliminate guesswork; you have thermometers that tell you just when food is ready to come off the top of the stove or out of the oven; and, you even have pans to which food won't stick.

But even more important than this equipment are the things that you can find at any corner grocery or supermarket: fresh and fragrant herbs and spices, gathered throughout the whole wide world; vegetables, fruit, meat, and poultry of such magnificent quality that the chefs of yesterday never dreamed that anything so fine could ever be grown; pungent condiments that make seasoning child's play; and flour, salt, baking powder, soda, sugar, etc., of a grade many times superior to anything that mama ever knew. Furthermore, you live in a world where transportation is so swift that you can have fresh Maine lobsters or Louisiana crayfish within a few hours after they are caught no matter where you may be, and last, but certainly not least, our world is one where food processors spend millions of dollars each year not only to improve their products, but also to find ways for you to cook exciting, succulent dishes with the greatest of ease.

You have many advantages that mama never had, but she had one advantage you don't have. She probably had someone in to do the cooking or to "help" (and oh, how much that word "help" could cover), so when she didn't feel like cooking, she didn't have to. The domestic, however, is fast disappearing from the American scene, and unless you are one of that very small minority, the exceptionally wealthy, if the day hasn't already come, it may not be too long before—if you and your family want to keep on eating—you are going to have to take on the chore of cooking.

Inasmuch as you won't have much choice about doing this chore, you might as well learn to do the job properly, with a minimum of labor, so that failures and unnecessary work won't drive you into a nervous breakdown or an early grave. You may even grow to enjoy cooking since every normal human being gets pleasure out of something in which he or she excels and for which he or she is praised—and nobody gets more praise than a good cook.

There is no valid reason why *you* can't cook superbly; old wives' tales to the contrary, there are no "secrets" insofar as fine cuisine is concerned, but you do need a few tools. Most of these tools are quite inexpensive, and actually, many can be "bought" with trading stamps. Also, it is necessary that you make up your mind that you can cook just as well as anybody living and that you can get pleasure out of doing it. On the other hand, if you have made up your mind that there is something mysterious about cooking and that these mysteries are beyond your ability to penetrate, and also, should you decide that cooking is sheer drudgery, then skip the whole thing, and buy a can opener or find a good psychiatrist who will help you get rid of a mental block.

You didn't start your education by writing a thesis for a doctorate; you began in the first grade and then went through grammar school, unless, of course, you are a genius. Unfortunately, most of us must delay the excitement of writing a thesis for a Ph.D. degree until we have a background of general knowledge, and what is true of a formal education is also true of cooking.

This book is being written because we need a few more "grammar schools" for prospective cooks, both male and female, young and old, instead of the "post graduate" courses that far too often are all that are available.

Fortunately, this grammar school course in cooking doesn't take eight years. It really takes only a very short time, for you'll be ready for graduation when you have read and absorbed the few hundred pages in this book. This is possible because there are a handful of recipes that are the basis of most other recipes, and if you learn the proper (and easiest) way of preparing these recipes, insofar as cooking is concerned, you have it made. For example, probably the finest of all butter cakes is the old and reliable *1–2–3–4 Yellow Layer Cake**. In this book you will find a recipe for this cake and a step-by-step explanation of the simplest way of successfully making it and then you will make an amazing discovery—by learning how to make this one cake, you have also learned, since only very slight changes are necessary in each case, to make delicious chocolate cakes, marble cakes, spice cakes, silver cakes, fruit cakes, cookies, upside-down cakes, pound cakes, loaf cakes, cupcakes, and so on. As for sauces, if you can make a good *White Sauce**, and you can't fail if you take the few minutes needed to study the simple procedure explained in this book, you will also be expert in the preparation of at least thirty-six other sauces.

You will discover that the recipes in this book do not follow the ordinary cookbook arrangement, but this is not primarily a collection of recipes, although I hope that you will find that those it contains are worthy of any collection. It is, instead, a "kitchen textbook" and the recipes are arranged according to the method of cooking, which will, I trust, make learning to cook easy for you; therefore, if a chop, a fish, a steak, an egg, a tomato, or a piece of chicken can all be cooked in just about the same way, these recipes are grouped together. That's why you'll find *Angel Food** cakes in the Meringue chapter, since, in reality, they are meringues with flour added.

It will be noted that in certain cases I have mentioned specific products (trade names) because I personally have used them. However, there may be other similar products which will prove equally successful.

I hope that through this book you will learn to prepare successfully the handful of *"key"* recipes, for if you do, it follows as the night the day that you cannot fail on their hundreds and hundreds of variations, many of which are included in this volume.

                                        ELISE LANDAUER MEYER

Contents

YOU CAN BE A BETTER COOK
THAN MAMA EVER WAS

1

The Tools You Need

What could Rembrandt van Rijn have done without a brush and what can you do without the proper tools in a kitchen?

The right equipment not only makes it possible for you to do a good job, it also enables you to do the job faster and with a minimum of work. It must be wonderful to be able to buy all the labor-saving appliances and devices that are available for a kitchen, but, since I must count pennies, I get along very well— and so can you—without a great many of the very fine tools that are on the market today. If you can afford them, by all means buy them, but if you can't, don't give them another thought. You can still be an outstanding cook!

I. The Stove: You must, of course, have a good stove, and it would be well to remember that the word "good" is not necessarily synonymous with "expensive." It is, however, quite important that the oven of your stove be equipped with a dependable thermostat control, since it is, in part, your ability to control temperature when baking or roasting that makes it possible for you to be a better cook than mama ever was. If for some reason or other you don't have a thermostat for your oven, there is a thermostatically controlled roaster-oven, which is sold for about fifty dollars, and with this appliance—and I write from experience since I used a roaster-oven for many years while I lived in an efficiency apartment that was equipped with a small stove whose oven had no control—you can bake excellent cakes, pies, and biscuits as well as roast poultry or meat. This appliance doesn't take up much room, but if you have to utilize every inch of space, when the roaster-oven is not being used for cooking, it can be lined with aluminum foil or heavy brown paper and used for storing clothes, linens, or pots and pans.

II. The Refrigerator-Freezer: The second "must" for every kitchen is a refrigerator-freezer for proper food storage. The freezer is quite important for the person who lives alone or who has a very small family, since he or she can cook a roast or even a fairly large turkey and can then slice the meat that was not used, wrap quantities just big enough for 1 meal in aluminum foil or freezer paper or put the meat in freezer bags and store in the freezer section until desired. This eliminates having to eat the same thing day after day (so it can all be used before it spoils) until everyone concerned begins to feel slightly ill at the sight of the meat or fowl. The refrigerator-freezer also enables us to prepare congealed and frozen foods properly. Refrigerator-freezers come in many sizes so that they can be fitted into a cubbyhole apartment or a mansion and there is a wide range of prices.

III. Table or Counter: There must be a table or counter on which to work, and this table or counter must, of course, be big enough and strong enough to hold table appliances and also there must be space on which to work with a little elbowroom to spare.

IV. Table Appliances: There are 2 table appliances that I highly recommend and would not like to do without. They are the food mixer (preferably on a stand) and the electric frying pan. With these 2 tools you can create magnificent dishes with little effort on your part. Insofar as the frying pan is concerned, it can do the job while you do something else in another part of the house and it will only be necessary for you to drop into the kitchen occasionally to turn the food or cut down the temperature, should you be preparing something that is first browned and then cooked at a lower heat. Also, if you don't have a chafing dish, the electric frying pan can be used, in many instances, as a substitute, and food can actually be prepared on the table where it is to be served. Should you wish to go gourmet for some special occasion, you can do a wonderful flambé in this appliance. As for the mixer, it can do the really tiring jobs while you watch.

V. Pots, Pans, Bowls, Tools, Cutlery, Etc: There are a number of pots, pans, bowls, tools, cutlery, and miscellaneous items that you will need if you are to do a good job of cooking with a minimum of effort. If you've never taken the time to browse at the kitchen counters of Woolworth's or your department store, you have something to live for. It can be as fascinating for an even slightly adventurous adult as a circus is for a six-year-old boy. Here are some of the things you will find and which every well-equipped kitchen should have:

1 roaster with lid (porcelain preferred, as it browns better; stainless steel is second choice)

1 double boiler (rounded bottom inset pan is a necessity if you are going to do any of the hollandaise sauces)

1 coffeepot

1 teakettle

1 12-quart aluminum pot with lid (for soup, principally)

1 1-quart saucepan with lid (Teflon preferred)

1 1-pint saucepan (for heating or cooking the very small quantities which all of us occasionally use)

1 3-quart saucepan with lid (Teflon preferred)

1 iron frying pan

1 deep iron frying pan with lid

1 egg poacher pan

2 9-inch round aluminum or Teflon layer cake pans[1]

1 8-inch round aluminum or Teflon layer cake pan[1]

1 8×8×2-inch square aluminum or Teflon pan

2 9×5×3-inch loaf pans[1]

1 13×9×2-inch oblong pan[1]

1 10-inch tube pan with metal legs (this should be reserved for *Angel Food** cakes and never greased)[1]

1 10-inch tube pan that can be greased and used for things other than *Angel Food**

[1] If you are not going to bake cakes, skip these items, but you will miss out on one of the most satisfying and gratifying experiences one can have in the kitchen.

2 10½×15½-inch cooky trays with ½- to ¾-inch rim—Teflon preferred (these can also double for jelly roll pans)

1 9×1½-inch aluminum pie pan

1 9-inch Pyrex pie pan

2 muffin pans—Teflon preferred—large size cups

or

4 muffin pans ("tea size")—small cups

1 1-quart casserole or baking-serving dish

1 2-quart casserole or baking-serving dish (larger, if desired)

8 6-ounce Pyrex baking cups (baking-serving cups may be substituted)

1 ring mold—8 inches suggested, but on this item you will be the best judge of your own requirements

1 2-quart mold (or larger if that fits your requirements better) for congealed desserts or salads

1 large mixing bowl (bowl from food mixer may be used)

1 small mixing bowl (bowl from food mixer may be used)

4 1-pint plastic refrigerator or freezer cartons with lids

4 1½-pint plastic refrigerator or freezer cartons with lids

2 ½-gallon plastic refrigerator or freezer cartons with lids

2 1-gallon plastic refrigerator or freezer cartons with lids

1 rolling pin with stockinette cover

1 pastry cloth

1 pastry blender

2 wire cake testers

1 wooden spoon

1 plastic spoon (if you have Teflon pots)

1 plastic fork (if you have Teflon pots)

1 plastic spatula (if you have Teflon pots)

1 plastic knife (if you have Teflon pots)

1 kitchen spoon with long handle

1 slotted metal spoon

1 2-prong kitchen fork

1 rubber spatula

1 metal spatula

1 pancake turner

1 small paring knife
1 large sharp knife
1 grater-grinder (hand crank or electric)
1 hand grater (for fruit rinds, etc.)
1 vegetable parer
1 mincer
1 cooky or biscuit cutter
1 set of graduated metal or plastic standard (16 tablespoons to the cup) measuring cups for dry ingredients—if there is any question in your mind as to whether or not the measure is standard, ask the person who sells it to you
1 glass standard 1-cup measuring cup for liquids
1 glass standard 2-cup measuring cup for liquids
1 set (¼, ½, and 1 teaspoon, 1 tablespoon) standard measuring spoons
1 sifter (should hold a minimum of 6 cups)
1 rotary egg beater
1 wire whip
1 potato masher
1 breadboard or cutting board
1 colander
1 large strainer
1 small strainer
1 funnel
1 candy thermometer
1 meat thermometer
1 basting syringe
2 cake racks[1]
1 meat rack
1 knife sharpener
1 bottle opener
1 can opener (electric or manual, but get a good one)
2 thin brushes
2 pot holders
1 asbestos mat
1 pair padded kitchen mittens or gloves

2

Ladies' Choice—Then Handle with Loving Care

In this day of scientific wonders, none can doubt, old saw to the contrary, that the day will come when we shall have silk purses made out of sows' ears, but we shall probably never be able to make good apple pies out of bad apples. It therefore behooves us, when we do our food shopping, to pick the "good apples." It may take a few more minutes at the store to pick and choose, but since these few minutes will result in better food on your table and help to eliminate waste, this is well worth while.

And then: during that period, be it minutes, hours, or days, between the time that food is delivered to your home and the time it goes into a pot or onto a plate (if it's something you don't have to cook), in the best interests of your continued good health, your pocketbook, and your taste buds, it should be properly handled and stored. Don't, however, let the advice, "handle with loving care," frighten you. The right way of doing something usually takes no more time or effort than the wrong way. I'm lazy, so I found out at a relatively tender age that I could eliminate the (to me, serious) risk of having to do work a second or third time, and additionally, I didn't have to spend energy and time explaining and/or placating, if I just did things right in the first place.

If you have the slightest ambition to be a "good" cook, there are a few facts you should know about the storing and preliminary handling of the more common food items.

BERRIES, OTHER FRUITS, MELONS, AND VEGETABLES

BERRIES

Buying

Blackberries, Boysenberries, Dewberries, Loganberries, Raspberries, Youngberries: SEEK those that are large, bright, clean, and have a uniform rich hue. AVOID those that are soft, dirty, crushed, and wet, with stems and adhering caps (a sign of immature fruit), even the slightest sign of mold, or having green (in some cases red) drupelets. Always check the bottom and sides of a berry container as a stained carton may indicate berries of poor quality.

Blueberries: SEEK those that are well rounded out, clean, and have a good purplish-blue color (ripe berries may be covered with a natural wax overlying the true darker color). AVOID those that are sticky, soft, lackluster, watery, or even slightly shriveled.

Cranberries: SEEK those that are fresh, firm, large, and bright. AVOID those that are discolored, shriveled, soft, or show any evidence of sticky juice.

Strawberries: SEEK those that are bright red, fresh, and clean, with caps and stems, since strawberries without caps are subject to rapid decay and to mold. AVOID those that are soft, misshapen, dirty, wet, or show any sign of mold. Examine the sides and bottoms of the containers, as stained cartons indicate berries of poor quality. Also, if possible, tip the container until you can see some of the berries near the middle of the box, as far too often the decayed berries are hidden.

Handling

Berries are highly perishable. Don't keep them more than 1 or 2 days after buying. Store them in a shallow dish in the refrigerator without washing, and, in the case of strawberries, without hulling. Approximately 30 minutes before they are to be used, wash and sort (this is the time to hull the strawberries) the quantity needed in ice water. The sorting (and hulling) should be done in cold water because the heat of the hands softens berries. Drain on a rack or in a colander and then pat as dry as possible with paper or other soft towels. If desired, slice, halve, or quarter the fruit after it has been dried. Return to refrigerator, preferably in the large bowl or individual dishes in which the berries are to be served, and store until ready to use.

FRUIT, OTHER THAN BERRIES

Buying

Apples: *For eating as is:* Delicious; Golden Delicious; Jonathan; McIntosh; Stayman; Winesap. *For baking:* Northern Spy; Rhode Island Greening; Rome Beauty; Winesap. *For other cooking, including pies and tarts:* Gravenstein; Lodi; Newtown (Albemarle Pippin); Yellow Transparent.

Regardless of the intended use, SEEK apples that are firm, free of dirt, and richly colored for their particular type. AVOID those that are shriveled, dull in appearance, and those that have soft, brown spots, cuts, insect damage, or yield to a light pressure.

Handling

Store ripe, mellow apples in the refrigerator. Don't cover them, and use within a week. Hard apples and those that are not yet ripe should be kept in a room with a temperature of between 60° F. and 70° F.

Buying

Apricots: Seek reasonably firm fruit with a rich, uniform gold color. Avoid soft, hard, lackluster, greenish-yellow, and/or slightly shriveled fruit.

Avocados: Seek fruit that is weighty in proportion to size and just beginning to soften. The edible portion should have a buttery texture, so if avocado is ripe, a toothpick should slide into the stem end with ease. Avoid discolored and very soft fruit. Watch for dark, soft spots, bruises, cuts, or broken surfaces. A light brown "scab" on the skin has no effect on quality.

Figs: Seek slightly soft figs with a syruplike juice in the tiny opening in the bulbous end. Avoid fruit with bruises, broken skins, the least trace of mold, and/or an even slightly sour odor.

Grapes: Seek lustrous, firm, clean berries, which remain attached to bunch when it is lightly shaken. Some green grapes are best when they are turning amber. Avoid shriveled, soft, lackluster, or wet grapes. Watch out for any sign of mold.

Nectarines: Seek firm, richly colored, well-filled-out fruit, with a slight softness along the small ridge that appears on one side of the fruit. Avoid lackluster, shriveled, soft, or hard fruit with skin cracks or any sign of mold.

Peaches: Seek fairly firm, well-filled-out fruit with a creamy or yellowish hue and a pink to rosy-red "blush." Avoid shriveled, badly discolored fruit. Watch for dark brown spots, cuts, bruises, or mold.

Pears: Seek reasonably firm, well-filled-out fruit. Avoid pears that are lackluster, have an even slightly unpleasant odor, bruises, or light-colored areas on sides.

Plums: Seek just slightly soft, well-filled-out fruit. Avoid very soft or hard, shriveled plums. Watch for signs of moisture or mold, brown or brownish-red on the sides of the fruit and growth cracks that are not well healed.

Handling

Ripe apricots, avocados, figs, grapes, nectarines, peaches, pears, and plums should be kept in the refrigerator. They need not be covered and with the exception of figs, which should not be kept over a day or two, the fruit can be stored for 4 or 5 days. If the fruit is not ripe, it should be kept out of the sun but at room temperature until ripe. Darkening of these fruits after they are peeled and/or sliced can be prevented by dipping them into citrus or pineapple juice or by covering them with gelatin, either before or after it is congealed.

Buying

Bananas: For eating as is, SEEK fruit whose skin is deep yellow with brown flecks. For cooking and pies, SEEK firm fruit with slightly greenish ends. AVOID bananas that are lackluster or have broken or discolored skins.

Handling

Bananas should not be stored in a refrigerator unless they are fully ripe (yellow peel flecked with brown), and then only for a very, very short time. If bananas are all yellow or have green tips, ripen at a comfortable room temperature. The low temperature of a refrigerator prevents proper ripening. If fruit is peeled or cut before cooking or serving time, sprinkle liberally with lemon or orange juice or cover fruit with gelatin, either before or after it is congealed.

Buying

Cherries: For eating as is, SEEK firm, well-rounded-out sweet fruit (dark mahogany colored Bings or Lamberts, purplish-black Tartarians, Republicans, and Windsors, purplish-red Schmidts and light, golden Royal Anns). For cooking, including pies, SEEK tart, reasonably firm, and bright fruit (medium shade red Montmorencys and Early Richmonds or blood-red English Morelles). AVOID soft, hard, bruised, and/or cut fruit.

Handling

Store cherries uncovered in refrigerator. Don't keep more than 2 or 3 days and don't wash or remove stems until ready to use.

CITRUS FRUIT

Buying

Grapefruit: SEEK firm, well-rounded, smooth-skinned fruit that is weighty in proportion to size and "springy" when lightly touched. A reddish-brown or reddish-yellow overcast on skin will probably not affect flavor. AVOID soft, light-in-weight-for-size fruit. Also watch out for any sign of mold.

Lemons: SEEK those whose skins have a fairly smooth texture and that are firm and weighty for size. If acid fruit is desired, select light yellow or greenish-yellow fruit, but if juicy, though less acid, fruit is wanted, select deep yellow colored fruit. AVOID soft, shriveled fruit, and watch out for soft spots at stem ends.

Limes: SEEK firm, lustrous, soft-green colored fruit. AVOID shriveled or soft limes.

Mandarin Oranges and Tangerines: SEEK those that are a rich golden-orange color and are weighty for size. AVOID those with soft spots at the stem ends or those that are dull-appearing or show any trace of mold.

Oranges: SEEK those that are firm, weighty for size, and of a rich bright hue. AVOID those that are shriveled or puffy, and/or light for their size. Watch for any mold.

Handling

Store citrus fruit at 60° F. to 70° F.; however, if chilled fruit is desired for serving, citrus fruit may be kept in refrigerator for a short time, either whole, or peeled and sliced or in sections. Don't store citrus fruit over a week.

Buying

Pineapple: SEEK those that are clean, weighty for their size, with dry bottoms, firm surface squares, and a pleasant fresh scent. Test ripeness by pulling leaf from tufted crown—the more white showing at the bottom of the leaf, the riper the pineapple. AVOID lackluster, bruised fruit and watch for light colored areas on sides and an unpleasant odor.

Handling

Store in room with temperature of 60° F. to 70° F. If you want to serve the fruit chilled, place in refrigerator, either whole or peeled and sliced, 8 to 10 hours before using. Pineapple should be used within a week of the time it is bought.

MELONS

Buying

Cantaloupes: SEEK those that are a creamy yellow with a coarse, yellow or ash gray "network of veins," a distinctive cantaloupe odor, and a slight softening at blossom end. Stem end should have a smooth, hollow, dime-sized cavity. AVOID those with widely separated or flat "veins," severe bruises, shriveling, soft sunken spots, or any sign of green showing along the "veins." Don't buy melons if stem ends are flat and hollows are rough.

Casaba: SEEK those with yellow rinds that have a slight softening at the blossom ends. AVOID those that have dark sunken areas and even the slightest trace of mold.

Crenshaw: SEEK those that are mainly rich golden-yellow in hue with the remaining areas a greenish-yellow that yield very slightly when lightly pressed at the blossom end, and also have a pleasing odor. AVOID those that have water-soaked or slightly sunken areas.

Honey Ball: SEEK those with very pale yellow rind and a distinctive, pleasing odor. The cavity in the stem end should be smooth and hollow. AVOID those with bruises, growth cracks, any hint of mold, and sunken dark spots.

Honey Dew: SEEK those that are creamy white or creamy yellow and have a pleasant sweetish odor. AVOID those with bruises, sunken spots, and with pink or black dots.

Mushmelon: Judge by same standards as *Cantaloupes.**

Persian: SEEK those that are firm, but not hard, with a somewhat dull gray-green or bronze-green rind and with a slight softness at the blossom ends. AVOID glassy green melons and those with soft, sunken spots or any sign of mold or moisture at ends.

Watermelons: It is advisable to buy cut melons. SEEK those whose flesh is firm and a bright red shade, with dark brown or black seeds. AVOID those with white streaks, dry mealy or stringy watery flesh. Also avoid melons whose flesh has a pale hue or those with white seeds.

Handling

Store uncut melons in a room with a temperature of between 60° F. and 70° F. Do not keep more than 4 or 5 days. Place in refrigerator 8 to 10 hours before serving to chill. If space is a problem, trim the rind from the edible part of the melon and then cut the pulp into small squares or balls. Place in a plastic refrigerator carton, which should then be securely covered and stored in refrigerator.

VEGETABLES

Buying

Artichokes, French or Globe: SEEK those that have large fresh-appearing green leaves that cling tightly to each other. The artichoke should be weighty for its size. AVOID those whose leaves are hard at the tips and beginning to open up. Watch out for worm injury, which can usually be detected on the artichoke bottom, discoloration, or any sign of mold.

Handling

Store in vegetable drawer of refrigerator. If artichokes are to be kept longer than a day or so, it is suggested they be "simmered," placed in plastic bags, and stored on the shelves of the refrigerator.

Buying

Asparagus: SEEK those that are firm and fresh-looking and whose green portions are easily broken and pierced. The tips should be closed. AVOID those whose tips are partially opened, wilted, or spread.

Handling

Before storing, discard the tough part of the stalk. Then put stalks in plastic bags and store in vegetable drawer of refrigerator.

Buying

Beans, Butter or Lima: SEEK pods that are a clean, dark green and well filled. AVOID those with sunken areas or those that are dried, shriveled, or discolored.

Handling

Do not shell until needed. Wash, drain, and pat as dry as you can with paper or other soft towels. Store in refrigerator vegetable drawer. If the limas must be shelled in advance, place in plastic bag and store in refrigerator.

Buying

Beans, Green, Snap: SEEK those that are tender, yet firm, and both clean and fresh-looking. Tender, crisp beans snap easily when broken. Immature seeds indicate tender pods. AVOID pods that are dull, wilted, soft, or show any sign of mold. If seeds are more than half grown, pods will usually be tough. Also watch out for stringiness, which can be checked by breaking the pod in two and carefully separating the 2 parts.

Handling

Pack in plastic bags and place in refrigerator vegetable drawer.

Buying

Beets: SEEK those that are firm and fairly smooth to the touch. AVOID those that are flabby or shriveled and have soft wet areas.

Handling

Remove the tops (greens) leaving a 1-inch stem, so that beets will not "bleed"; do not peel before cooking. Store in covered container in refrigerator.

Buying

Broccoli: SEEK broccoli that is dark green, purplish-green, or a sage green and that is clean with a fresh appearance. AVOID broccoli with bud clusters that have opened and/or yellowed or whose leaves are wilted, flabby, and/or bruised.

Handling

If vegetable is dirty, which is rare in these days, it should be washed and then thoroughly dried. Place in plastic bag and store in vegetable drawer of refrigerator.

Buying

Brussels Sprouts: SEEK those that are a clean, fresh green and are firm. AVOID those that are soft and have wilted leaves. Watch out for worm damage to the leaves.

Handling

Pack in plastic bags and store in refrigerator.

Buying

Cabbage: SEEK firm, clean heads that are weighty for their size. The stems should be cut close to the head and there should only be 3 or 4 outer leaves attached. AVOID those that are soft or have yellowing leaves or any sign of worm damage. Also watch out for burst heads or those whose outer leaves have separated from the stem at the base.

Handling

If cabbage is to be stored for a few days before it is used, wrap it and place it in the vegetable drawer of the refrigerator where humidity is high. If the cabbage is to be used for salads, it may be cut or shredded as long as several days before it is to be used if it is placed in a plastic carton and covered with salt water (½ teaspoon salt for each 1 cup of water). Carton should be securely covered before being placed in refrigerator. Before using, drain cabbage and pat as dry as possible with paper or other soft towels.

Buying

Carrots: SEEK those that are fresh in appearance, well shaped, smooth, and a bright yellow or rich orange-red in color. AVOID those that are soft or shriveled and watch out for water-soaked areas or any sign of mold.

Handling

Cut off the stems and leaves and remove the root tips. Pack into plastic bags and store in refrigerator.

Buying

Cauliflower: SEEK those with firm, clean, white or creamy-white centers, surrounded by fresh green outer leaves. AVOID those that are bruised or spotted. Also watch out for "spreading," which is the separation of the flowerets.

Handling

Store in a plastic bag in refrigerator.

Buying

Celery: SEEK stalks that are crisp and clean with branches that snap easily. AVOID those with soft or small hard branches. Also check by separating the branches to examine the heart for a brown or black discoloration of the small heart branches and for insect damage.

Handling

Cover celery with plastic wrap before storing it in the vegetable drawer of the refrigerator. If celery is to be served uncooked, wash and then scrape with a small knife, or, and this is much easier, cut away strings with vegetable parer. Again wash and chill for at least 30 minutes in ice water. Pat dry and serve.

Buying

Corn: SEEK well-filled-out ears with fresh green husks and kernels that are just firm enough to offer a slight resistance when gently pressed. AVOID ears with dry husks and either very small or hard kernels.

Handling

Only store corn for a very short time. Do not dehusk until ready to use. Corn should be kept during this short period of time in the vegetable drawer of the refrigerator.

Buying

Cucumbers: SEEK those that are clean, well shaped, firm, and a deep green in color (in some varieties there may be a very pale green at the tip and on the ridged seams). AVOID those that are shriveled and dull in appearance with soft spots.

Handling

Whole cucumbers should be stored in the refrigerator hydrator. If desired, the cucumbers may be sliced very thin crosswise— a vegetable parer makes this easy to do—and then placed in a plastic refrigerator carton. Cover slices with salt water (½ teaspoon salt to 1 cup water), securely cover the carton with a lid, and store on the shelves of refrigerator. The sliced cucumbers stored in this way will keep for 4 to 5 days.

Buying

Eggplants: SEEK those that are a very dark purple, firm, and weighty for their size. AVOID those that are scarred, gashed, soft, or shriveled. Watch out for worm damage and dark brown spots.

Handling

Since eggplants are injured by temperatures below 50° F., store in a room with a temperature of about 60° F.

Buying

Garlic: SEEK those cloves with clean, unbroken outer skins. AVOID those that are soft, spongy, or shriveled.

Handling

Store at room temperature, or if you have a place in your home —not the refrigerator—that is slightly cooler, store there. Garlic should be stored where cool, dry air can circulate freely. Place in a loosely woven or open-mesh bag.

Buying

Greens—Beet, Chard, Collard, Dandelion, Kale, Mustard, Sorrel, Spinach, Turnip: SEEK those with young, tender, clean green leaves. AVOID those with coarse stems, dry or wilted leaves, and watch out for any sign of insect damage.

Handling

Wash thoroughly in cold water. Lift out of water when the grit settles to the bottom of the pan. Drain on rack. Pat as dry as possible with paper or other soft towels. Place in plastic bags and store in refrigerator.

Buying

Leeks or Green Onions or Shallots: SEEK those that are tender and crisp with green tops and 2- to 3-inch-long blanched necks. AVOID those with wilted, discolored tops and soft or tough necks.

Handling

Store in plastic bags in refrigerator.

Buying

Lettuce, Crisp Head: SEEK firm heads that are clean, weighty for their size, and have whitish or pink butts. AVOID heads with heavy outer wrappings of leaves, dark red butts, discolored areas, and wide spaces between the base and portions of the outer leaves, and an unusual swelling of one side of the top of the head.

Lettuce, Loose Leaf, and Other Salad Greens: SEEK those with clean, bright, and tender leaves. AVOID those that are discolored or show any sign of insect damage.

Handling

Store in vegetable hydrator of refrigerator or wrap in plastic and store in other section of refrigerator. An hour or so before serving, wash in lukewarm water (barely warm on the wrist). The lukewarm water will not wilt the greens and it will get them cleaner than cold water. Drain in a colander or on a wire rack and then pat dry as possible with paper or other soft towels. Return to refrigerator until ready to use.

NOTE: If you wish to *separate a head of lettuce into cups,* using a sharp, pointed knife, cut out the core and then hold the opening under cold, running water until the leaves separate as a result of the pressure. They can then be removed from the head without difficulty.

Buying

Mushrooms: SEEK those that are clean, white to creamy white. AVOID those that are pitted, discolored, or have fully opened caps. If the caps are partially opened, watch out for brown or black gills, as an indication of an overaged mushroom.

Handling

Store in hydrator of refrigerator, but don't keep more than a few days.

Buying

Okra: SEEK clean and tender 2- to 4-inch pods that are easily pierced. AVOID those that are dull in appearance, shriveled, or discolored.

Handling

Store in refrigerator hydrator, but don't keep more than 2 or 3 days.

Buying

Onions, Dry: NOTE: The larger the onion, the sweeter it is, and the less strength it has. SEEK those with dry skins that crackle loudly when handled and are hard and well shaped. AVOID those that are discolored or show moisture at the neck, as this indicates decay, even when it is not visible. Watch out for the slightest sign of mold.

Handling

See storage instructions given for *Garlic**.

NOTE: *To chop or mince an onion quickly,* peel and cut a slice from stem end. Cut thin slices, downward from stem end, being careful not to cut through the bottom ½ inch of the onion. Give onion a quarter turn and cut thin slices that crisscross those already cut, again being careful not to cut through the bottom ½ inch, so that onion remains in 1 piece. Turn onion on its side and cut thin slices crosswise.

Buying

Peas, Green: SEEK those whose pods are clean, light green in color, smooth to the touch, and well filled out. Also check by opening a pod to see if peas are tender and well developed. AVOID pods that are dark green in color or a yellowish light green or are flecked with grayish marks. Also watch out for those that are either swollen or unusually flat.

Handling

The peas, if possible, should be left in their pods until needed. Wash pods, drain, and pat as dry as you can with paper or other soft towels. Store in refrigerator vegetable drawer. If peas must be shelled in advance, store in plastic bag in refrigerator.

Buying

Peppers, Green: SEEK those that are firm, clean, and well shaped. AVOID those that are shriveled or limp. Watch out for soft or bleached spots.

Handling

Store in vegetable drawer of refrigerator.

Buying

Potatoes, Sweet: SEEK those that are firm, clean, and well shaped. AVOID those that are shriveled or discolored or have any sign of worm damage or dry or wet rot.

Handling

Store in room with a temperature of about 60° F. Sweet potatoes are injured by storage where temperature is below 50° F.

Buying

Potatoes, White: SEEK firm, smooth, clean, and well-shaped ones. For baking, look for those with firm ends and those that are oblong in shape. AVOID those that are shriveled, spongy, or have sprouts, and watch out for any sign of decay.

Handling

White potatoes should be kept in darkness where cool, dry air (between 45° F. and 50° F.) can circulate freely. If the potatoes are peeled and/or sliced before cooking time, they should be kept in salt water (rounding ½ teaspoon salt for each cup water) and stored in the refrigerator. They should not, however, be stored for more than 2 to 3 hours in the salt water. If the potatoes are to be boiled, they may be cooked in the salt water in which they have been soaked, but if they are to be cooked in some other fashion, before using, drain in colander or on a rack and then pat with paper or other soft towels until as dry as possible.

Buying

Radishes: SEEK those that are well shaped, firm, and crisp. AVOID those that are spongy and show any sign of wilt or decay.

Handling

Store in refrigerator vegetable drawer or place in plastic bag and keep in refrigerator.

Buying

Squash, Summer: White or creamy-white white bush scallop, also known as cymling and patty pan, yellow straight or crook-neck, green zucchini, and Italian marrow. SEEK those that are fresh and weighty for size, as well as tender. AVOID those with hard rinds.

Squash, Winter: Green Des Moines, acorn, and Danish, green or gold delicious, and buff butternut. SEEK those with hard rinds. AVOID those with soft spots or any sign of mold.

Handling

Store the summer squash in the hydrator of the refrigerator. Winter squash should be stored in a room with a temperature of about 60° F. Temperatures below 50° F. may injure the squash.

Buying

Tomatoes: SEEK those that are well shaped, filled out, and firm. AVOID those that are soft, puffy, discolored, and that have un-healed growth cracks, any sign of worm damage, and/or mold.

Handling

If tomatoes are only partially ripe when purchased, they should be ripened at temperatures from 60° F. to 70° F. and should be kept in the shade. If temperature goes over 85° F., the bright red color will not develop. Only ripe, firm tomatoes should be stored in the refrigerator (use the vegetable drawer).

NOTE: *To blanch tomato,* stick the prongs of a fork through the stem end. Plunge into boiling water for 20 to 25 seconds. Remove from water and with the tip of a small sharp knife, break the skin at the blossom end and peel.

If tomatoes are cut in thin slices from the stem to the blossom end instead of the usual crosswise fashion, they will not lose as much juice.

CANNED FOOD

Handling

Canned foods should be kept in a cool, dry place and after a can is opened, the unused portion of food should be stored in a covered container in the refrigerator. Canned food should not be kept for an unlimited length of time, as there is, in most cases, a loss of nutrients, although there has been some reduction in these losses due to improvements in the methods of process.

CHEESE

Handling

Cheddar, Parmesan, Swiss and Other Hard Cheese: Wrap tightly so as to keep out the air and store in the refrigerator. If this is done, these cheeses may be kept for long periods of time.

Camembert, Cottage or Fresh Cream Cheese, Pasteurized Cream or Other Soft Cheese: Tightly cover and then store in coldest section of refrigerator. Cottage and fresh cream cheese should only be kept for 2 to 3 days. The others may be kept for 10 days to 2 weeks.

FISH AND SHELLFISH

FISH

Buying

For Baking, Broiling, Planking try to get a fish with oil running through all the flesh, such as catfish, herring, mackerel, pompano, redfish, salmon, shad, sturgeon, trout, tuna, or whitefish.

For Poaching, Steaming try to get a fish with drier flesh, such as bass, cod, croaker, flounder, haddock, halibut, perch, pike, red snapper, or whiting.

For Frying, any of the fish listed above is satisfactory.

Always SEEK fish with firm flesh, clear bulging eyes, reddish-pink gills, and AVOID fish with a strong odor.

Allow for Each Serving: *Whole fish* (as it comes from water) 1 to 1¼ pounds; *dressed fish* (scales, entrails removed) ½ to ⅔ pound; *fillets, steaks, and sticks:* ⅓ to ½ pound.

Handling

To Scale: Hold fish by tail. Using blunt knife and starting from tail and working downward to the head (against way in which scales grow), scrape off scales with steady, short strokes.

To Remove Entrails: Slit fish on underside and carefully remove entrails. After this is done, carefully wipe out opening with paper towels.

To Cut Fish into Fillets: If fish has scales, first scale and then remove entrails. Place fish on breadboard or chopping block. Using a very sharp knife, cut off head and starting from where it was removed, cut down entire length of back of fish as close to backbone as possible. Carefully cut flesh from rib bones. Skin fish, beginning at tail end, and, if desired, cut into serving-size portions.

Storage: If fish is to be eaten in 1 or 2 days, wrap securely enough so that odor will not permeate everything in refrigerator, but also loosely enough for fish to benefit from circulation of the air. Fish should be stored in coldest part of refrigerator—temperature of 30° F. to 35° F. is recommended. If fish is to be kept longer, wrap in freezer paper or aluminum foil or place in plastic bags and store in freezer.

SHELLFISH

Buying

Clams, crabs, crayfish, lobster, oysters, and turtles should be purchased live. It is, however, advisable to have oysters and possibly clams shucked and turtle meat dressed at time of purchase. Shrimp are not live when bought. They should be greenish-gray in color and you should be very sure they smell fresh. If any shellfish is bought frozen, the buyer should be well acquainted with the reputation of the packer or of the market from which purchase is made.

Allow for Servings:
   ½ peck (steamed) clams for 4 people;
   1 cup crab meat or 6 full, heavy hard-shell crabs for 3 people;
   2 small soft-shell crabs or 1 large one for each person;
   1 pound crayfish for each person;
   1 or 2 (according to appetites) 1- to 1¼-pound lobster(s) per person—while larger lobsters will serve 2 to 3 people, the small ones for individual servings are preferable;
   9 to 12 oysters per person (for main course), 4 to 6 for appetizer;
   1¼ to 1½ pounds shrimp (weighed with shells) for 2 people;
   1 pound dressed turtle meat for 2 people.

Handling

To Open Clams: (If you don't get them shucked at the market.) Lay clams in pan with water enough to cover. Sprinkle with handful of cornmeal. Let stand in water several hours and then drain. Place in kettle with 1 cup of cold water and 1 teaspoon salt. Bring to a boil, reduce heat, and cover. Cook until shells open (about 8 minutes).

Preparing Hard-shell Crabs for Cooking: Let the live crabs swim in cold, clear water about 5 minutes to cleanse themselves. If desired, this may be repeated several times. Then boil in seasoned water or a water and white wine mixture. The crabs are cleaned after being boiled. This is done by raising up the apron or *tablier* (the small pointed portion of lower shell) and then lifting off the upper shell. The crab meat is contained in light shell "cases" at each end and all that lies between these 2 "cases" should be removed (with the possible exception of the yellow fat, which some people regard as a delicacy). The halves may then be separated, and if desired the crab meat picked from the shell—but be very careful not to get any of the thin shells mixed with the meat. The large claws can then be broken with a nutcracker or a potato masher and the meat picked out, but again watch that you don't get the thin shell found on the inside of the claws mixed with the meat.

Preparing Soft-shell Crabs for Cooking: Wash carefully and remove all sand, but do not scald nor blanch. Remove the spongy substances under the side points, the sand bags from under the shells, just between the eyes, and that small pointed portion of the lower shell known as the apron or *tablier*. For maximum flavor, soak crabs in milk for 3 or 4 hours in a covered dish in the refrigerator after they are cleaned. When ready to cook, drain and pat dry.

Preparing Crayfish and Shrimp: Place in cold water and let stand for 5 minutes. Drain and continue rinsing until water runs off clean. Shrimp have a thin black vein that starts at the base of the head and runs down the middle of the back. If the shrimp are boiled, the heads should be detached, the shells peeled off, and the tiny veins removed with a small, sharp, pointed knife after they are cooked; however, there are recipes that specify raw shrimp, and in these cases, the heads should be removed, the shells peeled off, and the shrimp deveined before use.

Lobsters, Cleaning: Boiled lobsters are cleaned after they are cooked. Hold hard-shell side next to the palm of the left hand. With a very sharp knife or scissors split the lobster open from head through tail and remove the sac that is back of the head, the black vein, and spongy lungs. Broiled lobsters are cleaned before they are cooked. They should be placed on their backs and then killed by cutting down through the head with a very sharp knife. After that, follow instructions given above for removing sac, black vein, and spongy lungs.

Storage of Shellfish: If possible, shellfish should be used on the day purchased. The seafood should be kept in the coldest section of the refrigerator, at a temperature of between 30° F. and 35° F., and it should be wrapped well enough so that its odor does not affect the other food in the refrigerator, but at the same time loosely enough so that it benefits from the air circulating through the refrigerator. Crab meat, soft-shell crabs, crayfish, lobster, shrimp, and turtle meat can be successfully kept in a freezer for several months. The heads of the shrimp and crayfish should be removed before freezing. Should the crayfish heads be needed for a bisque later, they should be detached from the bodies, thoroughly cleaned, and frozen separately.

FROZEN FOODS

STORAGE

Unfortunately, frozen food like canned food cannot be kept indefinitely. In fact, it is wise not to store frozen foods too long, so it is advisable to be careful that first stored frozen foods are the first used.

If you are using a *freezer chest of a conventional refrigerator,* it is important that foods like ice cream or fruits with a high sugar content be kept on the bottom of the chest. Furthermore, ice cream, fish whose flesh has a high oil content (see *Fish, Buying**), ground meat, chicken à la king, chili, soup, and leftovers should be kept only for a relatively short period of time; however, most properly packaged fruits, vegetables, beef, and lamb may be kept up to 3 months.

Where a *freezer section is completely insulated,* so that *freezer temperatures are in the zero zone,* the following outside limits for storage are suggested:

	Months
Commercial Frozen Foods	1½ to 2½
Cooked Foods	
such as chicken à la	
king, chili, soup	2 to 3
Most Leftovers	1 to 1½
Fish (see *Fish, Buying**)	
Fat	1½ to 2½
Lean	4 to 5
Fruits (Most)	10 to 12
Ice Cream[1]	1 to 1½
Meat:	
Beef	10 to 12
Lamb	10 to 12
Ground	1½ to 2
Ham, Smoked	1½ to 2
Pork	4 to 6
Sausage, Fresh Seasoned	1 to 1½
Veal	4 to 6
Poultry	4 to 6
Vegetables	10 to 12

Don't refreeze food once it has been thawed, as it loses quality and flavor when this is done.

THAWING

Thawing may be successfully accomplished either by cooking or by removing food from the freezer and letting it stand, if time permits, in the refrigerator, or at room temperature. If food is

[1] In frost free freezers, ice cream should be covered with plastic wrap or foil once it has been opened, and the wrap or foil should be pressed onto the surface of the ice cream to prevent evaporation. Since the best dipping temperature for ice cream is 5° F. to 8° F., it is suggested that if the ice cream is very hard it be removed from the freezer and placed in refrigerator 20 to 30 minutes before it is served.

thawed at room temperature, as soon as it is defrosted, it should be placed in the refrigerator or used.

MILK

STORAGE

Keep covered and away from strong light. Store in coldest part of refrigerator.

MEAT

Buying

One of the cheapest and most valuable of all government services is rendered by the United States Department of Agriculture, whose men inspect all meat products that are sold interstate. At a cost of about 15 cents per person per year, experts from the department examine our meat and the purple round stamp (made from a harmless purple vegetable juice) that reads "U.S. Insp'd & P'S'D'" is our assurance that at the time of inspection, the meat was clean, good, and wholesome. This, however, has nothing to do with quality and it is only in those cases where the packer or processor is willing to pay for such a service to his customers that federal graders check the meat and using their purple vegetable juice and a roller stamp, which leaves a ribbon-like imprint of the grade name on almost, if not all, of the retail cuts[2], mark the meat so that available to you is the most expert of judgment on the quality of meat you purchase. It is therefore wise when marketing

[2] Unfortunately pork carcasses cannot be marked in this way, since when the meat is trimmed to prepare it for retail cuts, the marks would be cut off.

to look for the shield-shaped stamp that encloses the letters USDA" and the federal grade.[8]

TENDERNESS IN RELATION TO CUT

IDENTIFYING THE CUT BY THE SHAPE OF THE BONE

The tenderest and most expensive cuts of beef, lamb, pork, and veal are from the Loin. You can identify these cuts by the "T-Bone," which really doesn't look much like any "T" I have ever seen, but more like a fancy "Y" lying on its side.

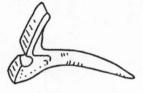

T-Bone

Next in tenderness and in price are the cuts from the Rib. The shape of the Rib Bone resembles that of a hammer.

Rib Bone

[8] See *Beef—U. S. Department of Agriculture Grades*, Lamb—U. S. Department of Agriculture Grades*, Veal and Calf—U. S. Department of Agriculture Grades.**

The cuts from the Sirloin are third in this scale of both tenderness and cost. They are identified by the Wedge Bone, but don't be confused by the name of this bone, since it is not even slightly similar to a wedge.

Wedge Bone

Next insofar as tenderness and price are concerned are the cuts from the Round. These cuts are identified by the Round Bone, and the name in this case is actually descriptive of the shape of the bone, since it looks like a ring.

Round Bone

The least tender and the least expensive of all cuts are those from the Shoulder, which are identified by the Blade Bone, whose shape is quite like that of the old-fashioned can opener with which mama had to cope.

Blade Bone

Marbling: The layman can judge the tenderness and juiciness of meat by the thin lines of fat that are interspersed in the lean, known as marbling. Meat with little or no marbling will be tough and it will not be juicy.

Beef—U. S. Department of Agriculture Grades: Beef that carries the purple shield reading "USDA Prime" is of top quality. Unfortunately, this beef, produced from young and well-fed cattle, is not often available to the average consumer since it is usually sold to restaurants. "USDA Choice" is of high quality and good flavor, but has less fat interspersed in the lean (marbling). "USDA Choice" Loin and Rib Steaks and Roasts, as well as Top and Bottom Round Roasts, are particularly tender. It is advisable that cuts such as Chuck be braised (this includes Pot Roasts). "USDA Good" is of fair quality, though it lacks the juiciness of Prime and Choice beef. It is particularly recommended for those, who because of a health problem, must have very little fat in their meat or for those who are trying to make both ends of the budget meet. "USDA Good" Sirloin, Porterhouse, T-Bone, Club, and Rib Steaks may be broiled and "USDA Good" Top Round, Sirloin Tip, and Bottom Round may be satisfactorily roasted. Other cuts of this grade of beef should be braised. There are 3 other federal grades of beef. They are "Standard," "Commercial," and "Utility." The "USDA Standard" has only a thin fat covering and is less juicy than the "Prime," "Choice," and "Good" grades. Braise beef that has been graded as "Standard." "Commercial" and "Utility" grades of beef are obtained from older cattle, and since mature beef has a rich, full flavor, very excellent soups and stews can be made from these grades if the meat is cooked for a long period at a low temperature.

BEEF—HOW TO ORDER JUST WHAT YOU WANT

ROASTS[4]

Oven Cooked (Preferably USDA grades "Prime" or "Choice," though "Good" may be used.)

CUT	RECOMMENDED THICKNESS OR WEIGHT	ALLOW FOR EACH SERVING
Rib Roast	At least 2 ribs thick	½ to ⅔ pound
Rump Equal to flavor of Rib Roast, but usually is not quite as tender.	At least 4 pounds	½ to ⅔ pound
Top and Bottom Round and Sirloin Tip While not quite as tender as the Rib or Rump, the fact that there is no bone gives these cuts some advantages.	At least 4 to 5 pounds	⅓ to ½ pound

Pot Roasts—Braised

Top and Bottom Round, Sirloin Tip	At least 4 to 5 pounds	⅓ to ½ pound
Round Bone Chuck (Shoulder Arm) While this cut is much less expensive than Top and Bottom Round and Sirloin Tip, it does not have a great deal of bone and is highly recommended for Pot Roasts.	At least 3½ to 4 pounds	⅓ to ½ pound

[4] Roasts and steaks are listed by order of tenderness and cost.

CUT	RECOMMENDED THICKNESS OR WEIGHT	ALLOW FOR EACH SERVING
Blade Chuck	At least 3½ to 4 pounds	½ to ⅔ pound
Good flavor but much more bone than Round Bone Chuck.		

Rolled Roasts—Braised

Cut from Plate or Brisket		⅓ to ½ pound
Flank Steak	2 to 2½ pounds	⅓ to ½ pound

STEAKS[4]

For Broiling (Preferably USDA grades "Prime" or "Choice," though "Good" may be used.)

CUT	RECOMMENDED THICKNESS OR WEIGHT	ALLOW FOR EACH SERVING
Porterhouse (Short Loin) If Filet Mignon is desired, the Tenderloin portion can be removed, as it is in the Porterhouse that much of the Tenderloin is found.	1 inch, 1½ inches, 2 inches	¾ to 1 pound
T-Bone (Short Loin) Does not have as much of Tenderloin as Porterhouse.	1 inch, 1½ inches, 2 inches	¾ to 1 pound
Club Steak (Short Loin) There is no Tenderloin in this cut, and it is particularly recommended for individual steaks.	1 inch, 1½ inches, 2 inches	½ to ⅔ pound
Rib Steaks (Rib Cut)	1 inch, 1½ inches, 2 inches	½ to ⅔ pound

[4] Roasts and steaks are listed by order of tenderness and cost.

CUT	RECOMMENDED THICKNESS OR WEIGHT	ALLOW FOR EACH SERVING
Sirloin (Loin End) Ask for steak with only a small amount of bone.	1 inch, 1½ inches, 2 inches	½ to ⅔ pound

For Braising (Including Swiss Steak)

CUT	RECOMMENDED THICKNESS OR WEIGHT	ALLOW FOR EACH SERVING
Round Steak and Flank The Swiss Steak is pounded before it is cooked.	¾ to 1 inch For Swiss Steak: 1½ inches	⅓ to ½ pound ⅓ to ½ pound

STEWS

CUT	RECOMMENDED THICKNESS OR WEIGHT	ALLOW FOR EACH SERVING
From Plate, Brisket, Chuck, Neck, or Round	1½- to 1¾-inch chunks	Boneless: ⅓ to ½ pound Bone-in: ½ to ⅔ pound

SOUP MEAT

CUT	RECOMMENDED THICKNESS OR WEIGHT	ALLOW FOR EACH SERVING
For rich, hardy broths, select the Brisket, Chuck, or Shank. The less expensive grades are excellent for soup. Use soup bone from Hind or Fore Shanks.	At least 4 pounds	½ pound

GROUND MEAT

CUT	RECOMMENDED THICKNESS OR WEIGHT	ALLOW FOR EACH SERVING
Use meat from Flank, Plate, Fore Shank, or Chuck. Add a small amount of fat to meat before it is ground; 2 thin slices of bacon can be added for each pound of lean beef.		¼ pound

LAMB—HOW TO ORDER JUST WHAT YOU WANT

LAMB—U. S. Department of Agriculture Grades

The grading of lamb is based on tenderness, juiciness, and the percentage of meat to bone. Since all lamb is obtained from young animals, most cuts are tender. Of course, "Prime" is the most tender, the juiciest, and has the largest ratio of meat to bone; "Choice" is second as to these qualities and "Good" is third. There are also 2 lower grades: "Utility" and "Cull."

ROASTS

Oven Cooked (Preferably USDA grades "Prime" or "Choice.")

CUT	RECOMMENDED THICKNESS OR WEIGHT	ALLOW FOR EACH SERVING
Leg	5 to 7 pounds	½ to ⅔ pound
Crown (Rib)	4¾ to 5¼ pounds	½ to ⅔ pound
Shoulder	3½ to 4¾ pounds	½ to ⅔ pound

Oven Cooked or Braised

Shoulder (Boned and Rolled)	3 to 4 pounds	⅓ to ½ pound

CHOPS

Broiling

Loin or Rib	¾ to 1 inch	½ to ⅔ pounds

The Loin Chops are more tender and have less bone than the Rib Chops, but are more expensive.

STEW

CUT	RECOMMENDED THICKNESS OR WEIGHT	ALLOW FOR EACH SERVING
Brisket, Shoulder, Neck, or Shank	1¼- to 1½-inch cubes	Boneless: ⅓ to ½ pound Bone-in: ½ to ⅔ pound

GROUND MEAT

Trimmings from Shank and Brisket		¼ to ⅓ pound

PORK—HOW TO ORDER JUST WHAT YOU WANT

Pork (Fresh) U. S. Department of Agriculture Grades Not Shown
Since pork in markets does not show the federal grades, this must
be a case of *caveat emptor* (let the purchaser beware).

ROASTS

Oven Cooked

Leg—Fresh Ham or Round	9 to 15 pounds	½ to ⅔ pound
Loin or Rib End	3½ to 10 pounds	½ to ⅔ pound
Shoulder Boston Butt—Upper Part —Less Bone Picnic—Less Expensive	5½ to 8 pounds	½ to ⅔ pound
Crown Roast Entire Rib Half		½ to ⅔ pound

BARBECUES

CUT	RECOMMENDED THICKNESS OR WEIGHT	ALLOW FOR EACH SERVING
Rib (sold in sheets)		½ to ¾ pound

STEAKS—BRAISED

From Boston Butt	½-inch thick	½ to ⅔ pound

CHOPS—BRAISED

Loin, Rib, or Shoulder	½ inch for chops that are to be breaded; ¾ to 1 inch for chops that are to be braised but not breaded	½ to ⅔ pound

STEW
(Brunswick or Chop Suey, etc.)

From Boston Butt	½- to 1½-inch chunks (depending on recipe)	½ to ¾ pound

GROUND MEAT

From Boston Butt		¼ to ⅓ pound

VEAL AND CALF[5]—HOW TO ORDER JUST WHAT YOU WANT

Veal and Calf[5]—U. S. Department of Agriculture Grades

The 3 top federal grades for veal and calf, "Prime," "Choice," and "Good" as well as the other grades, "Standard," "Utility," and "Cull" are based on the ratio of meat to bone and the amount of fat. Since this is very young meat, there will never be a great amount of fat marbling the lean, but the higher grades with more fat will be juicier and have more flavor than the lower grades.

ROASTS

Oven Cooked

CUT	RECOMMENDED THICKNESS OR WEIGHT	ALLOW FOR EACH SERVING
Rump or Round	5 to 8 pounds	½ to ¾ pound
Shoulder	4¾ to 7½ pounds	½ to ¾ pound

Oven Cooked or Braised

Shoulder—Boned and Rolled	4 to 6 pounds	⅓ to ½ pound

[5] Veal—bovine animals, 3 months or less when slaughtered, who lived principally on milk; calf—bovine animals, between 3 and 8 months old, who lived for some time completely or almost so on food other than milk.

STEAKS

Braised

CUT	RECOMMENDED THICKNESS OR WEIGHT	ALLOW FOR EACH SERVING
Round	½ to ⅔ inch	⅓ to ½ pound
Grillades (Loin End)	½ inch	⅓ to ½ pound
Swiss—Cut from Flank	1¼ inches	⅓ to ½ pound

CUTLETS

Breaded and Braised

Cut from Sirloin Tip In cutting veal, the round and Sirloin Tip are cut together	½ to ¾ inch	⅓ to ½ pound

CHOPS

Broiled or Breaded and/or Braised

Loin or Rib	For breading: ½ to ¾ inch. For broiling and braising without breading: ¾ to 1 inch	½ to ⅔ pound

STEW

CUT	RECOMMENDED THICKNESS OR WEIGHT	ALLOW FOR EACH SERVING
Cut from Round, Plate, Brisket, or Chuck	¾- to 1¼-inch chunks	Boneless: ⅓ to ½ pound Bone-in: ½ to ⅔ pound

GROUND MEAT

From Fore and Hind Shanks		¼ to ⅓ pound

LIVER

(veal, if you are very lucky; if not, calf)	½ inch slices	⅓ to ½ pound

Meat-handling

Fresh meat should be stored, if it is to be kept for a few days, in the coldest part of the refrigerator (temperature between 32° F. to 35° F.). While it should be covered with a wrapping, the wrapping should be loose enough to allow the meat the full benefit of air circulating in the refrigerator. Fresh beef can normally be stored 4 or 5 days in the refrigerator. Fresh lamb can normally be stored 3 or 4 days in the refrigerator. Fresh pork can normally be stored 2 or 3 days in the refrigerator. Fresh veal or calf can normally be stored 3 or 4 days in the refrigerator.

Cooked, sliced, fresh meats can normally be stored 3 to 4 days in the refrigerator, but they should be carefully wrapped in plastic wrap or aluminum foil, so they won't dry out. Liver, ground meat, hearts, and kidneys should be used the same day as they are purchased, unless they are stored in the freezer.

Ham, smoked, corned, salt-cured, pickled, and dried meats can normally be stored for 10 days in the refrigerator.

If meat is to be kept for longer periods than those shown above, it is advisable to store it in the freezer.

NUTS

Handling

Nuts that have not been shelled keep better than those that have been shelled. Keep nuts in airtight containers in the refrigerator. If nuts are ground to use in cookies or tortes, if possible, grind the nuts at least 24 hours before using. Should this not be possible, spread the ground nuts on a cooky sheet and place in a 325° F. oven for 5 to 10 minutes (according to how oily nuts are). Cool before using. To **BLANCH ALMONDS,** shell the nuts and then cover with boiling water. Let stand until the skins loosen—3 to 5 minutes. Quickly drain off water and add a small quantity of cold water. Slip off skins by pinching each nut between the index finger and the thumb. Place nuts on absorbent paper towels to dry. To prepare **TOASTED NUTS,** spread nuts on a cooky sheet. Place in 350° F. oven for 8 to 10 minutes. Stir nuts 2 to 3 times and watch carefully so they don't brown too much.

SALTED NUTS should be prepared shortly before they are to be used, since they become rancid quickly unless vacuum packed. To salt nuts, mix ½ pound of the shelled, and in the case of almonds, blanched, nuts with 2 tablespoons vegetable oil or melted butter or margarine. Spread out on a shallow pan. Brown in 350° F. oven, stirring from time to time. Sprinkle with salt immediately after removing nuts from oven and drain on absorbent paper.

POULTRY

Buying

If you are going to broil chicken, select young "springers," weighing 1½ to 2¼ pounds.

If you are going to fry chicken, select larger "springers," weighing 2½ to 3½ pounds.

If you are going to stew or fricassee chicken, select large, fat hens weighing 5 to 6 pounds or young "springers," weighing 2½ to 3½ pounds.

If you are going to roast (bake) chicken, select plump young chickens that weigh 4 pounds or more or select a capon that weighs at least 5 pounds.

When you buy Rock Cornish Hens, use the 16-ounce or smaller size. If over 16 ounces, the bird may not be the true tender Rock Cornish strain.

When you buy turkeys, choose the Tom over the hen, although this is contrary to popular practice. It is, however, a matter of plain common sense. Since the Tom grows faster and larger than the hen, if there are a Tom turkey and a hen turkey of equal size, the Tom will be younger and therefore should be more tender.

Since January 1959, the government has required that all poultry moving in interstate commerce be inspected. The round inspection seal, which carries the message "Inspected for Wholesomeness by U. S. Department of Agriculture," denotes that the fowl has been inspected and that at the time this was done, insofar as health standards are concerned, the bird was fit for human consumption. This, however, is no mark of quality, and grading by the United States Department of Agriculture is something that the processor can "buy" or ignore as he so pleases. When the processor "buys" this service for the benefit of his customers, United

States Department of Agriculture graders then judge the poultry on the basis of the shape of the bird, the meatiness, the amount of fat distributed in and under the skin. They also check for bruises, tears, discolorations, and pinfeathers. There are three federal grades for ready-to-cook poultry and when the processor has availed himself of the grading service offered by the Department of Agriculture, the grade is shown on a small shield, which carries the letters USDA and the grade. The 3 grades are U. S. Grade A, U. S. Grade B, and U. S. Grade C. Birds that have been judged to be Grade A are of course superior insofar as the amount of edible meat is concerned. Also, they have been carefully processed so that there are no bruises, pinfeathers, and tears. While Grade B is quite satisfactory, it does not have as much edible meat as Grade A and there is a possibility that some defects were incurred during the cleaning, picking, and other dressing processes. Grade C denotes the least desirable poultry. There is less edible meat and the dressing defects may be much more serious than those found in the other 2 grades.

If the poultry you buy does not carry the United States Department of Agriculture grade stamp, and much ready-to-cook poultry does not, the only thing left for you to do is to find a butcher who cares—for your business—and who will, therefore, do his best to help you in the selection of fowl.

Handling

Poultry should be kept in the coldest part of the refrigerator—32° F. to 35° F., and it should not be stored more than 2 to 3 days. If it is to be kept longer, store in the freezer.

AND IN CONCLUSION, A WORD OF THANKS

My hat is off for their efficiency and my thanks go to the members of the New Orleans offices of the Department of Agriculture, particularly those in the Home Demonstration Agent's and the

County Agent's office, who helped me to get some of the information necessary to compile this chapter.

I am also very grateful to one of the nicest men and one of the best butchers I have ever known, Mr. Jimmy Ferraro of the Winn Dixie Stores, who shared with me (and thus, in turn, with you) some of his vast knowledge about meat and poultry.

3

Season to Taste, but Season

When I was thirteen, two of my younger cousins came to New Orleans for a visit. As a very special treat, an uncle, who had the respect for good food that is its due, took us to have lunch at Galatoire's, which was then, and still is, one of New Orleans' finest restaurants. As a start for our lunch, Uncle Martin ordered turtle soup. Unfortunately, one of my young cousins did not have an equal respect for, nor even very much knowledge of, gourmet cooking, and when the waiter, an elderly Frenchman, placed the wonderful concoction that is Galatoire's turtle soup before her, without even tasting it, she asked for Worcestershire sauce. To a man steeped in the tradition of haute cuisine, this was more than a faux pas; this was a crime. With great indignation and even greater pride, the old man, his voice shaking slightly, rebuked my cousin by telling her, "You do not need the sauce; here, we season our food in the kitchen." And that is exactly where seasoning should be done!

The dictionary says that to season is "to render palatable by adding a tasty ingredient; to give zest to or relish to"; and quite in line with this definition, insofar as I am concerned, a seasoning is "sugar and spice and everything nice," including many things that, like sugar, are usually considered as main ingredients. The "everything nice" covers: salt and the seasoned salts; pepper, from the fiery cayenne to the mild paprika; herbs, as well as spices, whose use can transform an ordinary dish into a culinary masterpiece; condiments and sauces; vegetables and fresh vegetable seasoning substitutes, including the oh, so important onion; salt, pickled, and smoked pork; fruit rinds and lemon juice; the extracts; and alcoholic spirits, which are indispensable ingredients of successful gourmet cooking.

SALT

Salt is undoubtedly the best known of all seasonings. So common has been its usage for so long that Homer in the *Odyssey* felt it worthy of comment that there were islanders who did not know the seas and used no salt in their food. Certainly, salt is no less important today than it was when a high tax on this seasoning was a contributing factor to the French Revolution.

While salt is used in every course from soup to nuts, too much or too little can ruin almost any dish. When food is cooked in a previously unsalted liquid, it is safe to use a rounded ½ teaspoon of salt for each cup of liquid. For roasting (or baking), broiling, or braising meat, fish, or poultry, you may allow, according to your taste, from ⅓ to ½ teaspoon salt per pound for meat and fish and from ¼ to ⅓ teaspoon per pound for poultry.

Onion, celery, and garlic salt are used when respectively, the flavor of onion, celery, or garlic is desired in addition to the salt. I would recommend that in most instances a combination of the flavored and regular salts be used.

PEPPER

If pepper is to do its best for food, it must be fresh. In fact, the real gourmet will grind the peppercorns when he is ready to season food.

Black Pepper is undoubtedly the most popular pepper. If a recipe does not specify the kind of pepper that is to be used, you may safely add black pepper. It is used in hors d'oeuvres, soup, meat, poultry, eggs, sauces, vegetables, stuffings, salad dressings, and gravies.

White Pepper is zesty, but milder than black, cayenne, or red pepper. It is used with seafood, vegetables, and sauces primarily.

Cayenne is the hottest of the red peppers and must be used sparingly. It lends excitement to eggs, sauces, a few meat dishes, vegetables, dips, and fish.

Red Pepper is zesty and sharp but is milder than cayenne, and is used in egg, meat, vegetable, and seafood dishes as well as in sauces and dips.

Paprika is cool, mild, and has a slightly sweet taste. It is valuable for both flavor and its lovely red color, which lends itself so well to garnishing food. It is used with seafood, salads, meat, poultry, eggs, vegetables, and sauces.

OTHER SPICES AND HERBS

Not so many years ago, while the more common spices could be easily found, you really had to search to find the vast majority of herbs, but today, even in small-town grocery stores you find well-stocked herb and spice shelves. This is definite evidence that Americans have decided that if they must eat, they might as well eat with pleasure.

To preserve the freshness of herbs and spices, and, if they aren't fresh, they will do more harm than good, they must be protected from air, dampness, and heat.

If dry herbs are specified in a recipe and only fresh ones are available, use 3 to 4 times the specified quantity; on the other hand, if fresh herbs are specified, and only dried ones are to be had, use ¼ to ⅓ of the specified quantity. Some herbs turn bitter if cooked for more than an hour, so in making soups and stews, add herbs in the final hour of cooking. For foods that are not cooked, such as vegetable cocktails, etc., add herbs at least 12 hours before using.

The following herbs and spices will add tantalizing and delightful flavor to the food you cook; however, you can always overdo a good thing, so, if you are new to herb and spice cookery and do not have a recipe from a reliable source, start your experiments cautiously—and by this I mean with as little as ⅛ teaspoon of a dried herb or spice[1]—if you find that you would like a little more of the seasoning, increase the amount in subsequent trials.

Allspice is a spice with a light, pleasing aroma. It is supposed to combine the flavors of cinnamon, cloves, and nutmeg.

Anise is an herb with a licorice flavor.

The herb *Basil* lends a zesty flavor to meat, shellfish, egg, and vegetable dishes. It blends magnificently with tomato.

Bay Leaf (Laurel) has a sharp, but delightful flavor; however, when using this herb, you will find that ½ a large leaf or 1 small leaf is usually enough.

Bouquet Garni is composed of a tablespoon of powdered herbs: 3 sprigs of parsley, 1 sprig of marjoram, 1 sprig of thyme, and 1 very small or ½ a medium-sized bay leaf, which are tied in a bag made of thin cloth and added to soup or pot roast during the last hour of cooking.

The *Caraway* seed is a must insofar as rye bread is concerned, but this fragrant herb with its pungent flavor can also be used to advantage with such diverse foods as cookies and calf liver.

The fruit of the herb *Cardamon* lends a lively and agreeably different flavor to many foods. The tiny seeds are sometimes used whole, sometimes ground, and the whole pod is used for pickles.

Celery Seed looks like another herb, parsley, but it's flavor is almost identical to that of celery.

The herb *Chervil* tastes much like mild parsley, and it has a most pleasant odor.

---

[1] This does not apply to cakes, but undoubtedly you won't start your experiments with cakes.

Chili Powder is a combination of chili peppers, garlic, and the herbs cumin and oregano, which lend a quite lively and unique flavor to many foods.

Chives is an herb with a flavor quite similar to that of the vegetables of the onion family.

Cinnamon, the inner bark of the tropical laurel, is used either whole or ground. The tantalizing flavor and aroma of this spice are real appetite arousers.

Cloves are the dried flower buds of a tropical tree. This spice, which can be used whole or ground, lends a sharp but delightful taste and odor.

The leaves of the *Coriander* are quite strong in flavor, and should never be used extravagantly, but the seeds of this herb, with their lemon rind-sage flavor, are milder.

Cumin seeds add a real tang to many dishes. The seeds of this herb are used whole or ground.

Curry Powder is a blend of the spices turmeric and cayenne and the herbs fenugreek and coriander. It is, of course, associated by most of us with (East) Indian cooking, but it can also add a tantalizing flavor to many completely Western dishes.

Both the leaves and the seeds of *Dill* add zest to a number of foods. Mankind owes a great debt to the person who first combined the seeds of this herb with pickles.

The herb *Fennel*, like anise, has a licorice flavor. It is often used in Scandinavian cooking.

Fenugreek is the only leguminous herb. The seed, whose flavor has some similarity to that of burnt sugar, should definitely be used when making chutney.

Fines Herbes are a minced mixture of such herbs as parsley, basil, and chives, and are used in soup, eggs, and stews.

Ginger is a zesty spice that can be used cracked or ground.

Gumbo Filé is made from thyme and sassafras leaves. It is the magic ingredient for New Orleans oyster and crab gumbo. It should never be added until food is removed from the stove, and once it has been added, the food should never be reheated.

Horseradish is a bitter herb, so strong when it is fresh it can bring tears to the eyes. It is often used as an accompaniment for boiled beef.

Mace is the outer covering of the nutmeg seed and there is some similarity in the flavor of the 2 spices, although mace is not quite as pungent as nutmeg. Mace adds the perfect touch for the *1–2–3–4 Pound Cake**.

Marjoram can be used whenever oregano is specified and vice versa, since the flavors of the 2 herbs are quite similar. The marjoram, however, is slightly sweeter and not quite so strong.

Mint is perhaps the most "deliciously cool" of all the herbs, although it lends a certain tangy flavor to beverages and jelly. The odor is heavenly and there is no more lovely garnish.

Mustard seed is used whole, ground, and "prepared," but in whatever way it is used, this pungent herb adds zesty flavor.

Nutmeg is the kernel found under the mace. This spice lends a delightful and distinctive flavor and aroma to many different kinds of food.

Oregano is slightly bitter, but certainly not unpleasantly so. This herb is used in most Italian dishes, such as pizza and pasta sauce, and in many Mexican ones.

Parsley sprigs or the minced or dried and flaked leaves add a certain magic—used in moderation of course—to just about every food excepting desserts, and this herb is certainly a very beautiful garnish.

The herb *Rosemary* has a flavor and aroma that are slightly sweet, distinctive, and certainly intriguing.

The spice *Saffron* must be used sparingly. Usually ⅙ of a teaspoon dissolved in a tablespoon of hot water will be enough to add when 1 cup of raw rice is specified for a rice dish (its principal use).

Sage is so strong it can be overpowering. The most popular usage for this herb is in stuffing.

Savory is a herb whose flavor is best described by its own name.

The herb *Tarragon* has a slight anise flavor. It's really a must for *Béarnaise Sauce**.

Thyme is the indispensable herb, if you would cook well. A touch of thyme does wonders for most dishes, as it makes them distinctive and delicious.

The spice *Turmeric* has a slightly bitter flavor, which adds zest to prepared mustard, pickles, relishes, and many sauces.

MATCHING THE HERB AND/OR SPICE TO THE FOOD
(For Your Ready Reference)

FOR	USE
APPETIZERS	Mace; Mint; Nutmeg; Thyme; Turmeric
ARROZ CON POLLO	Saffron

BEVERAGES
Alcoholic and non-
  alcoholic
	Allspice; Cinnamon (sticks or ground);
	  Cloves (whole or ground); Mace;
	  Mint; Nutmeg

Café Brûlot	Cinnamon Sticks and Whole Cloves
Coffee	Cardamon Seeds

BREAD AND COFFEE CAKE (YEAST)	
Sweet Breads	Anise; Cardamon; Cinnamon; Cloves; Cumin; Mace; Nutmeg; Poppy Seed
Rye Bread	Caraway
BREAD (QUICK)	
Cinnamon Toast	Cinnamon
Doughnuts	Mace; Nutmeg
French Toast	Cinnamon
Muffins	Cinnamon
Pancakes	Cinnamon
Waffles	Cinnamon

CAKES	Allspice; Anise; Caraway; Cardamon;
	  Cinnamon; Cloves; Ground Ginger;
	  Mace; Nutmeg; Poppy Seed

Gingerbread	Ground Ginger
Pound Cakes	Mace

FOR	USE
CANDY	Anise; Cinnamon
CEREALS	
Cream of Wheat	Cinnamon
Oatmeal	Cinnamon
Rice	Curry; Saffron, Cinnamon in Sweet Rice
COOKIES	Allspice; Anise; Caraway; Cardamon; Cinnamon; Cloves; Coriander; Cumin; Ginger; Nutmeg; Poppy Seed
CUSTARDS	
Coffee-flavored	Cardamon; Cinnamon; Cloves; Nutmeg
Custard Toppings	Cinnamon; Cloves; Nutmeg
EGGS	Basil; Chervil; Chili Powder; Chives; Cumin; Curry; Dill; Fines Herbes; Parsley; Oregano; Tarragon; Thyme; Turmeric
Creamed	Cumin; Turmeric
Deviled	Cumin; Turmeric
Hard-cooked	Curry
Omelets	Basil; Chives; Parsley; Thyme
Poached	Curry
Scrambled	Basil; Chives; Parsley; Thyme
FRUIT	
Baked Apples, Bananas, Peaches, Pears	Whole or Ground Allspice; Cardamon; Cinnamon; Cloves; Nutmeg
Bananas Flambé	Cardamon; Cinnamon; Nutmeg
Jellies	Cardamon; Mint
Melons, Chilled	Cardamon
Preserves	Cinnamon Sticks; Whole Cloves; Cracked Ginger; Whole Mace
Stewed Apples, Peaches, Pears, Prunes	Allspice; Cardamon; Cinnamon; Ground Ginger; Nutmeg
Stewed Cherries	Whole Mace
GRAVIES	Basil; Chili Powder; Ground Mustard; Thyme

FOR   USE

MACARONI, NOODLES AND SPAGHETTI

Noodles, Spaghetti,   Caraway: Poppy Seed
  or Macaroni with
  Cheese

MEAT

For	Use
Chili con Carne	Chili Powder
Creamed	Cumin; Turmeric
Croquettes	Thyme
Hamburger	Chili Powder; Savory; Thyme
Meatballs	Anise; Chili Powder; Savory; Thyme
Meat Loaf	Chili Powder; Cumin; Mace; Savory; Thyme
Meat Pies	Basil
Roasts	Whole Allspice; Bay Leaf (crumbled); Bouquet Garni; Poultry Seasoning; Thyme; Ground Ginger
Stews	Basil; Bay Leaf; Chili Powder; Chives; Fines Herbes; Marjoram; Oregano; Parsley; Savory; Thyme
Sausage	Marjoram; Sage
With Beef:	
Boiled	Horseradish
Kidneys	Caraway
Tongue (boiled)	Whole Cloves
With Lamb	Basil; Dill; Mint; Oregano; Savory
With Pork	Caraway; Chives; Whole Cloves; Marjoram; Rosemary; Savory
With Veal and Calf	Basil; Ground Ginger; Sage; Savory; Tarragon; Thyme
Calf Liver	Caraway

MINCEMEAT

Allspice; Cloves; Cinnamon; Mace; Nutmeg

PICKLES AND RELISHES

Whole Allspice; Bay Leaf; Cardamon
Pods; Celery Seed; Cinnamon Sticks;
Whole Cloves; Coriander; Cracked
Ginger; Turmeric

For	Use
Chutney	Fenugreek
Pickles, Sweet	Fennel

FOR   USE

PIES:
  Apple   Cinnamon; Cloves; Fennel; Nutmeg
  Custard   Nutmeg
  Fruit Other Than   Allspice; Cinnamon; Cloves; Ginger;
    Apple   Nutmeg
  Pumpkin   Allspice; Cinnamon; Cloves; Ginger;
                             Mace; Nutmeg

PIZZA   Oregano

POULTRY   Bay Leaf; Chives; Cloves; Cumin;
                             Curry; Dill; Marjoram; Nutmeg;
                             Parsley; Rosemary; Sage; Savory;
                             Tarragon; Thyme; Turmeric
  Chicken   Curry; Marjoram; Rosemary; Savory
  Chicken, Broiled   Poultry Seasoning
  Chicken or Turkey,
    à la King   Cumin; Turmeric
  Ducks   Marjoram; Sage
  Geese   Marjoram; Sage
  Stews or Fricassees   Bay Leaf; Chives; Dill; Parsley;
                             Tarragon; Thyme
  Turkey   Marjoram; Rosemary; Savory

PUDDINGS
  Bread and Rice   Allspice; Cardamon; Cinnamon; Cloves;
                             Ginger; Nutmeg
  Chocolate   Cinnamon
  Indian   Cinnamon; Ginger
  Plum   Allspice; Cinnamon; Cloves; Mace;
                             Nutmeg

SALAD DRESSINGS   Basil; Celery Seed; Chervil; Chives;
                             Curry; Dill; Horseradish; Ground
                             Mustard; Prepared Mustard; Parsley;
                             Savory; Tarragon; Thyme; Turmeric

SALADS   Basil; Celery Seed; Chervil; Chives;
                             Coriander; Dill; Horseradish; Prepared
                             Mustard; Whole Mustard Seeds;
                             Parsley; Poppy Seeds; Rosemary;
                             Savory; Thyme; Turmeric

FOR	USE
Beets	Whole Mustard Seed
Chicken	Cumin; Turmeric
Crab Meat	Cumin; Turmeric
Green	Coriander
Pork	Cumin
Potato	Chives; Cumin; Prepared Mustard; Turmeric
Shrimp	Cumin; Turmeric
Tomato	Thyme
Turkey	Cumin; Turmeric
SAUCES	Basil; Bay Leaf; Celery Seed; Chervil; Chili Powder; Chives; Horseradish; Mace; Marjoram; Mint; Ground Mustard; Nutmeg; Oregano; Parsley; Rosemary; Savory; Tarragon; Thyme
Béarnaise	Tarragon
Cocktail	Horseradish
Pasta	Oregano
Remick	Ground Mustard
Remoulade	Ground Mustard
Tomato	Basil; Bay Leaf; Oregano; Parsley; Rosemary; Thyme
SEAFOOD	Ground or Whole Allspice; Basil; Bay Leaf; Chervil; Chives; Cloves; Cumin; Curry; Dill; Fennel; Marjoram; Nutmeg; Oregano; Parsley; Sage; Savory; Thyme; Turmeric
Salt Fish	Sage
Seafood Salads	Cumin; Turmeric
SOUP	Basil; Bay Leaf; Bouquet Garni; Celery Seed; Chervil; Chives; Dill; Fines Herbes; Marjoram; Oregano; Parsley; Poultry Seasoning; Saffron; Thyme
Bean	Dill
Bouillabaisse	Allspice; Bay Leaves; Parsley; Saffron; Thyme

FOR	USE
Chowder	Oregano
Cream	Mace; Nutmeg
Cream of Tomato	Dill
Gumbo (Chicken, Seafood)	Gumbo Filé
Pea	Dill
SPICY SYRUPS	Whole Cloves
STUFFINGS	Basil; Coriander; Marjoram; Oregano; Parsley; Poultry Seasoning; Rosemary; Sage; Savory; Tarragon; Turmeric
TARRAGON VINEGAR	Tarragon
TURTLE STEW	Chives; Parsley
VEGETABLES	
Beans, Green	Basil; Marjoram; Sage; Savory
Beans, Lima	Marjoram
Beans or Peas, Dried	Parsley; Rosemary; Thyme
Beets	Basil; Caraway; Coriander; Whole Mustard Seed; Parsley
Carrots	Basil; Mint; Nutmeg; Parsley; Savory; Thyme
Cauliflower	Chervil; Chives; Nutmeg; Parsley
Creamed Vegetables	Chervil; Chives; Curry; Parsley
Eggplant	Basil; Thyme
Greens	Rosemary
Peas	Basil; Marjoram; Mint; Savory
Potatoes, Sweet	Cinnamon; Cloves; Mace; Nutmeg
Potatoes, White	Chives; Cumin (for salad); Parsley; Rosemary (for boiled); Turmeric (for salad)
Radishes	Chives
Sauerkraut	Caraway; Cumin
Spinach	Curry; Nutmeg; Thyme
Squash	Basil
Squash, Yellow (Pudding)	Cinnamon; Cloves; Mace; Nutmeg
Tomatoes	Chives; Parsley; Rosemary; Tarragon; Thyme
Vegetable Pears	Basil

SUGAR

Small amounts of sugar are used to season such vegetables as peas and cooked tomatoes, as well as to season meat, sauces, and salad dressings. The new sugar substitutes can be used quite successfully for seasoning.

MONOSODIUM GLUTAMATE (ACCENT)

Monosodium glutamate adds no flavor of its own to food, but it enhances to a marked degree the natural flavor of soups, meats, seafood, poultry, vegetables, sauces, gravies, and stuffing.

VINEGAR

While vinegar is one of the main ingredients when it is used for most dressings and for pickling, it also does great service as a seasoning. The more popular types of vinegar are cider, distilled, pepper, malt, tarragon, and wine. The cider, distilled, and wine vinegars are used to season sweet and sour, barbecue, and other sauces; tarragon is a must for some sauces (Remick and Béarnaise, in particular); a dash or two of pepper vinegar does marvels for cooked greens and just a small amount of distilled or wine vinegar adds a great deal to potato and meat salad, when mayonnaise is used as the salad dressing, and also to many aspics. Vinegar is also used as a seasoning for New Orleans' famous *Grillades** (veal steaks).

Vinegar has another important use, which many cooks overlook. To tenderize meat, about 6 hours before cooking steaks, chops, or a roast, brush the meat with a small amount of vinegar or soak these meats for 1 to 2 hours in French dressing, made of equal parts vinegar and salad oil. If desired, 1 tablespoon Worcestershire sauce may be added for each cup of the vinegar and oil mixture. Meat should be stored in the refrigerator after it is brushed with vinegar or placed in French dressing. In the event the French dressing does not cover the meat, turn chops, roast, or steak several times while in the marinade.

CONDIMENTS

Ketchup—I guess there are many children who like ketchup as much as they like ice cream, and with most of us, throughout our lives, this spicy, slightly sweet tomato sauce is a favorite. In addition to its use at the table, Ketchup, used as a seasoning in the kitchen, adds tremendously to some soups, stews, barbecued meats, salad dressings, sauces, and seafood dishes.

Other condiments that are worth their weight in gold as seasonings are

Chili Sauce—a little thicker and less smooth than ketchup, but it too is a spicy tomato sauce. For a slight variation in flavor, it may be substituted in most dishes where ordinarily ketchup is used for seasoning.

Kitchen Bouquet—adds a slightly smoky or charcoal flavor to meats, seafood, and poultry. Used with honey, it makes a magnificent glaze for poultry. A little Kitchen Bouquet brushed on meat, poultry, or seafood is a guarantee that the food will be appetizingly browned when it is served.

Soy Sauce—a must for many oriental dishes. It is particularly good with many pork and chicken dishes, whether they be cooked in oriental or American fashion.

Tabasco—This sauce is aged naturally in wood for a number of years. It is fire-hot and when using it as a seasoning for sauces, soups, eggs, seafood, cheese biscuits, meat stews, and vegetable juice cocktails, it is wise to measure by the drop.

Worcestershire—Lends a spicy, tantalizing flavor to soups, meat, fish, sauces (particularly barbecue, cheese, or cocktail), toasted cheese sandwiches, and vegetable juice cocktail.

VEGETABLES

Onions, Shallots and Leeks: It is the onion, green or dry, or members of the onion family, shallots and leeks, that lend great zest to many salads, gravies, sauces, soups, stuffings, and meat, poultry, fish and egg dishes, as well as to other vegetables; however, when using onions, shallots, and leeks as a seasoning, don't be a spendthrift. They are best when used to blend in with and supplement the flavor of the main ingredients and care should be taken so that the seasoning does not dominate the dish. Many prefer the more subtle flavors of the shallot or leek to that of the dry onion.

The leek, which is milder than the onion, is almost a must for *Vichyssoise**, although in an emergency, onions or shallots may be substituted.

While I prefer to use the members of the onion family in their fresh state, the dehydrated flakes, purée, powder, or juice of the onion may be substituted and results will be most satisfactory.

Garlic: The flavor and odor of garlic can be overpowering. Used correctly, garlic can do much for certain foods, but if you add the garlic with a "heavy hand," the food that you have so badly treated may wind up in the garbage can. For some salads and steak sauces, instead of adding the minced garlic, peel and cut a clove in half and rub the wooden bowl in which the salad is to be served or a wooden or plastic container in which the steak sauce is to be mixed with the cut sides of the garlic halves. Garlic is a required seasoning for many Italian dishes. It is used with meat, seafood, gravies, and sauces. Garlic purée and powder may be substituted for fresh garlic and the purée is actually preferable for garlic or garlic-cheese bread.

Mushrooms, Green Pepper, Celery, Cabbage, and Carrots: Small amounts of cooked or canned mushroom pieces or slices, chopped green pepper, and chopped celery add tremendously to the flavor of soups, sauces, stews, meats, seafood, and stuffings. The green pepper and celery also add much to many salads and aspics. A small amount of finely chopped cabbage adds a distinctive flavor to a vegetable or beef-vegetable soup. As for the carrot, use it for seasoning sauces, soups, and stews. A few thin slices of raw carrot add both a touch of color and flavor to cabbage salad (slaw).

SALT, PICKLED, OR SMOKED PORK

I am a Southerner, so, for me, salt, pickled, or smoked pork is an indispensable seasoning for greens, cabbage, or dried beans and peas. And no matter where you come from or where you are, you probably associate beef fillets with the thin strip of bacon in which they are wrapped. Salt, pickled, and smoked pork also add a delightful flavor to many fish and poultry dishes. The fat that is fried out of the bacon when it is cooked lends a marvelous flavor to stuffings, some sauces, meat, poultry, and fish.

CITRUS FRUIT RINDS AND LEMON JUICE

Lemon and orange rinds (either in strips or grated) add intriguing flavors to many poultry and game sauces, custards, cheese cakes, pies, cooked fruits, candied vegetables, such as carrots and sweet potatoes, and ice cream.

Lemon juice adds dash and sparkle to vegetable juice cocktails, beverages, seafood, meat, poultry, sauces, cooked fruits, cakes, pies, sherbets, and other desserts.

EXTRACTS

Vanilla, almond, lemon, maple, peppermint, and rum extracts are used to flavor cakes, custards, both vegetable and dessert puddings, ice cream, frostings, and candy. The vanilla bean is growing harder and harder to find although it's still available in a few grocery and drugstores, but to those of us who had the wonderful experience of licking a dasher when it was removed from an old-fashioned crank freezer, there is nothing so good as vanilla-bean flavored custard ice cream. The scraped pulp of the bean also adds a pleasing flavor to powdered sugar when the sugar is used to coat cookies or dust cakes.

SPIRITS (ALCOHOLIC)

More and more Americans are beginning to appreciate what spirits such as rum, wine, gin, whisky, and cordials do to improve the flavor of food. To the real gourmet, most food that can be cooked in water can be cooked even better in a dry white wine or in equal parts of white wine and water. As for the other and stronger spirits, quite often a little can do a lot. If you want a glass of brandy, sniff and then sip it, but don't add so much brandy to food that all you can taste is the spirit. The gourmet cook takes full advantage of the magnificent flavor of the spirits without overdoing things to a point where other excellent flavors are completely drowned.

A few suggested uses: rum or sauterne adds much to French (salad) dressing; anisette and sauterne give mayonnaise an intriguing flavor; kirsch transforms Roquefort dressing into something fit for the gods on Mount Olympus; as for gin, add a small amount with a little ketchup or chili sauce to mayonnaise or tartar sauce.

Meats, poultry, seafood, desserts, and dessert sauces are often flavored by being flambéed in rum, brandy, gin, or whisky and the beauty of a flambé can certainly make life more exciting. Incidentally, *flambées* are not difficult to do. The secret is to have everything very hot. Just pour all but a couple of tablespoons of the very hot spirit you are using over hot food in a hot utensil or serving dish. Quickly ignite remaining hot spirit and pour burning liquid over previously added spirit.

Cordials, brandy, and rum add much to the flavor of cakes and keep them fresh and moist for weeks when properly stored. Kirsch, Cointreau, Triple Sec, and rum work magic with fruit, including berries and melons, ice cream, frostings, puddings, dessert sauces, meringues, and soufflés.

Also, a marinade of wine (used for 6 or 7 hours before cooking) is a wonderful meat or poultry tenderizer, and the meat and poultry so treated are deliciously moist when cooked. And try sprinkling beef with gin about 6 hours before it is cooked!

4

For a Better Understanding

Like most of the other woes of the world, bad cooking is quite often the result of a complete breakdown in communications— the recipe-receiver just doesn't understand the recipe-giver. It would do little good if you were given the world's best recipe for an *Angel Food** if you didn't understand the directions in the recipe about beating egg whites until they reached the soft peak[1] stage and didn't have the slightest notion of how to fold the flour-sugar mixture into the egg white-sugar-extract mixture.

MEASUREMENTS

It takes real genius to measure ingredients with the eye and come up with something worth eating. Since very few people are so gifted, use standard measuring cups and spoons.

The ¼-, ⅓-, ½-, and 1-cup measures for dry ingredients are usually made of plastic or metal and if you fill them to the top, they hold, respectively, exactly (and that's the important thing) ¼, ⅓, ½, and 1 cup. Cup measures for liquids are usually made of glass or clear plastic, so that you can see when the liquid is exactly level with the line that marks the particular measurement you want, be it ¼, ⅓, ½, ⅔, ¾, 1, 1¼, 1⅓, 1½, 1⅔, 1¾, or 2 cups. Above the line showing the 1-cup or 2-cup level, depending on the capacity of the measure used, there is room for additional liquid, so as to prevent spilling; however, the measurements to be accurate must be level with the lines on the cup.

Occasionally, ⅛, ⅜, ⅝, or ⅞ of a cup of some ingredient

[1] See *Whipping Stages of Egg Whites**.

will be specified in a recipe. For ⅛ cup, use a tablespoon measure and measure 2 tablespoons; for ⅜ cup, measure ¼ cup and add 2 tablespoons; for ⅝ cup, measure ½ cup and add 2 tablespoons; and for ⅞ cup, measure ½ cup and ¼ cup and then add 2 tablespoons.

Should your recipe call for ⅛ teaspoon, measure ¼ level teaspoon. With the blade of the knife, cut the ingredient into 2 equal parts and with the side of the knife remove ½ of the ingredient from the spoon. Should the recipe specify ⅓, ½, or ⅔ tablespoon, measure 1, 1½, or 2 level teaspoons respectively.

Unless a recipe specifies otherwise, you may safely assume that measurements should be level. As a matter of convenience, few recipes of this day specify "rounded" or "heaping," as was once common practice. In order to get a level measurement when using dry ingredients, fill your measure and then place your knife or spatula on the rim of one side of the cup or spoon; quickly pass it across the ingredients in the measure to the rim of the opposite side, thus cutting away any excess. Should you find a direction for a rounded measurement, and it's only common sense that perfection doesn't always come in convenient level measurements, fill your cup or spoon so that the ingredient is slightly rounded above the rim. If you are using a very old recipe and find a heaping measurement specified, substitute 1⅛ level teaspoons for 1 heaping teaspoon, 1¼ level tablespoons for the heaping tablespoon (for the ¼ tablespoon measure, use a level ½ teaspoon plus a level ¼ teaspoon), and for 1 heaping cup, use 1 level cup plus 1 level tablespoon.

Usually flour is sifted before it is measured. Flour and confectioners' or granulated sugar should be spooned into a cup. Don't pack, knock down, or shake these ingredients when measuring. Brown sugar, shortening, margarine or butter, coconut, dried fruit, and nuts should be packed into a cup.

RELIABLE SUBSTITUTES

From time to time you are going to want to cook something and find yourself out of one of the ingredients, so:

IF YOU NEED, BUT DON'T HAVE:	*USE:*
1 whole egg for cookies	2 egg yolks and 1 tablespoon water
2 egg yolks for cookies	1 whole egg
1 whole egg for custard	2 egg yolks
2 egg yolks for custard	1 whole egg
Cake flour (for each cup)	⅞ cup all purpose flour
All purpose flour (for each cup)	1⅛ cups cake flour
Cornstarch for thickening (for each tablespoon)	2 tablespoons all purpose flour
All purpose flour for thickening (for each tablespoon)	½ tablespoons cornstarch
Unsweetened cooking chocolate (for each ounce)	3½ tablespoons cocoa, plus 1½ teaspoons butter or margarine
Cocoa (for each 1⅔ tablespoons)	½ ounce unsweetened baking chocolate and reduce quantity of fat specified in recipe by ¾ teaspoon
Sour milk (for each ½ cup)	½ cup fresh sweet milk plus 1½ teaspoons lemon juice or vinegar—let stand in warm spot for short time before using

SEPARATING EGG WHITES FROM YOLKS

Eggs separate better when cold; however, let the egg whites stand until room temperature before beating for best results. To separate the white from the yolk, crack the shell as near to the center as possible on the rim of a cup. Holding the egg above a bowl, separate the shell into 2 parts—one of which should hold the yolk and most of the white. Hold the part of the shell with the yolk, allowing as much white as possible to "spill" into the bowl. Also pour any of the white that remained in the other part of the shell into the bowl. When most of white has drained off yolk, transfer yolk and remaining white to other half of shell, continuing to hold both parts of the shell just above the bowl. This must be done carefully so as not to break the yolk. Repeat transferring yolk carefully from one part of shell to other until practically all of white has drained into bowl.

ADDING RAW EGGS OR EGG YOLKS TO HOT FOOD

When adding raw eggs or egg yolks to hot food, such as sauce, gravy, vegetable, stuffing, etc., beat the eggs slightly. Remove food from heat and add a small amount of it to the beaten eggs. Mix until well blended and then stir the mixture into remainder of hot food.

WHIPPING STAGES OF EGG WHITES

If your recipe specifies a particular whipped stage at which egg whites should be used, this is how to recognize it:

Frothy: Air bubbles of all different sizes can be seen.

Beginning to Hold Shape: Minute air bubbles are close together and eggs are whiter. When the beaters are lifted through whites, their "path" can be seen on surface.

Soft Peak: When beaters are lifted up through whites, a peak will be raised on surface; however, the tip of peak will bend—

this means tip and not collapse of whole peak a few seconds after it is lifted.

Stiff, but Not Dry: Peaks lifted on surface will be stiff and sharply pointed; eggs will be gleaming white and will cling to bowl if it is turned upside down.

Stiff and Dry: Peaks will be stiff and sharply pointed. Whites will be dull-looking with white spots on surface.

WHIPPING CREAM

Use very fresh heavy (40 per cent) cream for whipping. Before starting to beat, thoroughly chill cream, bowl, and beater(s), preferably those of electric mixer, but rotary egg beater may be used. If possible, whip shortly before using and then store in refrigerator. If you wish to sweeten, after cream is stiff stir in for each ½ pint cream 1 to 2 tablespoons sifted confectioners' sugar (to taste) and if in addition you wish to flavor, for each ½ pint cream use 1 teaspoon vanilla or desired extract or 2 tablespoons desired alcoholic spirit. Stir in flavoring after sugar is added.

CREAMING INGREDIENTS OR
BEATING BATTER WITH SPOON

To cream butter or margarine or a combination of fat and sugar (and other ingredients), hold spoon so its bowl is sideways and move it rapidly through the batter from one side of mixing bowl to other, then bring spoon up side of bowl and over fat or combination of ingredients back to side from where you started. Repeat until fat is consistency of stiff mayonnaise or batter is smooth, creamy, and light.

FOLDING IN INGREDIENTS

In order to prevent loss of air, it is sometimes necessary to "fold in" such ingredients as beaten egg whites or whipped cream. Dry ingredients also must sometimes be folded into a batter. Egg whites should be folded into a batter with a wooden spoon while dry ingredients should be folded into the batter on the lowest possible food-mixer speed or with a spoon. For complete directions for folding beaten egg whites into a batter, see Section 8, *Mixing Batter with Food Mixer** (*General Rules for Making Butter Cakes**). This same process may be used to fold dry ingredients or whipping cream into another ingredient or combination of ingredients.

CUTTING IN

In order to make flaky pastry, biscuits, cookies, etc., fat and flour are combined by literally cutting the fat into the flour with knives or a pastry blender. For complete directions for "cutting in," see Section 6, *General Rules for Preparing Biscuits**.

KNEADING

Some biscuit and most yeast bread doughs are kneaded to make them smooth. We have all seen the word "knead" so often when reading of the women who helped settle this country that most of us think we know what it means up to the time we find the direction "to knead" in a recipe.

There is no difference between the method for kneading biscuit and yeast doughs, except that the quick bread is usually kneaded 10 to 15 times, while the yeast dough is kneaded until it is elastic and doesn't stick to a board—usually about 10 minutes. Directions for kneading are given in Section 10, *General Rules for Preparing Biscuits**.

FRIED FOODS—
CHECKING THE TEMPERATURE OF THE FAT

Depending on what is to be cooked, the fat should be heated from 360° F. to 390° F. before food is placed in it. If you do not have an electric frying pan, a candy thermometer may be used to check the temperature of the fat or it can be checked with cubes of bread. At 360° F., a cube of bread will brown in 1 minute; at 370° F., a cube of bread will brown in 50 seconds; at 390° F., a cube of bread will brown in 40 seconds.

DEEP FAT FRYING

Food that is cooked in fat that is too hot will brown without being cooked through; food that is cooked in fat that is not hot enough is apt to be so grease-soaked that it's distasteful and an invitation to a bad case of indigestion. Fat should be heated in a heavy kettle or a deep fat fryer and the liquid or melted fat should be 3 or 4 inches deep Usually fish, meat, or poultry is deep fat fried at 360° F.; dough is fried in most cases at 370° F. and food is French fried at 390° F. Food that is being fried is much easier to handle when a deep fat frying basket is used. As the fried food is removed from the skillet in the frying basket or with a slotted spoon, place it on heavy brown paper or absorbent paper towels so that it will drain and not be greasy.

BREADED (AND FRIED) FOOD

A number of foods are breaded and then fried. The breaded fried food has much to recommend it. It usually absorbs less fat than other fried foods and in addition to this, under the crisp, delicious, and beautifully browned crust, the food remains moist.

Southern fried chicken is "breaded" by placing a disjointed fryer (2½ to 3½ pounds) in a bag containing seasoned (salt and, if desired, pepper, and/or poultry seasoning) flour, and shaking until each piece is thoroughly coated. The chicken is then browned on all sides in melted shortening or salad oil, which should fill pan to a depth of ½ inch and which has previously been heated to 360° F. This takes from 12 to 15 minutes. The heat is then reduced to 260° F. and the chicken is cooked until tender, about 15 to 20 minutes longer.

Fried breaded chops are prepared by first sprinkling the meat on both sides with salt and, if desired, pepper. Then they are dipped in cracker, fine bread, cornflake, or Rice Krispies crumbs. The crumb-coated meat is dipped in slightly beaten egg, which may be diluted with a small quantity of milk or water, and then it is again dipped in the crumbs until completely covered. The breaded chops may be cooked in fat that has been preheated to 360° F. until tender—about 15 minutes on each side (there will be no sign of "pink" when a slit is made near the bone of the chop if meat is cooked through).

Breaded croquettes are dipped in crumbs, eggs, and again in crumbs in the same way as the fried breaded chops; however, they should be fried in deep hot fat at 385° F.

Fish (fillets, steaks, or small fish) can be sprinkled with salt and pepper and then dipped in cornmeal or crumbs or the sea-food, minus salt, can be dipped in equal parts seasoned flour and cornmeal, then in a slightly beaten mixture of 1 egg and 1 tablespoon water or milk, and again in the flour-cornmeal mixture.

The breaded fish is cooked only until it will flake easily with a fork in ¼ to ½ cup of melted fat or salad oil, preheated to 380° F. It is browned first on one side, then turned and browned on the other. This should take between 5 and 8 minutes.

SAUTÉED FOOD

To sauté is to fry lightly and quickly in a small amount of hot fat, turning the food at frequent intervals.

BOILING, SIMMERING, POACHING, AND SCALDING

While in most cases liquids are brought to a boil before food is added, we long ago, with a handful of exceptions, gave up boiling all the nutrients and flavor out of food. Today, once the liquid reaches the boiling point after food has been added, we reduce the temperature to allow the food to simmer over a low heat. When a liquid reaches a "slow" or "gentle" boil it is still agitated by small bubbles that rise to the surface; when it reaches a "rolling boil" the whole top is agitated by very large bubbles; when heat is reduced so that food will simmer, there should be no bubbles on the surface of the liquid and the heat should be lowered just to the point where the bubbles disappear.

There is actually no difference in the process of simmering and poaching, since in both processes the food is cooked in a liquid that is kept slightly below the boiling point (212° F. is boiling point for water under ordinary conditions).

When a liquid is scalded, it is brought to a temperature just below the boiling point by being steamed, that is, cooked over boiling water, usually in a double boiler, or by being cooked over direct heat, which can be adjusted so that the liquid will not reach the boiling point. Milk is the liquid most often scalded and when it or cream is cooked in this manner, a skinlike coating forms on the top when the milk or cream is ready for use.

OVEN COOKING

Success with what is cooked in an oven depends a great deal on keeping the proper temperature constant. Therefore, it is of the utmost importance to set the temperature control and light the gas or turn on the electricity and preheat for 10 minutes before food is put in the oven. Also, oven doors should be kept closed during this period and opened as little as possible while food is cooking.

PROPER WAY OF SERVING CHILLED AND HOT FOOD

If at all possible, chilled food should be served on cold dishes and hot food on heated dishes.

5

Sauces—the Key to Becoming a Success in the Kitchen the Easy Way

Many a chef has become world-famous because of a sauce. And yet, the novice in the kitchen who learns just a few simple "tricks of the trade" can make a smooth and perfect *White Sauce** in less than 15 minutes. This, however, is only the beginning: there are at least 36 other sauces that are variations of the *White Sauce**, and if you know how to do one well, you can do very nicely with all of them. In addition to this, there is a quite important bonus for the person who masters the *White Sauce**, for in this one sauce and its variations there is a key to the serving of hundreds of different dishes—soups, meat, poultry, seafood, eggs, cheese, vegetables, and even desserts. In some instances all you have to do is pour the sauce of your choice over the food of your choice; in other cases, the sauce is used in the actual preparation of a dish such as cream soup, croquettes, creamed meat, poultry, seafood or eggs, hash, or an au gratin casserole. In fact, the *Chocolate Soufflé**, which many regard as the height of the kitchen art, has its beginning in a variation of a *Thick White Sauce**.

Then there is the hollandaise family of sauces! For far too long this sauce has been regarded as something to be ordered in a restaurant that boasts a great chef, but whose making should be strictly avoided at home. And again, just learn a few "tricks of the trade" and the odds are 100 to 1 in your favor that you'll have no more trouble with a *Hollandaise Sauce** or any of its variations.

THE WHITE SAUCE FAMILY

Here then are the "secrets" you must know to make a good *White Sauce** or any of its variations:

GENERAL RULES FOR MAKING WHITE SAUCE* OR ANY OF ITS VARIATIONS

1. Before adding any ingredient, excepting one used for seasoning, remove pan in which sauce is being made from heat, thoroughly blend in the new ingredient with what is already in the pan, and then return pan to the stove. To elaborate: Once the fat has been melted in a heavy skillet over low heat until it is bubbling, but not brown, or in the inset pan of a double boiler over rapidly boiling water and is thoroughly heated, remove skillet or inset pan from the heat before adding the flour. Blend the fat and flour (this mixture is known as a *roux*) with a spoon or wire whip, preferably the latter, and then return to the heat, continuing to stir until very thick. Again remove pan from heat and gradually add the liquid that is to be used to the still hot roux. Stir vigorously after each addition and when all of liquid is added to roux continue stirring until there are no lumps of flour in the mixture and it is completely smooth. Again return to heat to complete cooking. If beaten raw eggs or alcoholic spirits are added to the sauce after the liquid has been added, remove pan from heat before making the addition.

2. The sauce must be cooked at least 8 minutes after it thickens following the addition of the liquid in order to eliminate a floury taste. When the mixture of roux and liquid is returned to the stove, if cooking in a skillet, increase heat to medium and stir constantly until sauce thickens. It should be bubbling. Then reduce to low heat. If sauce is being cooked over boiling water, stir until it thickens. Once the sauce thickens, it is only necessary to stir from time to time during the 8-minute (or longer, if desired consistency has not been reached) cooking period.

3. Stir in salt and, if desired, pepper to taste.

4. Should you need more sauce than can be made from your recipe, do not hesitate to double the quantity of each ingredient specified. If you don't use all the sauce for any one meal, it will keep beautifully for several days in the refrigerator or for a much longer period in the freezer. If sauce is frozen, when ready to use, thaw and stir vigorously and continuously when heating.

WHITE SAUCE

    2 tablespoons butter or margarine
    3 tablespoons sifted flour
    2 cups boiling, strained, grease-free broth[1] or scalded milk
      and/or cream, or 1 cup boiling broth and 1 cup scalded
      milk and/or cream
    Salt and pepper to taste

Melt butter or margarine in heavy skillet over direct low heat or in inset pan of double boiler over boiling water. When the fat begins to bubble in the skillet or, if a double boiler is used, when the fat is thoroughly heated, remove from heat and stir in the flour until it is blended with the fat. Return to heat and cook, stirring constantly until roux is thick. Again remove from heat and add the hot liquid(s) of your choice, very gradually, stirring vigorously after each addition. When all of liquid has been added, continue stirring until there are no lumps of flour in mixture and it is completely smooth. Return to heat. If using skillet, increase heat to medium and stir until sauce bubbles and thickens; if using double boiler, stir until sauce thickens. When sauce in skillet

[1] See *Beef Broth** or *Chicken or Veal Broth**.

thickens, the temperature should be reduced to a low heat. Cook until sauce reaches desired consistency—a minimum of 8 minutes after it thickens—stirring from time to time. Add salt and pepper to taste. *Yield: Approximately 1½ cups.*

GOURMET TOUCH FOR WHITE SAUCE AND ALL ITS DERIVATIVES

If you desire, 2 minutes before you are ready to serve the sauce, remove from heat and stir in 2 tablespoons dry sherry or 3 tablespoons dry white wine. Stir until wine and sauce are blended and then return to low heat for 2 minutes.

SUGGESTED USES FOR WHITE SAUCE AND VARIATIONS

1. Serve as topping for hot cooked fish, poultry, or eggs.

2. Combine just enough *Thick White Sauce** with finely minced or ground cooked meat or poultry or fish flakes to hold mixture together for croquettes. This mixture should be thoroughly chilled before croquettes are shaped. See *Breaded Croquettes**.

3. Serve with hot drained vegetables (artichoke hearts from which "chokes" have been removed, asparagus, broccoli, Brussels sprouts, carrots, cauliflower, celery, green beans, green peas, lima beans, small white onions, white potatoes) that were cooked by simmering—see *Simmered or Poached Vegetable Chart**, *Oven Broiled Mushrooms**, and *Oven Broiled Tomatoes**.

4. Use for **CREAMED MEAT OR POULTRY, CREAMED EGGS,** and **CREAMED SEAFOOD:** Combine 1½ cups (approximate) of sauce with any of the following and cook over medium heat, stirring constantly until hot:

2½ cups simmered or roast poultry or meat, cut in ¾-inch chunks, *or*

8 coarsely chopped hard-cooked eggs, *or*

2½ cups cooked crab meat, flaked cooked fish, or deveined, shelled cooked shrimp, *or*

36 *Poached Oysters**, which have been drained. A combination of the oyster "water," in place of broth, and milk makes an excellent *White Sauce**.

5. Use for **CHICKEN OR TURKEY FLORENTINE, SEAFOOD FLORENTINE, OR EGGS FLORENTINE:** Combine just enough of the sauce of your choice with cooked or canned, finely chopped drained spinach to hold the spinach together. Heat. Make bed of vegetable on hot serving platter. If making the Chicken or Turkey Florentine, cover with slices of hot cooked poultry; if making Seafood Florentine, cover with fillets of hot *Oven Broiled Fish** or fillets of hot *Poached or Simmered Fish** or hot, cooked, shelled, and deveined shrimp or hot cooked crab meat, and if making Eggs Florentine, cover with hot *Poached or Simmered Eggs.** Top with remainder of sauce.

VARIATIONS ON A WHITE SAUCE

Yield for each of these recipes is the same as for *White Sauce** unless otherwise specified.

A. BY SIMPLE SUSTITUTION

Tan Sauce—Substitute 2 cups boiling bouillon—see *Bouillon or Consomme**—for 2 cups liquid specified in *White Sauce**.

White Wine Sauce—Substitute 1 cup boiling white wine for 1 of 2 cups boiling liquid specified in *White Sauce**.

B. BY SIMPLE ADDITION

Cream Sauce—Add to heated *White Sauce**, *Tan Sauce**, or *White Wine Sauce** 2 well-beaten eggs. To do this, first add small amount of hot sauce to beaten eggs and stir until blended. Then beat egg mixture into remainder of sauce. Season to taste with salt and pepper. *Yield: 1⅔ cups.*

Mock Hollandaise—Stir into heated *Cream Sauce** that has been removed from stove: 1½ tablespoons melted butter or margarine; 1 to 1½ tablespoons, according to taste, lemon juice; salt if needed. Cayenne, black, or white pepper may be added to taste if desired. *Yield: 1¾ cups.*

A la King Sauce—Add to *White Sauce**, *Tan Sauce**, *White Wine Sauce**, or *Cream Sauce**:

    1½ tablespoons drained, coarsely chopped pimiento
    ¼ cup coarsely chopped green pepper
    ½ cup drained cooked or canned peas
    2 coarsely chopped hard-cooked eggs
    ⅓ cup hot milk or cream
    ⅓ cup cooked or canned mushroom slices, pieces or
       buttons, if desired
    ⅛ teaspoon turmeric, if desired
    ⅛ teaspoon cumin, if desired
    Salt and pepper if desired
    2 tablespoons dry sherry, if desired

Combine ingredients, including sauce, and heat thoroughly. (If you use the sherry, it does not have to be stirred into the sauce until just before the sauce is removed from stove.) *Yield: Approximately 2⅔ cups.*

Artichoke Sauce—Add to *White Sauce**, *White Wine Sauce**, or *Cream Sauce** the pulp scraped from the bases of the warm leaves of 8 medium-sized cooked artichokes and, if desired, ⅓ cup cooked artichoke hearts cut into ½-inch cubes. Heat thoroughly, stirring gently, until sauce is piping hot. If needed, salt and pepper may be added to taste. *Serves 4.*

Asparagus Sauce—Combine *White Sauce*, *White Wine Sauce*, *Cream Sauce*, or *Mock Hollandaise* with ⅔ cup puréed or sieved cooked or canned asparagus. Heat thoroughly, stirring constantly, and add salt and/or pepper to taste. *Serves 4.*

Bordelaise Sauce—Prepare *Cream Sauce* using 2 cups of following mixture as substitute for 2 cups liquid used in the *Cream Sauce*. Scald 1½ cups milk and 1 cup breakfast cream. Add to scalded milk ⅓ cup minced shallots, leeks, or onion and ½ cup scraped, finely chopped carrots. Allow to simmer until vegetables are tender. If there is less than 2 cups of mixture after it has simmered, additional heated milk or cream may be added to make up the 2 cups. *Yield: Approximately 2¼ cups.*

Caper Sauce—Add 3 tablespoons capers to *White Sauce* or *White Wine Sauce*. Heat. Particularly recommended for fish or lamb.

Caviar Sauce for Fish—Spread hot *White Sauce*, *White Wine Sauce*, *Cream Sauce*, or *Mock Hollandaise* over 4 small, hot cooked fish or fish fillets (approximately 6 inches long) or 1 4- to 5-pound hot cooked fish. Sprinkle with 3 tablespoons (black) caviar or (red) salmon roe.

Cheese Sauce—Combine *White Sauce* or *White Wine Sauce* that has been thoroughly heated and removed from the stove with ½ cup grated American cheese and 1½ tablespoons Worcestershire sauce. Return to low heat and cook, stirring constantly, until cheese is melted and all ingredients are blended. *Yield: Approximately 1¾ cups.*

Chive Sauce—Combine hot *White Sauce*, *White Wine Sauce*, or *Cream Sauce* with 2 tablespoons finely chopped chives and 2 teaspoons minced parsley or dehydrated parsley flakes. Cook over low heat 2 minutes, stirring constantly.

Crab Meat Sauce—Combine hot *White Sauce**, *White Wine Sauce**, *Cream Sauce**, *Cheese Sauce**, *Chive Sauce**, *Herb Sauce**, or *Mushroom Sauce** with ⅔ cup cooked crab meat. Cook over medium heat, stirring constantly until piping hot. *Serves 4.*

Egg Sauce—Gently stir 3 coarsely chopped hard-cooked eggs into hot *White Sauce** or *White Wine Sauce.** Cook over medium heat, stirring from time to time, until eggs are piping hot. *Serves 4.*

Herb Sauce—Bring *White Sauce**, *White Wine Sauce**, *Cream Sauce**, *Cheese Sauce**, *Crab Meat Sauce**, *Egg Sauce**, *Lobster Sauce**, *Mushroom Sauce**, or *Shrimp Sauce** just to boiling point. Stir in ¼ teaspoon turmeric, ⅛ teaspoon cumin, and 2 teaspoons fresh dehydrated parsley, and cook several minutes, continuing to stir.

Lobster Sauce—Heat *White Sauce**, *White Wine Sauce**, *Cream Sauce**, *Chive Sauce**, *Cheese Sauce**, *Herb Sauce**, or *Mushroom Sauce** and remove from stove. Stir in ⅔ cup cooked small lobster chunks and cook until seafood is thoroughly heated, stirring from time to time. Recommended particularly as topping for hot cooked fish or eggs. *Serves 4.*

Mushroom Sauce—Combine hot *White Sauce** or variation of your choice with ⅔ cup cooked or canned mushroom pieces, slices, or buttons. Cook, stirring from time to time, over medium heat until piping hot. *Serves 4.*

Shrimp Sauce—Heat *White Sauce**, *White Wine Sauce**, *Cream Sauce**, *Chive Sauce**, *Cheese Sauce**, *Herb Sauce**, or *Mushroom Sauce** and remove from stove. Stir in ⅔ cup cooked, shelled, deveined shrimp, cut into ½-inch segments. Continue cooking, stirring from time to time, until shrimp are piping hot. Particularly recommended as topping for hot cooked fish or eggs. *Serves 4.*

Tomato Cream Sauce—Prepare *Cream Sauce** or *White Wine Sauce**, and set aside. Combine and bring to a boil:

¾ cup tomato juice
½ crumbled small bay leaf
1½ teaspoons minced parsley
1½ tablespoons minced celery
1 tablespoon finely chopped onion, shallots, or leeks
1 tablespoon finely chopped green pepper, if desired
1 tablespoon tomato ketchup
3 dashes Tabasco sauce, if desired
¼ teaspoon thyme, if desired
¼ teaspoon oregano or rosemary, if desired
½ cup water or white wine
Salt and pepper to taste

Reduce heat and allow tomato juice mixture to simmer 8 minutes. Heat sauce that was set aside and remove from stove. Stir in tomato juice mixture gradually. *Yield: Approximately 2½ cups.*

Whipped Cream Sauce—Thoroughly heat *White Sauce** or desired variation. Remove from stove and fold in ⅓ cup stiffly whipped cream. *Yield: Approximately 1⅔ cups.*

C. VARIATIONS THROUGH CHANGES IN MEASUREMENTS AND/OR ADDITIONS

a. (Less than 2 cups liquid)

Velouté Sauce—Follow recipe for *White Sauce** making these changes: Use 2 tablespoons flour first measured then sifted instead of 3 tablespoons sifted flour and substitute 1 cup boiling, strained, grease-free *Chicken or Veal Broth** for the 2 cups of liquid specified for *White Sauce**. When salt is added, also add ⅛ teaspoon nutmeg, and if pepper is used, it should be the white variety. *Yield: 1 cup.*

Béchamel Sauce—Prepare *Velouté Sauce** and add ⅛ teaspoon paprika. Fold ⅓ cup stiffly whipped cream into the hot sauce. *Yield: 1¼ cups.*

Normandy Sauce (for Fish)—Follow recipe for *White Sauce** making these changes: Substitute 1 cup boiling strained fish stock for 2 cups of liquid specified in *White Sauce** recipe. Stir 1 tablespoon of sauce into 2 well-beaten egg yolks and then combine yolk mixture with remainder of sauce. Stir in 1½ tablespoons melted butter or margarine, 1 tablespoon lemon juice, and, if desired, cayenne pepper to taste. Heat thoroughly. *Yield: 1¼ cups.*

Sauce Bienville (a topping for oysters baked on half shells[2])— Follow recipe for *White Sauce**, using a double boiler and making these changes: Substitute 1 cup scalded heavy cream for 2 cups liquid specified in *White Sauce** recipe and use only 2 tablespoons of flour. Stir gently during entire cooking period. Blend 1 tablespoon sauce into 2 well-beaten egg yolks and then combine yolk mixture with remainder of sauce. Add following:

⅛ teaspoon thyme
1½ tablespoons grated Parmesan cheese
½ cup minced, deveined, cooked, shelled shrimp
2 tablespoons dry sherry, if desired
1½ tablespoons minced parsley or 1 tablespoon dehydrated
    parsley flakes
1 tablespoon minced chives, shallots, or leeks, if desired

Cook, stirring constantly, over boiling water until shrimp are thoroughly heated. *Yield: Approximately 1¾ cups.*

Thick White Sauce[3]—Follow recipe for *White Sauce**, making these changes: Use 3 tablespoons butter or margarine instead of 2 tablespoons, use 3 tablespoons flour, first measured and then sifted, instead of 3 tablespoons sifted flour, and use only 1 cup of liquid instead of 2. *Yield: Approximately 1 cup.*

[2] See *Baked Oysters on Half Shells**.
[3] See *Chocolate Soufflé** for which a *Thick White Sauce** is the first step.

b. (*More than 2 cups liquid*)

Cream Gravy for Fried Chicken—Follow recipe for *White Sauce** making these changes: Substitute 2 tablespoons strained fat in which chicken was fried for butter or margarine and use 1¾ cups boiling, strained, fat-free chicken broth[4], or canned chicken consommé if broth is not available, plus ⅔ cup scalded milk and/or breakfast cream instead of 2 cups of liquid specified for *White Sauce**. *Yield: Approximately 2 cups.*

NOTE: 2⅓ cups scalded milk and/or breakfast cream may be substituted for the 1¾ cups chicken broth plus the ⅔ cup scalded milk and/or breakfast cream.

Maître d'Hôtel Sauce—Follow recipe for *White Sauce** making these changes: Substitute 2½ cups boiling strained meat or vegetable stock for 2 cups liquid specified for *White Sauce**. Stir 1 tablespoon of sauce into 1 well-beaten egg yolk and then blend mixture with remainder of sauce. Stir in 1 tablespoon lemon juice, 2 teaspoons finely minced parsley or 1 teaspoon dehydrated parsley flakes, and, if desired, salt and pepper to taste. *Yield: Approximately 1¾ cups.*

D. VARIATIONS THROUGH CHANGES IN PROCEDURE WITH IN SOME INSTANCES A FEW ADDITIONS

Yield for each of these recipes is the same as for *White Sauce** unless otherwise specified.

Brown Sauce—(just a *White Sauce** in a dark disguise)—Follow recipe for *White Sauce** making these changes. Melt fat in skillet over direct medium heat and let it cook until it begins to turn brown. Remove from stove and stir in flour. Return to heat, and, stirring constantly, cook until mixture (roux) is a rich, dark

[4] See *Chicken or Veal Broth**.

brown (don't cook long enough to burn, but on the other hand, don't settle for a pale beige). Do not use milk or cream for liquid; however, boiling water or bouillon[5] as well as *Beef Broth** or *Chicken or Veal Broth** may be used. *Yield: Approximately 1½ cups.*

Onion Brown Sauce—When preparing *Brown Sauce**, add 2 tablespoons minced onion, shallots, leeks, or chives to melted fat and cook 1 minute before adding flour.

Game Sauce (a *Brown Sauce** with a fruit flavor)—Follow recipe for *Brown Sauce**, making this change. Mix ¼ cup black seedless raspberry, blackberry, grape, or currant preserves or jelly with enough bouillon[5], *Beef Broth**, or *Chicken or Veal Broth** to make 1 cup and combine with additional cup of bouillon[5] or broth or 1 cup tawny port or claret. Bring to boiling point and use for liquid in *Brown Sauce.**

Game Sauce with Rum and Spice—Prepare *Game Sauce** and add ⅓ cup rum, ⅛ teaspoon each cloves, nutmeg, cinnamon, and, if desired, cardamon. Cook, stirring constantly, for 2 minutes. If you've used port or claret to make the *Game Sauce**, you'll find that either blends beautifully with the rum and spices. *Yield: Approximately 1⅔ cups.*

A la Turke Sauce—Prepare *Brown Sauce** or *Onion Brown Sauce**. Set aside. Sprinkle 16 small tender chicken livers with salt and pepper and mix with 16 button mushrooms. Heat ¼ cup butter or margarine to 360° F. Stir in livers and mushrooms. Cook 6 to 8 minutes, turning livers and mushrooms from time to time so they can brown on all sides. Lift livers and mushrooms from fat with slotted spoon and place on heated dish. Heat sauce and add livers and mushrooms. Continue cooking over very low heat, stirring occasionally, for 5 minutes. This is a perfect sauce for *Roast (Baked) Eggs**. *Serves 4.*

Mushroom Sauce (Brown)—Combine hot *Brown Sauce** or *Onion Brown Sauce** and ¾ cup hot sautéed fresh or canned

[5] See *Bouillon or Consommé** or use canned bouillon or the tablets.

mushroom pieces or slices. Cook for several minutes, stirring from time to time. *Serves 4.*

Oyster Sauce—Prepare 16 small *Poached Oysters**. Drain and reserve liquid. Combine oysters with ¼ cup cooked or canned mushroom buttons or pieces, if desired. Prepare *Brown Sauce** or *Onion Brown Sauce** using liquid drained from oysters as a substitute for liquid specified in *Brown Sauce** recipe. If needed to make up the 2 cups of liquid, the oyster "water" may be combined with broth. Combine sauce with oysters (and mushrooms, if they were used). Serve piping hot. *Serves 4.*

Sweet and Sour Sauce—Combine *Brown Sauce** or *Onion Brown Sauce** with 2 tablespoons brown or granulated white sugar and 2 tablespoons vinegar or lemon juice. Cook over low heat, stirring constantly, until thoroughly heated. This is particularly good with green beans or cabbage.

Tomato Sauce—Prepare *Brown Sauce** or *Onion Brown Sauce** substituting the following mixture for the liquids used in those sauces. Combine and bring to the boiling point:

1¼ cups tomato juice
¼ cup tomato ketchup
½ cup water or white or red wine
1 bay leaf
¼ teaspoon thyme
¼ teaspoon oregano
¼ teaspoon rosemary, if desired
1 teaspoon sugar if desired
1 tablespoon chopped green pepper, if desired
1 tablespoon minced parsley or 2 teaspoons dehydrated parsley flakes
2 tablespoons finely chopped celery or celery flakes, if desired
⅓ cup cooked or canned mushrooms, if desired

THE HOLLANDAISE FAMILY

As every working woman knows, there are those times when you want to (or have to) roll out the red carpet for a dinner guest or two or three, but you also have to be away from home 7 or 8 hours a day, so things get a little involved. Therefore, for those of us who lead a double life—gainfully employed outside the home and cook and chief bottle washer in it, "company" recipes that can be done either ahead of time or in just a few minutes are a real boon, particularly if it's something so festive as a *Hollandaise Sauce** that can, when necessary, be made in the morning, stored in the refrigerator until about 30 minutes before serving time, and then reheated. Furthermore, with slight changes the *Hollandaise Sauce** recipe contained in this book is the basis for 13 other sauces.

GENERAL RULES FOR
MAKING HOLLANDAISE SAUCE
OR ANY OF ITS VARIATIONS

1. Use a double boiler with an inset pan that has a rounded bottom so that it will be several inches above the hot water and the sauce will actually be cooked by steam.

2. Beat your egg yolks until they are very thick and lemon-colored, preferably with a food mixer, but, if you must, with a rotary egg beater.

3. Bring 1 inch of water in the bottom pan of the double boiler to a boil; then lower the heat to reduce the temperature to just below the boiling point so that not a single bubble shows on top of the water, and keep your heat constant.

4. Melt butter in inset pan of double boiler over the very hot water.

5. Stir constantly while adding first the eggs to the melted butter and then while adding the boiling—and it should be boiling— liquid to the egg and fat mixture. The eggs should be added in a very slow stream and from time to time the stream should be stopped so that the mixture in the inset pan can be stirred until it is as smooth as velvet before additional egg is added. Add the boiling liquid slowly, approximately a tablespoon at a time, blending the addition with the mixture in the pan before any more liquid is added. For the first 5 minutes after all liquid has been added, stir constantly. Then allow the sauce to cook over hot, but never boiling, water until the desired consistency is reached, stirring every 3 or 4 minutes.

6. When sauce reaches this desired consistency, remove from over hot water and stir in lemon juice, cayenne, and salt. Beat vigorously with a spoon or wire whip for ½ minute or 45 strokes.

7. Should you desire to store and then reheat the sauce, reheat in the same (cleaned, of course) double boiler, using 1 inch of very hot, but never bubbling, water in the bottom pan. Beat the sauce 45 strokes with a spoon or wire whip before putting the inset pan that contains the sauce over the hot water. This should be done at the very last minute. The food with which the sauce is served should be just as hot as possible and the sauce should be added when it is thoroughly warm.

8. If at any time during preparation or reheating the sauce starts to separate, beat vigorously with a rotary egg beater.

HOLLANDAISE SAUCE

6 tablespoons butter[6]
3 well-beaten egg yolks
⅝ cup boiling water, fish, meat, or chicken stock
1 tablespoon lemon juice
Cayenne pepper and salt to taste

Bring 1 inch of water to a boil in bottom pan of double boiler
whose inset pan has a rounded bottom that will not touch the
surface of the water, but will, in fact, be at least 3 or 4 inches
above it. Lower heat so that water is just below boiling point and
not a single bubble shows on top of water. Place butter in inset
pan and put pan over the very hot water. When fat is melted—
and don't jump the gun, wait until all of it is melted—add the
yolks in a thin, slow stream, stirring constantly and holding up
the stream from time to time so as to blend completely the yolks
and butter already in inset pan. After all of egg has been added,
very slowly, about a tablespoon at a time, add the boiling liquid,
continuing to stir so that the ingredients are completely blended
after each addition. For first 5 minutes after all the liquid has
been added, keep on stirring constantly. Then allow sauce to cook
until it reaches desired thickness, stirring every 3 to 4 minutes.
When sauce reaches proper consistency, remove from over hot
water, stir in lemon juice, cayenne, and salt. Beat vigorously with
wooden spoon or wire whip 45 strokes. *Yield: Approximately
⅞ cup.*

[6] Let the gourmets moan and groan, but if you're fresh out of butter,
margarine can be used, although the sauce will not reach the true perfection
of a *Hollandaise Sauce** made with butter.

SUGGESTED USES FOR
HOLLANDAISE SAUCE AND VARIATIONS

Serve with hot cooked artichokes, asparagus, butter or lima beans, green beans, green peas, grilled tomatoes, broccoli, cauliflower, or with poultry or seafood.

VARIATIONS ON A HOLLANDAISE SAUCE

Yield for each of these recipes is the same as for *Hollandaise Sauce** unlesss otherwise specified.

White Wine Hollandaise—Substitute ⅝ cup boiling white wine for ⅝ cup liquid specified in *Hollandaise Sauce**.

Béarnaise Sauce—Combine 2 tablespoons minced shallots, leeks, or chives, 2 tablespoons tarragon vinegar, and 2 tablespoons water or white wine. Bring to boil; then lower heat. Cook until mixture is reduced to 1 tablespoon. Prepare *Hollandaise Sauce** and after salt and pepper are added, stir in tarragon vinegar mixture and, if desired, ½ teaspoon fresh tarragon or ⅛ teaspoon dried tarragon. Then as directed in recipe for *Hollandaise Sauce**, beat vigorously with wooden spoon or wire whip for 45 strokes.

White Wine Béarnaise—Follow directions for preparing *Béarnaise Sauce**, using ⅝ cup boiling white wine for the ⅝ cup liquid used to make the *Hollandaise Sauce** that is the basis of the Béarnaise.

Herb Hollandaise—Follow recipe for *Hollandaise Sauce** making these changes: For the ⅝ cup boiling liquid, use 2 teaspoons Worcestershire sauce plus enough stock to make ½ cup liquid and 2 tablespoons water or sherry. Omit lemon juice and add: ¼ teaspoon turmeric and ¼ teaspoon cumin with salt and pepper.

Tomato Hollandaise—Follow recipe for *Hollandaise Sauce** substituting the following for the ⅝ cup liquid specified in that recipe. Combine, bring to a boil and strain:

¼ cup tomato juice
¼ cup broth
2 teaspoons ketchup
¼ teaspoon onion powder
2 tablespoons white wine, stock, bouillon,[7] or water
⅛ teaspoon oregano

Omit lemon juice, specified in *Hollandaise Sauce** recipe.

Chive Hollandaise—Add 1 tablespoon minced chives to *Hollandaise Sauce**.

Crab Meat Hollandaise or Béarnaise—Add ¾ cup hot cooked drained crab meat and, if desired, ¼ cup drained hot canned mushroom buttons, pieces, or slices to *Hollandaise Sauce** or *Béarnaise Sauce**. *Serves 4.*

Cucumber Hollandaise—Let 1 small, firm, unpeeled cucumber stand until room temperature; cut crosswise into ¼-inch slices and then cut slices into pieces about ¼ × ¼ × ⅛ inch. Combine pieces with *Hollandaise Sauce**. This sauce goes well with seafood. *Serves 4.*

Lobster Hollandaise or Béarnaise—Add ¾ cup hot cooked small lobster chunks and, if desired, ¼ cup canned drained hot mushroom buttons, pieces, or slices to *Hollandaise Sauce** or *Béarnaise Sauce**. *Serves 4.*

Mousseline Sauce—Just before serving, fold ⅓ cup stiffly whipped cream into *Hollandaise Sauce** or *Béarnaise Sauce**. *Yield: Approximately 1⅛ cups.*

[7] See *Bouillon or Consommé**.

Seafood Hollandaise—Prepare *Hollandaise Sauce** using fish stock as liquid. Just before serving, stir in the following:

⅓ cup hot cooked, shelled, deveined shrimp, cut in small
   segments
⅓ cup hot cooked crab meat
¼ cup hot drained cooked or canned mushroom buttons,
   slices, or pieces
12 small hot drained *Poached Oysters**

Serves 4.

Shrimp Hollandaise or Béarnaise—Add ¾ cup hot cooked, shelled, deveined shrimp, cut in ½-inch segments and, if desired, ¼ cup hot drained canned mushroom buttons, slices, or pieces to *Hollandaise Sauce** or *Béarnaise Sauce**. *Serves 4.*

Sour Cream Hollandaise or Béarnaise—Just before serving, fold ⅓ cup commercial sour cream into *Hollandaise Sauce** or *Béarnaise Sauce**. *Yield: Approximately 1⅛ cups.*

6

Soup

Soup can, and often does, set just the right touch with which to start the most formal and perfect of dinners; on the other hand, the hearty, "peasant" variety can make, with the possible addition of a few crackers or a slice or two of bread, a complete meal, which is both delicious and satisfying for a family.

For those of us who are too thrifty not to suffer when we have to throw away leftovers, many a dab of vegetable, either cooked or raw, or of rice, macaroni, noodles, and/or spaghetti can add just what is needed for a pot of soup.

There is nothing really difficult about making a good soup, but it takes time. Certainly this doesn't mean you are confined to the kitchen or even the house the entire time a broth is simmering, but you should plan to be available occasionally to skim off the foamy-looking scum that collects on top of the simmering soup. (And so that you will have your terminology straight, a *broth* is the thin liquid in which meat or chicken *with* vegetables was cooked, whereas a *stock* is the thin liquid in which meat, fish, chicken, *or* vegetables was cooked. *Bouillon* is clarified[1] brown beef broth and *consommé* is clarified[1] whitish chicken or veal broth.)

GENERAL RULES FOR MAKING SOUP

The quality of the soup is dependent on the broth and the quality of the broth is dependent on:

1. Not skimping on the quantity of meat or chicken. To make 2¼ quarts of a good brown beef broth, at least 1½ pounds of

[1] This is done with egg white and shell. See *Bouillon or Consommé*.

cracked shank bones and 4½ pounds of shank, brisket, or chuck should be used; to make the same quantity of chicken or veal broth, you need, respectively, at least a 5- to 6-pound stewing hen or veal knuckle. Remember, however, that for soup, the cheaper USDA Standard, Commercial, and Utility grades of beef and the USDA Standard, Utility, and Cull grades of veal are quite satisfactory and a stewing hen is usually much cheaper than a hen that is to be used for baking.

2. Preparing broth at least a day before it is used so that it can be stored in a covered bowl or carton in the refrigerator, thus permitting the fat to solidify on top so that it can be easily removed. The fat, however, should not be removed until just before the broth is used, since the solidified fat helps preserve the broth.

3. Sprinkling the meat or chicken very, very lightly with salt and, if desired, with pepper before cooking.

4. Cooking in a covered pot over quite low heat long enough and slow enough to get all flavor possible from the meat or chicken and vegetables and into the broth. This takes from 3¾ to 4¼ hours.

5. Skimming the scum from the surface of the broth from time to time during the entire cooking period.

6. Adding herbs such as bay leaf, celery seed, chervil, dill, fine herbes, marjoram, oregano, and thyme an hour before cooking time expires.

7. Adding salt and, if desired, pepper to season broth to taste during last 30 minutes of cooking. Since the liquid cooks down, adding seasoning, with the exception of the small quantity sprinkled on the meat or chicken, before the last 30 minutes of cooking may result in a salty broth or one with too much pepper.

Incidentally, it is not necessary to use all of the broth at one time or for any one kind of soup, and, if desired, different kinds of soup can be made from it if and when you wish. Furthermore, even though a great part of the flavor has been cooked out of the meat or chicken, don't waste either.[2]

BEEF BROTH

Marrow
1½ to 2 pounds cracked beef shank bones
4½ pounds (approximate) beef shank, chuck, or brisket
Salt and, if desired, pepper
14 cups water or 12 cups water and 2 cups dry white or red wine
¾ cup coarsely chopped onion or shallots
1¼ cups coarsely chopped celery
¾ cup scraped carrot, cut in ⅓-inch chunks
12 sprigs parsley
1 large or 2 small bay leaves
¼ teaspoon dried thyme and/or, if desired, ¼ teaspoon any or all of following: celery seed, chervil, dill, marjoram, oregano
Fine herbes, if desired
Salt and pepper to taste

Remove marrow from cracked beef shank bones. Cut beef into 2 equal parts and then cut 1 of these parts into small chunks. Very lightly sprinkle meat with salt and, if desired, pepper. Melt marrow in deep, heavy soup kettle or a frying pan. Add meat chunks and brown on all sides. If frying pan is used for browning, the chunks and as much marrow as possible should be placed in a deep, large heavy pot with lid when browning is completed. Add shank bones and remaining (uncooked) beef to browned meat and marrow. Cover with water or water and wine. Bring to a boil. Skim foamy scum from surface. Add vegetables and parsley. Again bring to boil. Reduce to very low heat. Cover pot or kettle and allow to simmer 2¾ to 3¼ hours, occasionally remov-

[2] See *Hash**.

ing scum from top of soup. Add bay leaf and desired herbs. Continue cooking over low heat 30 minutes. Season to taste with salt and pepper and allow to simmer 30 minutes more. Strain into large container. Cover and cool. Place in refrigerator so fat can solidify on top. When ready to use, remove fat from top. *Yield: Approximately 9 cups.*

CHICKEN OR VEAL BROTH

5- to 6-pound whole cleaned and dressed stewing hen or veal
    or calf knuckle with bone
Salt and white pepper
14 cups water or 12 cups water and 2 cups dry white wine
¾ cup coarsely cut shallots or leeks (if not available, use ½
    cup coarsely chopped onion)
1¼ cups coarsely chopped celery
¾ cup scraped carrot, cut in ⅓-inch chunks
12 sprigs parsley
1 large or 2 small bay leaves
¼ teaspoon thyme
Salt and white pepper to taste

NOTE: The only major difference between making *Beef Broth** and either of these broths is that for these two, marrow is not used and neither chicken nor veal is browned.

Lightly sprinkle hen or meat with salt and white pepper. Place in large heavy pot or soup kettle. Cover with water or water and wine. Bring to a boil. Skim foamy scum from surface. Add vegetables and parsley. Again bring to a boil and then reduce to very low heat. Cover pot or kettle and allow to simmer for 2¾ to 3¼ hours, removing scum from time to time. Add bay leaf or leaves and thyme and continue cooking over low heat for 30 minutes. Season to taste with salt and pepper. Again cover pan and cook 30 minutes more. Strain into large container. Cover and cool. Place in refrigerator so fat can solidify on top. When ready to use, remove fat from top. *Yield: Approximately 9 cups.*

BOUILLON OR CONSOMMÉ

2 egg whites
2 tablespoons water
9 cups (approximate) strained and fat-free *Beef Broth** for bouillon, or *Chicken or Veal Broth** for consommé
2 egg shells broken in pieces

Beat egg whites slightly and then combine and beat whites and water just until blended. Add to broth, from which solidified fat has been removed, with the pieces of shell. Heat, stirring until broth reaches boiling point. Cook at rapid boil for 2 minutes. Remove from heat and let stand, preferably in warm place, for 15 minutes. Strain through a fine sieve or through 3 layers of cheese-cloth. Serve hot. *Yield: Approximately 8 cups.*

VARIATIONS

Jellied Bouillon or Consommé—Soak 2 tablespoons unflavored gelatin in ½ cup water or dry white wine for 5 minutes. Pour 4 cups boiling *Bouillon or Consommé** over gelatin and stir until the latter is completely dissolved. Place in refrigerator and when firm, or at any time thereafter, spoon into 4 cups (bouillon cups preferably) and garnish with lemon slices. Serve at once.

Tomato Bouillon—Combine 4 cups of *Bouillon**[3] and 3 cups tomato juice. Bring to boiling point. Reduce heat, cover, and simmer 5 minutes. Season to taste with salt and pepper. Serve in 6 bouillon cups or, for informal meals, mugs, and, if desired, garnish with lemon slices.

Madrilene—Follow recipe for *Tomato Bouillon**, but use only 2¼ cups tomato juice and ¾ cup light dry sherry in place of 3 cups tomato juice.

[3] Canned bouillon may be used.

CHICKEN GUMBO

⅓ cup (approximate) margarine or butter
Salt and pepper
1 4½- to 5-pound cleaned, dressed disjointed hen
1 cup fresh or thawed frozen okra, cut in crosswise slices
¼ cup scraped and coarsely chopped celery
⅓ cup finely minced shallots, leeks, or onion
1½ cups (approximate) hot *Onion Brown Sauce** or *Tomato Sauce**
9 cups (approximate) fat-free chicken broth or consommé[4]
2 tablespoons minced parsley

Heat margarine or butter to 360° F. in skillet. While fat is heating, sprinkle salt and pepper lightly over chicken pieces. Brown chicken on all sides in hot fat and when browned set aside on warm plate. Stir okra into fat and when it begins to brown add celery and shallots, leeks, or onion. Okra should be stirred from time to time and if extra margarine or butter is needed while chicken or vegetables are cooking, it may be added. When okra is lightly browned, remove from heat. Put heated sauce in deep heavy pot or soup kettle and gradually stir in broth or consommé, which has been brought to a boil. Add chicken, vegetables, and parsley. Return to medium heat and bring to boil. Reduce heat, cover pan, and simmer until chicken is tender—about 2 hours—stirring from time to time. Should additional liquid be needed, broth or consommé or, if necessary, water may be added. Season to taste with salt and pepper. *Serves 10.*

[4] See *Chicken or Veal Broth** or *Bouillon or Consommé**.

BROTH AND VEGETABLE SOUP

6 cups fat-free *Beef Broth**, *Chicken or Veal Broth** or
   Bouillon or Consommé*[5]
1½ cups canned or stewed tomatoes
¼ cup ketchup, if desired
2 small raw potatoes, cut in ¾-inch cubes
½ cup scraped celery, cut in ½-inch pieces
2 medium-sized carrots, scraped and cut in thin slices
2½ cups of any combination of the following: beans (butter,
   green, or lima); tiny Brussels sprouts; shredded cabbage;
   small amount of cauliflower; corn kernels; thin slices okra;
   sliced or chopped onion, leeks, or shallots; green peas;
   sliced turnips
Salt and pepper, if desired

Bring broth, bouillon, or consommé, tomatoes, and, if desired, ketchup to boiling point. Add remaining ingredients with exception of salt and pepper. Again bring to boil; cover pan and reduce to low heat. Simmer for 15 minutes. Add salt and pepper to taste, if desired. Cover and continue cooking over low heat until vegetables are tender. *Serves 8.*

VARIATIONS

Corn Soup—Prepare *Broth and Vegetable Soup** making following changes: Omit potatoes and 2½ cups vegetables. Instead add to liquid kernels cut from 4 large ears corn and 4 cobs. Bring to boil; then reduce to low heat. Cover pan and simmer 15 minutes. Add salt and pepper to taste, and cook, still covered, 10 minutes more. Remove cobs and serve.

[5] Canned bouillon or consommé may be substituted.

Thick Old-fashioned Vegetable Soup—Prepare *Broth and Vegetable Soup**, substituting 2 medium-sized (peeled, boiled) potatoes that have been mashed and then put through sieve for 2 small, raw cubed potatoes. Add mashed potato to liquid and stir until well blended before adding other vegetables.

CHICKEN AND NOODLE SOUP

8 cups fat-free boiling chicken broth or consommé[6]
1 tablespoon minced parsley
1 tablespoon minced chives, leeks, shallots, or onion, if desired
2 tablespoons minced celery, if desired
1 cup noodles
Salt and pepper, white preferably, if needed

Combine boiling liquid with parsley, and chives, leeks, shallots, or onion, and celery (if desired). Add noodles and cook over medium heat for 15 minutes. Season to taste with salt and pepper. *Serves 6.*

VARIATIONS

Chicken and Noodle Soup with Cream—Prepare *Chicken and Noodle Soup** and just before serving, add 1 cup scalded breakfast cream to piping hot soup. Stir until blended and serve at once. *Serves 8.*

Chicken and Rice Soup—Follow recipe for preparing *Chicken and Noodle Soup** with these changes: Substitute ⅓ cup raw rice for noodles and after rice is added cook in covered pan over medium heat 25 to 30 minutes until cereal is tender. *Serves 6.*

[6] See *Chicken or Veal Broth** or *Bouillon or Consommé**.

CREAM OF VEGETABLE SOUP

1 cup (approximate) hot *Thick White Sauce**
2⅓ cups boiling *Beef Broth*, Chicken or Veal Broth*,
    Bouillon or Consommé**
1 cup scalded milk and/or breakfast cream
1¼ cups hot, drained, and cooked pulp (which has been put
    through a sieve) of any one of following vegetables:
    asparagus; carrots; cauliflower; celery; corn; mushrooms;
    peas; potatoes; spinach; tomatoes
Salt and pepper to taste
⅛ teaspoon nutmeg, if desired

Remove sauce from heat and blend with broth, bouillon, or consommé. Then stir in scalded milk and/or cream. Return to medium
heat and stir until soup begins to thicken. Remove from heat and
stir in vegetable pulp. Cook over very low heat for 20 minutes,
stirring from time to time. Season to taste with salt and pepper
and, if desired, add nutmeg. *Serves 6.*

VARIATIONS

Cream of Chicken Soup—Follow recipe for *Cream of Vegetable
Soup** making these changes: Use chicken broth or consommé and
the 1 cup milk and/or cream as liquid; substitute ½ cup ground
or finely minced cooked chicken for vegetables. Just before seasoning with salt and pepper, stir 1 tablespoon hot soup into 2
slightly beaten egg yolks and, when blended, stir mixture into
remainder of soup. Omit nutmeg.

Cream of Shrimp Soup—Follow recipe for *Cream of Vegetable
Soup** using boiling fish stock and the 1 cup milk and/or cream as
liquid; substitute 1 cup ground, boiled, shelled, and deveined
shrimp and ⅔ cup raw, shelled, and deveined shrimp, cut in ½-
inch segments for vegetables. Omit nutmeg.

POTATO SOUP

2 tablespoons butter or margarine
½ cup chopped leeks, shallots, or onion
3¾ cups boiling chicken broth or consommé[7]
5 cups raw peeled potato, sliced very thin[8]
1¾ cups equal parts scalded milk and breakfast cream (half
  and half may be used)
¼ teaspoon nutmeg
Salt and pepper (white, if possible), if desired
Minced chives or parsley, if desired

Melt fat and heat until it bubbles (360° F.). Add leeks, shallots, or onion. Brown lightly, stirring from time to time. Add broth or consommé and potatoes. Cook over low heat 35 to 40 minutes, stirring occasionally. Mash entire mixture through fine sieve and then stir in milk and cream and nutmeg. Season to taste with salt and pepper if desired. Bring to boil; reduce heat and simmer 3 to 4 minutes. Strain. If desired, garnish with minced chives or parsley. *Serves 8.*

VARIATIONS

Potato Tomato Soup—Follow recipe for *Potato Soup** substituting 1 cup boiling tomato juice and ¾ cup scalded breakfast cream for the 1¾ cups milk and cream. Serve hot or cold. If cold, chill at least 4 to 5 hours in refrigerator.

Vichyssoise—Prepare *Potato Soup** preferably with leeks. Chill 4 to 5 hours. Just before serving, fold in ¾ cup stiffly whipped cream. *Serves 9.*

[7] See *Chicken or Veal Broth** or *Bouillon or Consommé**.
[8] Unless you have some special slicing device, this is most easily done with vegetable parer.

7
Roasted Food

Faced with the necessity of feeding from 2 to 10 people on any day when I feel like doing practically nothing, I have found a way to have my cake and eat it too. I serve a roast of beef, lamb, pork, or veal, which looks like a lot of work, but involves at the most 15 minutes of very light labor on my part.

First, of course, the approximate time it will take the roast to cook must be calculated, but even a bad mathematician can do this in a couple of minutes. Then I preheat the oven for 10 minutes. During this time, I sprinkle the meat with salt and pepper, insert the thermometer, place the meat on a rack in my roasting pan, and since this takes about 10 minutes, I am ready to pop the meat into the oven. Then I'm free to fry other fish—at home or where I please—for at least an hour and a quarter, even if I'm cooking a small rare beef roast. Of course, if it's a larger piece of beef or if it's lamb, pork, or veal, I have a much longer vacation from the kitchen. I check the thermometer 20 or 30 minutes before the estimated cooking time expires, and if the meat isn't done—and I really don't expect it to be done—I repeat the checking at frequent intervals until it's ready.

Since a roast should stand, if you are to carve to the maximum advantage, for about 15 minutes after it comes out of the oven, during this period, I prepare a *Tomato Bouillon** or *Madrilene**, using canned bouillon if necessary, or a simple fruit cocktail, open a can or two of vegetables or cook a package or two of the frozen ones, heat French bread or rolls, make coffee, and top off the meal with fruit and cheese or ice cream (either homemade[1] or bought), which I usually keep in the freezer.

[1] See *Country Custard Ice Cream** and *Top of the Stove Custard—Frozen**.

The roast, however, is the *pièce de résistance* and the thing that makes it possible for you to loaf while dinner cooks. A ham can be baked with just as little trouble unless you want to serve it with a glaze, which will take a few minutes more of your time.

There's a bit more trouble involved in roasting poultry or fish, particularly if a stuffing is made, but you certainly don't have to spend a day in the kitchen to cook either fish or fowl.

As for baked (roast) vegetables, it's a matter of putting them into a pan, then putting the pan into the oven, and letting the vegetables alone until the estimated cooking time is nearly expired. Once roasted, the corn does have to be husked and the onions peeled, but this is quickly and easily done and of course it's only a matter of seconds to add melted fat and sprinkle with salt and, if desired, pepper.

GENERAL RULES FOR ROASTING MEATS

ROAST BEEF — ROAST LAMB — ROAST PORK (FRESH) — ROAST PORK (CURED OR SMOKED) — ROAST VEAL

1. Allow for each serving: meat with bone—½ to ⅔ pound; boneless—⅓ to ½ pound. If you live alone or if there are only 2 or 3 people in your family, there is no reason you can't have roasts, since leftover meat can be sliced and meal-sized portions packed into heavy plastic bags. The meat can then be frozen for use whenever desired.

2. *If Gourmet Touch is desired* (and this is certainly no necessity) about 6 hours before cooking, place meat in deep bowl and brush all surfaces liberally with French dressing, made with either lemon or vinegar, or with a light white wine or claret, or with vinegar. If wine is used, pour an additional cupful over meat. Store in refrigerator and several times during storage period turn meat. When ready to use, pat dry with absorbent paper napkins or towels. This will help ensure a more tender and juicier roast.

3. Meat may be taken directly from refrigerator, or allowed to stand at room temperature until it loses chill, or taken directly from freezer for roasting. I prefer, on the basis of long experience, to let the meat stand until it loses chill. If frozen meat is roasted without first being thawed, allow an extra 10 to 15 minutes per pound, depending on thickness of cut.

4. Preheat oven 10 minutes to 325° F.

5. While oven is preheating, season meat:

(a) If you want *GARLIC-FLAVORED ROAST* make 8 to 12 slits in top of roast, number depending on size of roast. The slits, which should be approximately ⅓ inch long×⅓ inch deep, should be cut with a thin, sharp knife and should be at least 1¼ inches apart. Peel garlic cloves—number depending on number of slits—and cut small cloves into 2 parts and large cloves into 3 parts. Insert 1 piece of garlic into each slit. If you like only a faint flavor of garlic in your meat, remove garlic from slits with point of sharp knife after meat has roasted 1 to 1¼ hours; if you want a strong garlic flavor, don't remove garlic until meat is taken from oven.

(b) Sprinkle meat (smoked or salted excepted, of course) with salt and, if desired, with pepper so that entire surface is lightly and evenly covered. If you wish to measure, allow ⅓ to ½ teaspoon salt per pound, according to your taste, and ⅛ teaspoon pepper per pound.

6. Place a meat rack in bottom pan of roaster or on large shallow pan with 1- to 2-inch rim (cooky sheet with rim will do). Put meat on rack, fat side up. If it is a matter of necessity, the meat may be roasted without a rack, but it will cook resting in its own melted fat and results are superior when a rack is used.

7. If meat is not frozen, insert point of thermometer in side of roast at thickest part of meat that is free from bone, fat, and/or gristle and as near the center of the side as possible.

There may be thicker parts where if the thermometer were inserted it would touch bone or gristle or rest in fat, and, therefore, these places would be entirely unsatisfactory as "sites" for the insertion of the thermometer. The thermometer should be pushed into the meat so that about ¾ of the stem is in the roast and the base of dial, from which temperatures are read, is about 1 inch from surface.

If meat is frozen, do not insert thermometer until half of cooking time has expired.

8. Cook until thermometer registers the internal temperature at which meat should be removed from oven, as shown on the following chart. This chart also shows (1) length of time various cuts of varying weights should be cooked before it is necessary to check thermometer (this will free you from the kitchen during this time, since there is no reason for anyone to stand around the kitchen opening and closing an oven door while meat roasts) and (2) the entire estimated cooking time, just in case something happens to your meat thermometer at the last minute, but never forget this is just an educated guess at best and without a thermometer you can never be really sure that the desired degree of doneness has been reached or that the meat has not been overcooked, inasmuch as there are many factors, including the internal temperature of the meat when it is put in the oven, its shape, and the fat covering, involved in the time required to cook a piece of meat.

INTERNAL TEMPERATURE AND TIME CHART FOR ROASTING VARIOUS CUTS OF MEAT

REMOVE FROM OVEN WHEN THERMOMETER REGISTERS:

	RARE	MEDIUM	WELL DONE
BEEF	140° F. (1 to 13 pounds) 130° F. (13 pounds or more)	160° F. (1 to 9 pounds) 150° F. (9 pounds or more)	170° F. (only roasts weighing 8 pounds or less should be cooked to this stage)

	RARE	MEDIUM	WELL DONE
LAMB		175° F. (leg only)	180° F. (leg, if desired, and crown and shoulder roasts)
PORK (FRESH)			187° F. (pork must be cooked until well done)
PORK (CURED)			
Pre- and Fully Cooked Hams and Picnics			130° F.
Raw Ham			160° F.
Raw Picnic			170° F.
VEAL			180° F.

VARIOUS CUTS AND VARYING WEIGHTS (in lbs.)	CHECK THERMOMETER AFTER MEAT HAS COOKED (time in hours)	TOTAL ESTIMATED COOKING TIME (in hours)

BEEF

	rare	medium	well done	rare	medium	well done
Ribs with bone						
4½	1½	1¾	2⅙	1⅚	2⅓	2⅔
5	1⅔	2	2½	2⅙	2½	3
6	2¹⁄₁₀	2½	3	2⅔	3	3½
7	2½	3	3½	3	3½	4
8	2⅚	3½	4⅙	3⅓	4	4⅔
9	3⅓	4	—	3⅚	4½	—
10	3¾	4½	—	4¼	5	—

	rare	medium	well done	rare	medium	well done
13	4½	5	—	5	5½	—
15	4½	4¾	—	4¾	5¼	—
Rump						
4 to 5	2	2½	2¾	2¼	2¾	3
Top or bottom						
Round or						
sirloin tip						
4 to 5	1¾	2¼	2¾	2	2½	3

LAMB

	rare	medium	well done	rare	medium	well done
leg						
5	—	2⅙	2⅔	—	2⅔	3⅙
6	—	2⅔	3¼	—	3⅙	3¾
7	—	3¼	3⅔	—	3¾	4⅓
crown						
4¾ to 5¼	—	—	3¼	—	—	3¾
shoulder						
(with bone)						
3½ to 3¾	—	—	2¼	—	—	2¾
4 to 4¾	—	—	2¾	—	—	3¼
shoulder—bone-						
less and rolled						
3	—	—	1¾	—	—	2¼
4	—	—	2¼	—	—	2⅔

PORK (FRESH) (Must always be cooked through)

	rare	medium	well done	rare	medium	well done
leg (fresh ham)						
9	—	—	4¾	—	—	5¼
10	—	—	5	—	—	5½
12	—	—	6⅙	—	—	6⅔
15	—	—	6½	—	—	7
loin or rib end						
3½	—	—	2¼	—	—	2¾
5	—	—	2½	—	—	3
7	—	—	2⅔	—	—	3¼
10	—	—	3⅙	—	—	3⅔

	rare	medium	well done	rare	medium	well done
Boston butt or picnic						
(Bone-In)						
5½	—	—	3¾	—	—	4¼
6½	—	—	4¼	—	—	4⅔
8	—	—	4½	—	—	5
(Boneless)						
4	—	—	3	—	—	3½
5	—	—	3⅔	—	—	4⅙
6	—	—	4¼	—	—	4⅔

PORK (CURED OR SMOKED)[2]

	rare	medium	well done	rare	medium	well done
pre- or fully cooked hams						
6 to 8	—	—	1¾	—	—	2¼
10	—	—	2	—	—	2½
12	—	—	2½	—	—	3
15	—	—	3	—	—	3½
18	—	—	3½	—	—	4
20	—	—	3⅔	—	—	4¼
raw ham						
6 to 8	—	—	2¾	—	—	3¼
10	—	—	3	—	—	3½
12	—	—	3½	—	—	4
15	—	—	4	—	—	4½
18	—	—	4½	—	—	5
20	—	—	5	—	—	5½
pre- and fully cooked picnic						
4	—	—	1¼	—	—	1¾
6	—	—	1¾	—	—	2¼
8	—	—	2¼	—	—	2¾
10	—	—	2¾	—	—	3¼
raw picnic						
4	—	—	2	—	—	2½
6	—	—	2½	—	—	3
8	—	—	3½	—	—	4
10	—	—	4	—	—	4½

[2] See *To Glaze Roast Cured or Smoked Pork*.

VEL

	rare	medium	well done	rare	medium	well done
rump or round						
5	—	—	3	—	—	3½
6	—	—	3½	—	—	4
7	—	—	3¾	—	—	4¼
8	—	—	4	—	—	4½
shoulder with bone						
4¾ to 5	—	—	3⅙	—	—	3⅔
6 to 7	—	—	3⅓	—	—	3¾
shoulder boned and rolled						
4 to 5	—	—	3	—	—	3½
6	—	—	3½	—	—	4

9. When roast reaches desired degree of doneness, remove pan from oven and lift meat out of pan—on the rack if one was used. Place meat on platter or tray with rim, as some of the juices will run out of meat. Let roast stand for at least 15 minutes before carving, if at all possible, as meat will cut to better advantage when slightly cooled.

10. If gravy is desired, prepare as soon as meat is removed from pan.

FOR UNTHICKENED GRAVY

Stir 1½ to 1⅔ cups boiling water or water and wine, quantity depending on amount of fat drippings, into drippings in bottom of pan. If needed, add salt and pepper to taste. It is possible that additional boiling water may have to be added to drippings if gravy is too salty. Heat thoroughly before serving. *Yield: 1½ to 1⅔ cups gravy.*

FOR THICKENED GRAVY

Measure 1 tablespoon all purpose flour, sift into a small skillet, and cook over medium heat, stirring constantly, until a rich brown; however, don't overcook. Blend 2 tablespoons water with browned flour and beat until smooth. Stir 1½ cups boiling water into fat drippings in roasting pan and then blend ½ cup of this mixture with browned flour mixture gradually, stirring until smooth. Combine with remainder of water and drippings mixture. Cook over medium heat, stirring constantly, until desired thickness is reached. Season to taste with salt and pepper. Heat thoroughly before serving. *Yield: Approximately 1 cup.*

11. If there is an emergency and the serving of a meal must be delayed for a short time, this is no cause for any concern about the roast (even a rare beef). When the meat thermometer registers 10° below a reading that would indicate the desired degree of doneness has been reached, or, if you are not using a thermometer, when all but about 15 to 20 minutes of the estimated cooking time has elapsed, pull roast out of oven and place pan in a warm (not hot) spot. When the emergency is over, the roast may be returned to the oven. Because the meat will have cooled somewhat while standing out of the oven, the total cooking time will be slightly longer than if the meat had not been removed from the stove— just how much longer will depend on several factors, so an exact time cannot be specified; however, the roast will not be hurt and a short wait is certainly better than ruining a good roast.

12. To summarize: BRIEF RECIPE FOR ROAST BEEF— ROAST LAMB—ROAST PORK (FRESH, CURED, OR SMOKED)—ROAST VEAL. Let meat stand at room temperature until it loses chill.[3] Preheat oven 10 minutes to 325° F. Sprinkle meat, smoked or salted excepted, so that it is evenly and lightly covered with salt and, if desired, with pepper.[4] Place it, fat side up,

[3] If frozen meat is to be cooked, see Sections 3 and 7 of foregoing.
[4] If garlic flavor is desired, see Section 5 of foregoing.

on rack resting in bottom pan of roaster or on large shallow pan. Insert thermometer in meat. Place pan in oven. When roast reaches desired degree of doneness—see Section 8 of foregoing for estimated cooking times—remove pan from oven and lift meat out of pan.

ROAST POULTRY

There are only a few major differences between the methods for roasting poultry and meat. Of course, for best results, the poultry should be stuffed and it is advisable to brush the breast and sides of a capon, chicken, or turkey with salad oil or melted butter or margarine, but the other differences are really minor.

GENERAL RULES FOR ROASTING POULTRY

ROAST CAPON—ROAST CHICKEN—ROAST DUCK
ROAST GOOSE—ROAST TURKEY

1. For each serving, allow ½ to ⅔ pound. Leftovers can be sliced, packed in meal-sized portions into heavy plastic bags, and frozen for use when desired, or the whole carcass may be covered with aluminum foil and placed in the refrigerator for use within the next day or so.

2. Frozen poultry should be completely defrosted before it is cooked; on the other hand, if using fowl that has not been frozen, after feathers have been plucked and entrails removed, it should be refrigerated at least 6 hours.

3. Wipe inside and outside of bird with cloth or paper towels before seasoning, and if the poultry is to be brushed with an alcoholic spirit, it should be wiped before spirit is applied.

4. *For the Gourmet Touch,* 6 hours before roasting, if you desire, brush inside and outside of fowl with sherry. Store in refrigerator and several times during the period before bird is cooked, repeat brushing with spirit. (This is an added touch to ensure a juicier and more tender fowl, but is certainly not a must.)

5. According to your desires, poultry may be taken from refrigerator just before roasting or allowed to stand at room temperature until it loses chill. I prefer the latter, but do whatever is more convenient for you.

6. Preheat oven 10 minutes to 325° F.

7. Rub body and neck cavities lightly with salt and, if desired, with pepper; lightly sprinkle back, wings, and legs with seasoning and then liberally sprinkle breast. If you prefer to measure, use ¼ to ⅓ teaspoon salt (according to taste) and ⅛ teaspoon pepper per pound.

8. Fill body and neck cavities with stuffing of your choice. Stuffings baste the poultry from the inside and using one results in a more moist and tender bird. The stuffing should be loosely packed into the cavities as it will expand while cooking. If you don't have time or inclination to make one of the traditional stuffings (*see Stuffings [or Dressings]**) you can use either of the following, allowing ½ cup for each pound of poultry:

APPLE AND CELERY STUFFING

Combine:

  2 parts cored peeled cooking apples, cut in eighths and, if desired, brushed with honey, sugar and water syrup or artificial sweetener
  1 part scraped, coarsely cut celery
  For each 4 cups apple and celery used, stir in: 2 tablespoons minced onion
  1 tablespoon pineapple juice, apricot nectar, wine, brandy, rum, or Cointreau

SWEET POTATO STUFFING

For each 2½ cups peeled, cooked, and well-mashed sweet potato, add and mix well:

¼ cup white or brown sugar
½ teaspoon each: cloves, nutmeg, cinnamon
2 tablespoons melted butter or margarine
⅓ cup canned drained pineapple chunks
½ cup toasted almond slivers or pecan pieces, if desired
½ cup raisins that have been simmered in water or water and
    sauterne until they puffed (5 to 8 minutes), if desired
⅓ cup of any of the following: pineapple or orange juice,
    apricot nectar, almond Marsala wine, sherry, rum, brandy,
    or Cointreau

9. When the neck cavity has been loosely filled, fasten neck skin to back with skewer or if skewer is not available, close cavity by sewing skin of neck to skin of back with coarse thread. If there is band of skin at tail end, the body cavity may be closed after it also has been loosely filled by pushing the ends of the legs through this band; if there is no band of skin, close opening by sewing with coarse thread or skewer the skin around the opening together and then skewer or sew this skin to tail, if it has not been removed. After this is done, tie ends of legs together with thread or skewers.

10. If there are wing tips, lift them up and over so that the back of the bird rests on them.

11. For Capon, Chicken, and Turkey Only. Brush breast and sides with salad oil or melted butter or margarine. For 4- to 8-pound capon or chicken, use 2 to 4 tablespoons (liquid) fat; for 8- to 12-pound turkey, use ½ cup fat: for 13- to 15-pound turkey, use ¾ cup fat; for 16- to 22-pound turkey, use ⅞ to 1⅛ cups fat.

12. Place meat rack in bottom of roaster or on large shallow pan with 1- to 2-inch rim. Place bird, breast side up, on rack.

13. If using a meat thermometer, insert point either inside the thigh where meat is thickest and also where thermometer is next to body or in thickest part of breast. Do not allow to touch bone.

14. For Capon, Chicken, or Turkey Only. Loosely cover with a tent of aluminum foil.

15. Place in oven.

16. For Duck or Goose Only. Remove fat from bottom of pan at frequent intervals either by using a spoon with a long handle or by using a basting syringe.

17. If using thermometer, when it registers 175° F., remove aluminum tent from capon, chicken, or turkey. If not using thermometer, remove "tent" 20 to 25 minutes before estimated cooking time expires.

18. If bird is not the rich dark brown you desire, 15 minutes before estimated cooking time expires, brush with Kitchen Bouquet or *HONEY GLAZE,* made by mixing 2 tablespoons strained honey and 1 teaspoon Kitchen Bouquet. Return poultry to oven to complete cooking.

19. Cook until thermometer shows an internal temperature of 187° F. ESTIMATED COOKING TIMES FOR BIRDS of various kinds and weights are:

	Pounds	*Hours*
Capon	5 to 6¼	2½ to 3¼
	6½ to 8	3½ to 4½
Chicken	4 to 5	2½ to 3
	5¼ to 6½	3¼ to 4
Duck	3½ to 4	2 to 2¼
	4¼ to 5¼	2⅓ to 3¼
Goose	9 to 11	3¼ to 3¾
	11¼ to 13	4 to 5
Turkey	8 to 10	3 to 3½
	10 to 14	3½ to 4
	14 to 18	4 to 4½
	18 to 20	4½ to 5
	20 to 22	5 to 6

As further checks for doneness, place paper or cloth between thumb and index finger, being careful that the ends of the fingers are well protected, and then press the meat at the thickest part of the drumstick between the protected thumb and forefinger to ascertain if soft. Also, check to see if drumstick can be easily moved up and down, using care not to break it off from the body.

20. If gravy is desired, follow directions in Step 10 of *Roast Beef—Roast Lamb—Roast Pork (Fresh)—Roast Pork (Cured or Smoked)—Roast Veal (General Rules for Roasting Meats)**.

21. Let poultry stand from 15 to 45 minutes after it is removed from oven, depending on size, so that it can be carved to best advantage.

22. To summarize: BRIEF RECIPE FOR: ROAST CAPON—ROAST CHICKEN—ROAST TURKEY: Wipe inside and outside of bird with cloth or paper towels. Preheat oven to 325° F. for 10 minutes. Rub body and neck cavities lightly with salt and, if desired, with pepper; lightly sprinkle back, wings, and legs with seasoning and liberally sprinkle breast. Fill cavities with desired stuffing.[5] Brush breast and sides with salad oil, melted butter, or margarine. Place, breast side up, on rack in bottom of roaster or large shallow pan. If using meat thermometer, insert in thickest part of either breast or thigh, next to body if thigh site is used. Loosely cover bird with tent of aluminum foil. Place in oven. Remove foil 20 or 25 minutes before estimated cooking time expires—see Section 17. When desired degree of doneness is reached (187° F.), if possible, remove pan from oven and let stand 15 to 45 minutes, depending on size.

BRIEF RECIPE FOR: ROAST DUCK—ROAST GOOSE: Follow instructions given in *Brief Recipe for: Roast Capon—Roast Chicken—Roast Turkey** with these exceptions: (1) do not brush with fat; (2) do not cover with aluminum foil; (3) remove fat from bottom of pan at frequent intervals while bird is roasting.

[5] See *Apple and Celery Stuffing**, *Sweet Potato Stuffing**, or *Stuffings (or Dressings)**.

GENERAL RULES FOR ROASTING OR BAKING FISH

CATFISH—FLOUNDER—HERRING—MACKEREL—POMPANO—
REDFISH—SALMON—SHAD—STURGEON—TROUT—TUNA—
WHITEFISH

1. For each serving, figure ½ to ⅔ pound dressed (scales and entrails removed) whole fish and ⅓ to ½ pound fillets or steaks.

2. Refrigerate fish until just before cooking time.

3. Wash fish and pat dry.

4. Preheat oven for 10 minutes to 350° F. (this is 25° higher than oven temperature when cooking meat or fowl).

5. Sprinkle entire surface lightly with salt, and, if desired, with white pepper, although in an emergency the black variety may be used. If you prefer to measure, use ⅓ to ½ teaspoon, depending on your taste, salt and ⅛ teaspoon pepper per pound.

6. Brush fish liberally with melted butter or margarine.

7. Line bottom of roasting pan or large shallow pan with 1-inch rim with aluminum foil. Use enough foil so that when fish is done, it can be removed without difficulty from pan by grasping the foil on each side of fish and lifting foil and fish from pan. (No rack is used for fish.)

8. Place fish on foil and arrange a "tent" of aluminum foil over fish. Completely enclose the fish in foil by pressing together edges of the bottom of the "tent" and edges of foil on which fish rests.

9. Put fish into oven.

10. Since no thermometer is used when cooking fish, test for doneness by lifting off tent and pulling off a small amount of the fish with a fork. If it is firm and yet flakes easily, fish is ready to eat. Estimated cooking times are

Whole Fish	Minutes per pound 15 to 18
Fillets	Total cooking time 18 to 22 minutes
Steaks	30 to 45 minutes

11. If fish is not done when tested, replace foil tent and continue cooking until it is done.

12. As soon as fish is done, remove tent, and lift fish by holding foil on which it rests with both hands—one on each side—and either turning fish out on hot platter or arranging it on foil on which it was baked on the platter. It is suggested that the hands be protected with pot holders or kitchen mittens.

13. *For a Gourmet Touch,* if you wish, as soon as fish is transferred to platter, sprinkle the fish liberally with hot, but not boiling, dry white wine or sherry.

14. Serve at once, either as is, or with hot melted butter or commercial sour cream that has been heated over hot but not boiling water just until it is warm. If you wish, add chopped chives or parsley to taste to butter or cream. Or if you prefer, instead of butter or cream, serve with *White Sauce** or *Hollandaise Sauce** or any desired variation of either.

VARIATIONS

Fish Baked on Bed of Vegetables and Herbs—Before placing fish on foil in baking pan, combine the following and arrange in a bed about the size of the fish on foil: 3 parts coarsely chopped celery; 1 part coarsely chopped parsley; 1 tablespoon minced onion for each cup celery; ¼ teaspoon sweet basil and ¼ teaspoon thyme for each cup celery. Place fish on herb bed and cover with foil "tent."

Stuffed Baked Fish—Before fish is seasoned with salt, loosely fill (about ⅔ full) cavity of whole fish with stuffing of your choice—see *Stuffings (or Dressings)**. Close opening by sewing edges together with coarse thread. If you wish, fish may be baked on bed of vegetables and herbs—see *Fish Baked on Bed of Vegetables and Herbs**.

Baked Fish Creole—Prepare *Tomato Sauce**. Combine with an equal amount of water or white wine. Use at least 2 layers of heavy duty aluminum foil to cover bottom of pan. After fish is placed in pan, spoon diluted sauce over it and instead of using a tent of the foil over the fish, completely cover the top of the pan with foil. It is advisable when fish is done to spoon as much of the gravy as possible into a receptacle and then when fish is in the platter to pour the gravy over it.

Baked Fish Creole with Crab Meat and/or Shrimp—Prepare *Baked Fish Creole** and when fish is done spoon gravy into pot. Add 1 cup cooked crab meat and 1 cup cooked, shelled, and deveined shrimp to the gravy or 2 cups of the crab meat or 2 cups of the shrimp. Heat thoroughly and pour over fish in platter.

ROAST (BAKED) EGGS

1. Allow 2 eggs for each serving.

2. Preheat oven to 325° F. for 10 minutes.

3. Grease individual baking dish(es), preferably large enough for 2 eggs. For 6 or more eggs, a large greased very shallow baking dish may be substituted for the individual dishes.

4. While eggs are still cold, break into baking dish. If convenient, let stand until chill is off eggs.

5. Sprinkle with salt and pepper to taste.

6. Place in oven.

7. Cook until whites set (they should no longer be transparent); yolks should still be runny, however. Cooking time will vary according to how cold eggs are when placed in oven and how thin the whites have spread out in baking dish. Allow approximately 6 to 10 minutes for eggs cooked in individual baking dish and approximately 15 to 20 minutes for eggs cooked in large baking dish.

8. If desired, top eggs with hot *White Sauce** or *Hollandaise Sauce** or any desired variation of either. Particularly recommended are *White Wine Sauce**, *Artichoke Sauce**, *Cheese Sauce**, *Crab Meat Sauce**, *Lobster Sauce**, *Shrimp Sauce**, *A la Turke Sauce**, *Tomato Sauce**.

If there is no time to make above-mentioned sauces, the following is suggested:

KETCHUP SAUCE FOR EGGS

For each egg, combine and bring just to boiling point:

    1 tablespoon tomato ketchup
    1 teaspoon Worcestershire sauce
    1 tablespoon water or sherry
    Tabasco sauce to taste, if desired

Serve both eggs and sauce piping hot.

GENERAL RULES FOR ROASTING OR BAKING VEGETABLES

CORN—ONIONS—SWEET POTATOES—WHITE
POTATOES—SQUASH—TOMATOES

1. Preheat oven for 10 minutes to 400° F.

2. With the exception of washing in lukewarm water, drying by draining, and then patting with paper towels, roast vegetables in the state that they come from the fields, that is, in their jackets, skins, or husks.

3. Place in open roaster pan—neither rack nor thermometer is used.

4. Put pan in preheated oven.

5. Cook from 40 to 60 minutes, depending on size of vegetable, until the vegetable tests done. The test is made by plunging a wire cake tester into the center of the vegetable and when it can be pushed through without effort the vegetable is ready to eat.

6. Remove from oven and prepare for table. The husks and silk should be removed from the corn; the onions should be peeled; the white potatoes cut; the squash cut and any seeds and fibers removed, and the tomatoes halved.

7. Sprinkle vegetables, with the exception of sweet potatoes, with salt and, if desired, with pepper, and brush or top with butter or margarine.

ROAST CORN

For each serving:

    1 large or 2 medium ears corn
    1 tablespoon melted butter or margarine
    Salt and, if desired, pepper to taste

Roast corn in its husks, according to *General Rules for Roasting or Baking Vegetables** until wire cake tester can be inserted through husks and pushed through niblets up to the cob without effort. Remove husks and silk. Brush niblets with melted fat and sprinkle to taste with salt, and, if desired, with pepper.

ROAST (WHITE) ONIONS

For each serving:

    1 large or 2 medium white onions
    1 tablespoon melted butter or margarine
    Salt and, if desired, pepper to taste

Roast onions without peeling according to *General Rules for Roasting or Baking Vegetables**. When wire tester can be pushed with ease through onion, it is ready to eat. Remove from oven and holding it gently with fork, cut away roots and skin with sharp knife. Brush with melted butter or margarine and sprinkle with salt and, if desired, with pepper.

ROAST OR BAKED SWEET POTATO

For each serving:

    1 large or medium sweet potato, according to appetite
    Butter or margarine, if desired

Roast potato in jacket according to *General Rules for Roasting or Baking Vegetables**. Test for doneness with wire tester and when it can be easily pushed through jacket and pulp (from 40 to 60 minutes) potato is ready. Serve at once in jacket with, if desired, butter or margarine (preferably in side dish).

ROAST OR BAKED WHITE POTATO

For each serving:

    1 medium or large white mealy potato
    Salt and pepper, if desired, to taste
    1 tablespoon butter or margarine

Roast potato in jacket according to *General Rules for Roasting or Baking Vegetables**. Test for doneness with wire tester and when it can be easily pushed through jacket and pulp (from 40 to 60 minutes), potato is ready. Cut potato in half lengthwise or cut a large, deep "X" on top and then gently squeeze until potato pulp pops up through the crisscrossed cuts. Sprinkle pulp with salt and, if desired, with pepper, and top with butter or margarine, broken into small pieces.

SERVING VARIATIONS

Baked Potato with Sour Cream—For each potato, substitute 2 heaping teaspoons commercial sour cream for butter or margarine. If you wish, sprinkle cream with finely minced chives, or parsley, and/or paprika.

Stuffed Baked Potato—As soon as potatoes are removed from oven, cut in half lengthwise. Reserve half of jacket "shells." Scoop out pulp with small spoon and push it through sieve. For each potato, add 1 teaspoon butter or margarine and 1 tablespoon hot cream or milk. Beat with fork until light and fluffy. Season to taste with salt and, if desired, with pepper. Also, if desired, any of following may be mixed with potato. For each potato allow:

1 tablespoon grated Parmesan, American, or Swiss cheese
1½ tablespoons chopped ham and ½ teaspoon chopped white
  or green onion
1 teaspoon French (dry) vermouth

Stuff mixture back into the reserved jacket shells and bake about 30 minutes in 425° F. oven until golden brown. If desired, potato may be sprinkled with paprika before it is placed in oven.

ROASTED OR BAKED SQUASH

Acorn squash, allow 1 for each 2 servings[6]

2 teaspoons melted butter or margarine for each squash
Salt, and, if desired, pepper

Roast squash according to *General Rules for Roasting or Baking Vegetables.** Test for doneness with wire tester and when it can be pushed with ease through squash (approximately 1 hour), it is ready. Remove from oven; cut in half lengthwise. Brush hollows with melted fat and sprinkle to taste with salt and, if desired, pepper.

ROASTED OR BAKED TOMATO

For each serving:

1 large or 2 medium very firm tomatoes
1 tablespoon melted butter or margarine
Salt and, if desired, pepper to taste

[6] If only 1 person is to be served, half of the cooked squash may be covered with plastic wrap or aluminum foil and stored in refrigerator for 1 or 2 days.

Roast tomatoes without peeling according to *General Rules for Roasting or Baking Vegetables**. When wire cake tester can be pushed with ease through tomato (15 to 20 minutes), it is ready. Remove from oven. Place on individual serving dishes or platter and cut each tomato in half (from blossom to stem end) with sharp knife. Brush cut surfaces with melted fat and sprinkle with salt and, if desired, with pepper.

8

Oven Broiled Food

When it comes to cooking, I am much like Baby Snooks, and unless you are among the very young, you will remember that she was the delightful and exasperating little girl created by the great Fanny Brice, whose answer to just about everything was a whining "Why, Daddy?" The great difference between us is that I usually want to know "Why not?"

This does not mean that I will discard a good method unless I can substitute what is, in my opinion, a better one, but I do not stick to something just because that's the way it has always been done. If you are a confirmed conformist, you should be warned, this book is not for you.

I bring this up at this particular point because I oven broil, and most successfully, a few foods that others don't usually cook in this manner, and also, I brush my meats before cooking them with melted butter or margarine. I do this because for a long time many great cooks have immersed beefsteaks in olive oil for 5 minutes before cooking, and, of course, broiled chicken is always brushed or rubbed with fat before it is cooked. So if steaks and chicken were better when broiled in this way, why not do the same thing with chops, seafood, and vegetables? I tried the oil and found that while it was ideal for steaks, particularly if you want one with an almost charred outside and a very rare inside, it doesn't do as good a job with other food; however, it's an entirely different story when you brush these foods with melted butter or margarine! Furthermore, I check frequently while broiling and reduce the heat when food is cooking too quickly, as I am more concerned with good food than with semantics.

GENERAL RULES FOR OVEN BROILING

1. Remove food from refrigerator just long enough to get the chill off it. This is particularly important for steaks that are to be served rare, since meat taken from refrigerator to broiler isn't even apt to be warm in the center, due to the short cooking period.

2. Cut through fat edge of meat in 2 or 3 places to prevent curling while broiling. If desired, some of fat may be trimmed from meat.

3. Place broiler pan as close to source of heat as possible. The food when it is placed in the broiler (later) may be put: (1) on the pan itself, particularly if broiler is equipped with a sizzling platter; (2) on a rack that fits into broiler pan, although this is not recommended for hamburger, chicken livers, shrimp, oysters, vegetables, eggs, or bacon.

4. Preheat broiler and broiler pan (with rack if it is to be used) 10 to 15 minutes for steaks and 8 to 10 minutes for other food —the length of preheating period will depend on type of stove being used, so consult instruction booklet furnished with your stove for this information.

5. Immerse beefsteaks for 5 to 6 minutes in olive or vegetable oil. Brush or immerse other foods in melted butter or margarine. Let the excess fat drain from food before broiling, but reserve this excess to use for brushing or basting food while cooking.

6. When the broiler has been properly preheated, the pan should be moved so that the surface of the food will be approximately 3 inches from heat source.

7. Place food on broiler pan or rack resting in pan.

8. Check at frequent intervals and at any time outside appears to be browning too quickly, lower heat.

9. With the exception of steak, hamburger, grapefruit, or oranges, if food is broiled longer than 5 minutes on a side, baste or brush with melted butter or margarine from time to time.

10. At the halfway point of cooking (estimated cooking times are shown in following recipes), with the exception of tomatoes, grapefruit, and oranges, turn food so that second side may cook, and, with the exception of beefsteak, brush or baste this second side with melted butter or margarine. (While in some cases, turning the food may not be absolutely necessary, I think the results are better and recommend that it be done.)

11. Check doneness of meat or chicken by cutting a small slit near the center of meat (if there is a bone, the closer to the bone, the better) and in the thickest part of the chicken, cutting deep enough to reveal a small portion of bone. You will then be able to judge by color if meat and chicken have reached desired degree of doneness. Rare meat will be red to pink, depending on degree of rareness; medium-done meat will be very light pink; and no trace of blood should show in well-done meat or in properly cooked chicken. Check fish by pulling a small amount off with a fork; if flesh is firm, yet flakes easily, fish is done.

12. When food is broiled to your taste, sprinkle both sides with salt and, if desired, with pepper before removing from broiler. This does not apply to bacon, tomatoes, grapefruit, and oranges. While the exposed surface of the tomato should be sprinkled with desired seasoning, it is not turned over, and of course salt and pepper are not used with bacon, grapefruit, or oranges. If you wish to measure seasoning, allow ⅓ to ½ teaspoon salt per pound, according to your taste, for meat and seafood; ¼ to ⅓ teaspoon salt per pound for chicken; and ⅛ teaspoon pepper per pound for meat, chicken, and seafood.

13. If desired, pan juices may be poured over food, after it is transferred to platter.

14. *For a Gourmet Touch with Meat, Poultry, or Seafood,* sprinkle the food lightly on both sides with heated white wine or sherry before it is sprinkled with salt. Also, if desired, when oven broiling meat or chicken, immediately after heat is turned off, add approximately ¼ cup dry white wine or sherry to the very hot pan juices, stir until juices and wine are blended and pour at once over food.

15. With the exception of chicken, which is equally good hot or cold, and possibly chops, oven broiled foods should be served without delay and piping hot.

OVEN BROILED
LAMB CHOPS or VEAL CHOPS

¾- to 1-inch thick lamb or veal chops
1 tablespoon (approximate) melted butter or margarine for
  each chop
⅓ to ½ teaspoon salt per pound meat
⅛ teaspoon pepper per pound meat, if desired

For each serving: ½ to ⅔ pound.
Remove meat from refrigerator at least 15 minutes before cooking. Cut through fat or heavy membrane edge of each chop in 2 or 3 places. Preheat broiler unit, pan, and rack, if the last is to be used, as close to heat source as possible for 8 to 10 minutes. Brush chops lightly on both sides with melted fat. Put chops on pan or rack and place it so that their top surfaces are approximately 3 inches below heating unit of broiler. Check at frequent intervals to see if chops are browning too quickly and if so, lower heat.

APPROXIMATE THICKNESS	ESTIMATED COOKING TIME ON EACH SIDE IN MINUTES	
	medium	*well done*
lamb chops		
¾ inch	2½ to 3	4 to 5
1 inch	4 to 5	5 to 6
veal chops		
¾ inch	——	5 to 6½
1 inch	——	7 to 8½

If meat is cooked for more than 5 minutes to a side, halfway through estimated cooking time for each side, brush top with melted fat. When estimated cooking time for one side expires, turn chop and brush top with melted butter or margarine. Continue cooking until estimated cooking time for second side expires. At this point, make small slit in center of chop near bone to see if bloody, medium, or well done. When chops reach desired stage of doneness, sprinkle on both sides with salt and, if desired, with pepper.

OVEN BROILED BEEFSTEAK
PORTERHOUSE—T-BONE—CLUB STEAK—
RIB STEAK—SIRLOIN

1- to 2-inch thick steak
1 to 2 cups olive or vegetable oil, quantity depending on size of steak
⅓ to ½ teaspoon salt and, if desired, ⅛ teaspoon pepper per pound meat

For each serving: With Bone—½ to ⅔ pound; Without Bone—⅓ to ½ pound.

Remove steak from refrigerator about 20 minutes before cooking. Cut through fat edge of steak in 3 or 4 places. Place broiler pan and rack, if it is to be used, close to heat source. Preheat 10 to 15 minutes, according to manufacturer's recommendations for stove.

Place steak in oil 5 or 6 minutes before cooking; let stand 2½ to 3 minutes; turn and let stand 2½ to 3 minutes more. Drain off excess fat. Place meat on pan or rack and move pan so that surface of steak is approximately 3 inches from heat source. Check at frequent intervals, and if steak is browning too quickly, lower heat.

	ON EACH SIDE—(IN MINUTES)		
	ESTIMATED TIME		
APPROXIMATE THICKNESS	*rare*	*medium*	*well-done*
1 inch	4 to 5	5½ to 6	7 to 8
1½ inches	6 to 7	9 to 10	11 to 12
2 inches	12 to 13	14 to 15	19 to 20

Cook steak on one side, turn and cook on second side. Check doneness by making small slit in center of steak, near bone, if there is one, so that you can judge by color if steak has reached desired degree of doneness. When cooked to your taste, sprinkle on both sides with salt and, if desired, with pepper. Place on heated platter. Any pan juices may be poured over meat. Serve at once.

OVEN BROILED HAMBURGERS

For each hamburger (allow 1 to 2 to serving, depending on appetites):

¼ pound ground beef[1]
½ teaspoon ketchup
2 teaspoons melted butter or margarine
⅛ teaspoon salt
Dash pepper (approximately 1/16 teaspoon), if desired

Remove ground meat from refrigerator 15 to 20 minutes before cooking. Work ketchup into meat until thoroughly mixed. Place

[1] Request butcher to add small quantity of fat to lean, or if you grind lean meat at home, use 2 thin slices bacon for each pound lean beef and grind together.

broiler pan (don't use rack) as close as possible to heat source and preheat 8 to 10 minutes. Form meat into patty or patties ¾ to 1 inch thick. Lightly brush both sides with melted fat. Put hamburger(s) on pan and place pan so that surface of meat is approximately 3 inches from heat source. Check at frequent intervals and if browning too quickly, lower heat.

	ON EACH SIDE—IN MINUTES		
	ESTIMATED TIME		
APPROXIMATE THICKNESS	rare	medium	well-done
¾ inch	2 to 3	4	5 to 6
1 inch	3 to 4	4½ to 5	7 to 8

Cook on one side, turn and brush with remaining melted fat—hamburgers should only be brushed with fat before they are cooked and immediately after they are turned even when they are cooked more than 5 minutes to a side. Continue cooking until meat reaches desired state of doneness. Handling gently, sprinkle on both sides with salt, and, if desired, with pepper.

VARIATION

Pickled Onion Hamburger—When ketchup is added, mix in 1 tablespoon well-drained tiny pickled onions.

OVEN BROILED BACON

For each serving:

  2 strips of bacon when served with eggs, liver, or other
    protein food and 4 strips when served without eggs, etc.

Place broiler pan as close as possible to heat source and preheat broiler 8 to 10 minutes. When properly preheated, arrange bacon on pan so strips are straight and do not overlap. Place pan so surface of bacon is approximately 3 inches below heat source. Cook until brown on one side—2 to 4 minutes; turn and brown on other side—1 to 2 minutes approximately. Place bacon on absorbent paper towels and allow to drain until dry and crisp. Serve quickly.

VARIATION

Oven Broiled Bacon and Eggs (Cooked Together)—When bacon is brown on one side, turn and gently push to end of pan. Quickly, but carefully, break eggs, allowing 2 for each serving, on any well-greased portion of pan. Cook just until second side of bacon is brown and whites of eggs are no longer transparent. Drain bacon on the absorbent paper and transfer eggs to warm platter. Sprinkle eggs with salt and, if desired, with pepper, and arrange crisp bacon on platter. Serve at once.

OVEN BROILED EGGS

For each serving:

    1 teaspoon melted butter or margarine
    2 eggs
    Salt and, if desired, pepper to taste

Grease shallow individual baking dish(es) or 1 large baking dish (9-inch pie pan is ideal for 6 eggs) liberally with melted fat. Break each egg into a cup and then carefully transfer to baking dish. Place broiler pan as close to heat source as possible and preheat broiler 8 to 10 minutes. When properly preheated, place dish holding eggs on broiler pan and move so that tops of eggs are approximately 3 inches below heat source. Cook until whites are set—they should be opaque, that is, no longer transparent. Do not overcook, as yolks should be runny. Sprinkle with salt and, if desired, with pepper. Serve at once "as is" or with desired sauce.

OVEN BROILED CHICKEN

Quarters or halves of 1½- to 2¼-pound broilers OR breasts of 2½- to 3½-pound fryers

3 tablespoons (approximate) melted butter or margarine for each breast or quarter OR ¼ cup for each half

¼ to ⅓ teaspoon salt and, if desired, ⅛ teaspoon pepper for each pound chicken

For each serving: ½ to ⅔ pound.

Remove chicken from refrigerator about 20 minutes before cooking. Place broiler pan and, if desired, rack as close to heat source as possible. Preheat 8 to 10 minutes. Liberally brush bird with melted fat. When broiler is properly preheated, arrange chicken, skin side down, on broiler pan or rack and place in broiler so that top of chicken is approximately 3 inches from heating unit. Check at frequent intervals and if chicken is browning too fast, lower heat. Baste or brush chicken with melted fat after it has cooked 6 minutes; Cook 6 minutes more, turn chicken and again baste or brush with fat. Cook another 6 minutes and for the third time, brush or baste with the fat. At the end of a total cooking time of 25 minutes, make small slit in thickest part of chicken, cutting to the bone. If there is any sign of blood, continue cooking. When chicken is cooked through, sprinkle entire surface with salt and, if desired, with pepper. Serve hot or cold as you wish.

NOTE: If skin side is not browned to your taste 4 minutes before you are ready to remove chicken from stove, brush it with a small amount of Kitchen Bouquet and then complete cooking.

OVEN BROILED CHICKEN LIVERS

Young chicken livers
2 teaspoons melted butter or margarine for each liver
¼ to ⅓ teaspoon salt and, if desired, ⅛ teaspoon pepper per
    pound livers

For each serving: ⅓ to ½ pound.
Remove livers from refrigerator about 20 minutes before cooking. Place broiler pan as close to heat source as possible. Preheat 8 to 10 minutes. Liberally brush or immerse livers in melted fat; then drain off and reserve excess fat. When broiler is properly preheated, arrange livers on broiler pan and place pan so surface of livers will be about 3 inches from heat source. Cook 4 to 6 minutes on each side. After cooking on one side, turn livers and brush with remaining melted fat. When livers have been cooked a total of 8 minutes, make small slit in center of one and check color to see if desired degree of doneness has been reached. If not, continue cooking, until it is, and then sprinkle livers with salt and, if desired, with pepper on both sides. Place on hot platter (or toast, if you prefer) and, if desired, pour pan juices over them. Serve at once.

OVEN BROILED FISH

Small whole fish, 1¾ pounds or less, (entrails removed) OR
Fish fillets or steaks
Melted butter or margarine—approximately 3 tablespoons for
    each pound fish
⅓ to ½ teaspoon salt and, if desired, ⅛ teaspoon white
    pepper per pound fish

For each serving: Whole Fish (as it comes from water) 1 to 1¼ pounds; Dressed Fish—½ to ⅔ pound; Fish Fillets or Steaks— ⅓ to ½ pound.

Remove fish from refrigerator about 15 minutes before cooking. Preheat broiler unit and pan (with rack if it is to be used) as close to heat source as possible for 8 to 10 minutes. If whole fish is being used, with exception of flat ones such as 1- to 1¼-pound flounders or pompano, split and spread out flat. Liberally brush on both sides or immerse fish in melted fat; if immersed, drain and reserve excess fat. Put fish on pan or rack, skin side down, and place pan so that surface of fish is approximately 3 inches below heat source. (If you wish to facilitate turning, fish may be placed on aluminum foil or well-greased brown paper.) Check at frequent intervals to see if fish is browning too quickly and if so, lower heat.

THICKNESS	COOKING TIME ON EACH SIDE (IN MINUTES)
⅔ inch or more	10 to 13
less than ⅔ inch	6 to 8

Brush top of fish every 4 to 5 minutes with melted fat. When estimated cooking time for one side expires, turn fish and brush top with fat. Continue cooking until estimated cooking time for second side expires. Check doneness by pulling small amount of fish off with fork and if flesh is firm and yet flakes easily, fish is done. When fish is cooked through, sprinkle with salt and, if desired, pepper on both sides.

OVEN BROILED LOBSTER

For each serving:

   1 lobster—preferably weighing 1 to 1¼ pounds
   ¼ cup (approximate) melted butter or margarine
   ⅓ to ½ teaspoon salt and, if desired, ⅛ teaspoon white pepper
     per pound lobster

Remove lobster from refrigerator about 15 minutes before cooking. Place lobster on back and cut down through head with a very sharp knife. Then split lobster open from head to tail and remove sac at back of head, black vein, and spongy lungs. To prevent curling, cut tail crosswise in several places. Place broiler pan (with rack if it is to be used) as close to heat source as possible and preheat 8 to 10 minutes. Brush lobster liberally with melted fat and put it, heavy shell side up, on broiler pan (or rack in pan). Place pan so that top surface of lobster will be approximately 3 inches from heat source. Check at frequent intervals and if lobster cooks too fast, reduce heat. Broil 6 to 8 minutes, depending on size of lobster; turn and again liberally brush with remaining melted fat. Continue cooking 4 to 6 minutes until meat is pink. Sprinkle lobster meat with salt and, if desired, with white pepper.

OVEN BROILED OYSTERS

For each serving:

9 large, fat oysters with liquid
¼ cup (approximate) melted butter or margarine
Salt and, if desired, white pepper

Prepare *Poached Oysters*. Drain and pat as dry as possible with paper towels. Liberally brush or immerse oysters in melted butter or margarine. If oysters are immersed, drain off excess fat and reserve it. While oysters are draining, place broiler pan as close to heat source as possible and preheat broiler 8 to 10 minutes. Put oysters on pan, arranging them so that they don't overlap and place pan so that it will be approximately 3 inches below heat source. Check oysters after 1 minute to be sure they aren't cooking too fast, and if they are, reduce heat. Cook 2 to 4 minutes until rich brown; turn, brush tops with remaining melted fat and cook approximately 2 to 4 minutes more until second side is also a rich brown (oysters should be checked at least once during this second cooking period so that they won't brown too fast). In the event that oysters are not browned to your taste at end of 4 minutes, place them a little closer to heat source. Sprinkle seafood on both sides with salt and, if desired, white pepper to taste. It is a good idea to taste the oyster liquid to see how salty it is, and to season accordingly.

SUGGESTION FOR SERVING: Serve piping hot on toast with slices or quarters of lemon and sprays of parsley.

OVEN BROILED SHRIMP
OVEN BROILED SOFT-SHELL CRABS

Large, raw, shelled, deveined shrimp
   OR
Soft-shell crab(s)[2]
Milk to cover
Melted butter or margarine: For shrimp: about 1½ teaspoons
   each
   For crab:
   Small—1 tablespoon each
   Large—1½ tablespoons each
Salt and, if desired, white pepper
Lemon slices or quarters, if desired

For each serving: Shrimp—⅝ to ¾ pound (shelled); Crab— 2 small or 1 large.
Put seafood in container with lid and cover it with milk, 3 to 4 hours before cooking. Secure lid on container and store in refrigerator. Remove from refrigerator 15 minutes before cooking. Drain seafood and pat as dry as possible with paper towels. Place broiler pan (rack may be used for crab) as close to heat source as possible and preheat 8 to 10 minutes. Liberally brush shrimp or crab(s) with melted fat. Arrange on broiler pan so that seafood does not overlap. Place pan so that surface of shrimp or crab(s) is approximately 3 inches below heat source. Check at frequent intervals to see if seafood is browning too rapidly, and if so, reduce heat.

[2] See *Preparing Soft-shell Crabs for Cooking*.

ESTIMATED COOKING TIME
ON EACH SIDE IN MINUTES

Shrimp	2 to 3
Soft-shell Crab(s)	
Small	4
Large	5 to 6

When estimated cooking time for one side expires, turn seafood and brush top(s) with remaining melted fat. Continue cooking until estimated cooking time for second side expires. When seafood is cooked through, sprinkle both sides with salt to taste and, if desired, with pepper. Turn out on heated platter and, if desired, pour pan juices over shrimp or crab(s). Garnish with lemon, if desired.

OVEN BROILED MUSHROOMS

For 4 servings (½ cup uncooked mushrooms each serving):

1 pint mushrooms
¼ cup melted butter or margarine
Salt and, if desired, pepper to taste

Wash mushrooms, drain, and pat dry. Only pare those with coarse skins. Place broiler pan as close to heat source as possible and preheat 8 to 10 minutes. Liberally brush or immerse mushrooms in melted fat. If they are immersed, drain off excess fat and reserve. Arrange mushrooms on broiler pan and place pan so that top surfaces of mushrooms are approximately 3 inches from heating unit. Check at frequent intervals and if mushrooms are browning too quickly, reduce heat. Cook 3 to 4 minutes, turn mushrooms and baste with remaining melted fat. Continue cooking 3 to 4 minutes more. Sprinkle with salt and, if desired, with pepper. Place on platter and, if desired, pour pan juice over mushrooms.

OVEN BROILED TOMATOES

For each serving:

1 large firm tomato
2 tablespoons melted butter or margarine
Salt and, if desired, pepper to taste

Cut tomato in half. Place broiler pan as close to heat source as possible and preheat 8 to 10 minutes. Liberally brush tomato halves with melted fat. Arrange halves on broiler pan, cut side up, and place pan as far as possible from heat source. Check every 2 to 3 minutes, and if tomato is browning too quickly, lower heat. Cook 5 minutes and baste with remaining fat. Continue cooking until tomato is thoroughly heated—about 5 to 7 minutes more, depending on size. Carefully place tomato halves on warm platter. Sprinkle with salt and, if desired, with pepper. Serve at once.

OVEN BROILED GRAPEFRUIT
OVEN BROILED ORANGE

For each serving:

½ grapefruit or large orange
2 teaspoons (approximate) melted butter or margarine
1 teaspoon brown sugar

Cut fruit in half. Remove seeds and center(s). Cut around sections to loosen. Place broiler pan as close to heat source as possible. Preheat 8 to 10 minutes. Brush top of fruit (cut side) with melted fat and then sprinkle with sugar. Arrange fruit on broiler pan, cut side up, and place pan as far as possible from heat source. Cook until fruit is thoroughly heated and starts to brown, approximately 10 to 15 minutes, depending on size of fruit. Check at frequent intervals while cooking and if fruit browns too quickly reduce heat. Serve at once.

Gourmet Touch: If you wish, sprinkle 1 teaspoon sherry, rum, Cointreau, or kirsch over each half before serving. If oranges are used, 1 teaspoon of curaçao may be used in place of fore-named spirits.

9

Braised (and Stewed) Food

If your knowledge of cooking meat and chicken had to be limited to one method—and certainly this is a ridiculous hypothesis —I would suggest, without hesitation, that you learn to braise. First, you can cook almost any cut of meat by braising (this includes stewing) and be reasonably confident that you are going to serve a good meal. Second, after a little attention at the start, braised foods, and this includes seafood and vegetables as well as meat and chicken, actually cook themselves, enabling you to cook and at the same time read, sew, chat on the phone, entertain guests, or even go out, without fear that the food will be ruined for lack of care. Of course, like all good things, this can be overdone and you should be around to check a short time before estimated cooking time expires. Third, there's an important fringe benefit, for when the liquid is added to the fat in which the food was browned, you stir until all the browned fat comes off the bottom of the pan to blend with the liquid (getting the fat off the bottom is a simple operation at this time), and as a result, when you are finished cooking, dishwashing is not very difficult.

There are really only 2 differences of any consequence between braising and stewing, since whether you braise or stew, you first brown the food in a small amount of fat; then you add the liquid and allow to simmer in a covered utensil until tender. The big difference is in the amount of liquid used. You use a small quantity for braised food, but for a stew, you must use enough liquid to cover the food. The second difference lies in the fact that the gravy for the stew is usually thickened and this is not done very often in the case of braised foods; however, whether the food is braised or stewed, to thicken or not to thicken must be a matter of personal taste.

GENERAL RULES FOR BRAISING AND STEWING

1. Remove food from refrigerator 15 to 20 minutes before cooking.

2. Sprinkle with salt and, if desired, with pepper, so that entire surface is lightly and evenly covered. If you prefer to measure:

For Meat and Seafood—⅓ to ½ teaspoon salt and ⅛ teaspoon pepper per pound.
For Poultry—¼ to ⅓ teaspoon salt and ⅛ teaspoon pepper per pound.

3. For *Meat or Chicken with a rich dark brown outside,* after food is sprinkled with seasoning, lightly brush with Kitchen Bouquet.

4. For *a golden "flour crust,"* roll unseasoned food in (or shake in a bag of) sifted flour, salt, and if you like, pepper. For each cup flour, use, depending on taste, 1¼ to 1¾ teaspoons salt and ⅙ to ¼ teaspoon pepper.

5. When preparing *Swiss Steak*, Grillades*, Breaded Veal Cutlets** or other food of this kind, flatten meat before cooking by pounding with mallet, back of heavy spoon, or rolling pin. The "breaded" meat is dipped in slightly beaten egg or egg and milk and in crumbs, so that it is completely coated with the crumbs.

6. Melt enough fat or use enough cooking oil to cover bottom of frying pan to depth of about ⅛ inch. For a 9×9-inch frying pan, about ¼ cup butter, margarine, vegetable shortening, or cooking oil will be required. Slightly more is needed for a larger pan and less for a smaller one.

7. Heat fat until it bubbles, about 360° F. (fat for rice excepted, since rice should be browned at 380° F.).

8. Add food to fat, being sure not to overcrowd the pan.

9. Keep the temperature as constant as possible. This is easy with an electric frying pan, but otherwise, you will have to watch carefully to see that food doesn't brown too quickly or perhaps even burn.

10. Keep the frying pan filled to a depth of approximately ⅛ inch with melted fat. When needed, additional fat should be added, but this should be done gradually so that the temperature of the grease won't drop too rapidly while food is cooking.

11. Brown food on one side, turn and brown on other side. If there are more than two sides, continue turning meat after each side is browned until all sides are evenly browned.

12. Add very hot liquid to food, quantity ranging from a ¼ cup for *Breaded Veal Cutlets** to enough liquid to cover food that is being stewed. Insofar as the liquid is concerned, there is a wide choice: water; stock; bouillon; milk; canned or stewed tomatoes; tomato juice (with, if you like, a small amount of ketchup); dry white wine; a combination of 1 part red wine and 4 parts water, stock, or bouillon; or 1 part of *White Sauce** or the variation of your choice and 3 parts of water, stock, bouillon, milk, or dry white wine.

13. Stir the liquid into the browned fat and continue stirring until all of fat is blended with liquid and there is none left sticking to the bottom of the pan.

14. Bring liquid to a boil, reduce to a slow simmer and cover pan, if cooking on top of stove. If cooking in oven, place food in baking dish, add boiling liquid, cover dish, and bake in 350° F. oven.

15. Cooking time for braising or stewing varies according to what is being cooked. A 5-pound *Beef Pot Roast** will take approximately 3¾ hours, while *Shrimp Stew (Shrimp Creole)**

will take from 20 to 25 minutes. When food can be easily pierced and is so tender that the fork goes through without any effort on your part and when, in the case of meat or chicken, there is no sign of blood, the food is ready for table.

16. If vegetables are to be added to a stew, scrape or peel those that need it. Cut large vegetables such as potatoes, onion, or big carrots into chunks or slices. Such vegetables as peas, mushrooms, or midget carrots, and/or onions should be cooked whole. When the fork test shows meat is starting to get tender, about 30 to 40 minutes before estimated cooking time expires, add vegetables and cook at a simmer until both meat and vegetables are tender.

17. If *Dumplings** are going into the pot, remove cover from stew about 20 minutes before estimated cooking time expires. Check food and if almost tender enough to serve, bring to boiling point. Add dumpling mixture by teaspoonfuls, dropping so that the dumplings rest on top of food and not in liquid. Cook uncovered for 10 minutes. Cover pan securely and cook additional 10 minutes at same temperature.

18. If you wish *to thicken gravy,* brown a thin layer of flour, without grease, in a skillet. Stir constantly while browning. Remove from heat and add twice as much cool water as there is flour. Beat with fork or rotary egg beater until paste is lump free. *Estimate Quantity of Liquid** in cooking food, and, depending on how thick you want the gravy, use 1 to 2 tablespoons flour paste for each 1½ cups (estimated) liquid. Stir some of hot liquid from stew into paste and then blend mixture into simmering stew. Keep stirring until gravy is smooth. To avoid a floury taste, cook food over low heat about 15 minutes, stirring from time to time.

19. About 8 minutes before serving, check food for seasoning. If needed, add salt and pepper to taste. If gravy is too salty, and you had not planned to thicken it, you can use the flour paste *to reduce salty taste;* however, if you prefer not to thicken, peel and cut 1 or 2 potatoes into small pieces; add to stew with a small quantity of cool water. Cook until potato can be pierced with a fork, but don't cook to pieces. If you wish, potato may be removed from stew with slotted spoon. As a last resort, if you had a really "heavy hand" with the salt, gradually add a small quantity of lemon juice, being careful not to add so much that the gravy tastes after the juice.

20. *When cooking large quantities,* if you have only 1 frying pan, brown just enough food at one time not to crowd pan. When browned, transfer to a heavy pan with cover for cooking on top of stove or to a baking dish, also with cover, for cooking in the oven. Keep in warm, not hot, place. Continue browning and storing food until all of it has been taken care of. As additional fat is needed while browning food, add it gradually to keep the fat level at around ⅛ inch. If cooking on top of stove, add very hot liquid to browned fat, stir until blended and then pour over food in pan. Bring to a boil, reduce to slow simmer, and cover pan. If cooking in oven, add liquid to fat in which food was cooked, stir until blended, and bring to a boil. Pour over food in baking dish. Cover dish and cook in 350° F. oven. Follow all other instructions as given above.

BRAISED LAMB LOIN OR RIB CHOPS
BRAISED PORK LOIN OR SHOULDER CHOPS
BRAISED VEAL LOIN OR RIB CHOPS
BRAISED CHICKEN—BRAISED QUAIL

¾- to 1-inch thick lamb, pork, or veal chops
   OR
Halved or quartered cleaned and dressed broilers (1½- to 2¼-
   pound chickens) OR fryer breasts (from 2½- to 3½-pound
   chickens)
   OR
Quail—drawn, plucked, and split down back
Salt:
   For Meat—⅓ to ½ teaspoon per pound
   For Chicken or Quail—¼ to ⅓ teaspoon per pound
⅛ teaspoon pepper per pound, if desired
Kitchen Bouquet, if desired
Melted butter or margarine to fill frying pan to depth of ⅛
   inch (approximately ¼ cup for 9-inch pan)
Enough of any of following boiling liquids to fill pan to depth of
   ¼ inch (approximately ⅔ cup for 9-inch pan): water; stock;
   bouillon; equal parts dry white wine and water, stock, or bouillon;
   1 part red wine and 4 parts water, stock, or bouillon

For each serving: Chops—½ to ⅔ pound; Chicken—¼ to
½ broiler or 1 breast; Quail—1.

Sprinkle chops, chicken, or quail so that entire surface is lightly
covered with salt, and, if desired, with pepper. If you want outside of cooked food to be a deep, rich brown, brush all surfaces
sparingly with Kitchen Bouquet. Heat margarine or butter until
it bubbles (360° F.). Add food, brown on one side (8 to 10
minutes), turn and brown on other side (8 to 10 minutes). Add
boiling liquid, and stir gently until blended with all fat and fat
drippings in pan.

   Complete cooking by either of following methods: (1) Reduce heat to low simmer (220° F.). Cover pan OR (2) Place
food in baking-serving dish and add liquid from frying pan.

Cover securely—aluminum foil may be used if dish does not have cover. Bake in 350° F. oven. Allow food to simmer or bake until tender and until when small slit is made in thickest part near bone, there is no trace of blood. Estimated simmering or baking time for chops and quail is 30 to 40 minutes and for chicken 35 to 45 minutes.

VARIATIONS

With Herbs: For each ⅔ cup (approximate) liquid add any or all of following to basic recipe after liquid is blended with fat:

1 tablespoon minced parsley
¼ teaspoon thyme
¼ teaspoon basil
½ small crumbled bay leaf
1 teaspoon minced chives

With Apples: Add to ingredients of basic recipe, for each 2 chops, pieces of chicken or quail:

1 large peeled, cored cooking apple cut lengthwise in 8 thick slices
Artificial liquid sweetener or sugar syrup (2 parts sugar dissolved in 1 part water)
⅛ teaspoon any or all following: cinnamon, nutmeg, cloves

Brush apple slices with artificial sweetener or sugar syrup and sprinkle with spice. After food has browned on one side, turn, and add fruit. Cook 4 to 5 minutes and turn fruit on other side. Finish browning (4 to 5 minutes more) and then proceed exactly as directed in basic recipe.

With Sweet Potatoes: Add to ingredients of basic recipe, for each 2 chops, pieces of chicken or quail:

1 large sweet potato
1½ tablespoons (approximate) sugar
Additional butter or margarine if needed

Simmer potato(es) in jacket(s) for 10 minutes. Chill, peel, and cut into ¾-inch thick slices. Heat butter or margarine specified in basic recipe until it bubbles (360° F.). Add potatoes and brown on both sides—about 10 minutes on each side. Remove to warm platter. Sprinkle all surfaces with sugar. If additional fat is needed to bring level in frying pan to depth of ⅛ inch, add butter or margarine gradually. Brown chops, chicken, or quail and, after liquid is added, pile sweet potatoes on top of meat, chicken, or quail in frying pan or place chops, chicken, or quail in baking dish, top with vegetable, and add liquid. Proceed as directed in basic recipe.

With Apples Flambé; with Sweet Potatoes Flambé: After liquid is added to browned food, arrange chops, chicken, or quail in baking dish. Top with fruit or vegetable and add liquid from pan in which food was browned. Bake in 350° F. oven as directed in basic recipe. When meat or bird is cooked through, immediately heat 3 tablespoons rum or brandy for each 2 chops, pieces of chicken or birds. Pour all but 1 to 1½ tablespoons over apples or potatoes. Ignite the very hot remaining 1 to 1½ tablespoons of spirit and pour burning liquid over food. Serve without delay.

BREADED VEAL CUTLETS

½- to ¾-inch thick veal cutlets
Salt—⅓ to ½ teaspoon per pound
⅛ teaspoon pepper per pound, if desired
1 whole egg for each 4 cutlets[1]
2 tablespoons milk for each egg[1]
¼ cup (approximate) crumbs for each cutlet (Rice Krispies, cornflakes, fine bread or cracker)
Butter or margarine to fill frying pan to depth of ⅛ inch (approximately ¼ cup for 9-inch pan)
Any of following boiling liquids to cover bottom of frying pan (approximately ¼ to ⅓ cup): water; stock; bouillon; 1 part dry white wine to 1 part water; 1 part red wine to 4 parts water

[1] If cooking 1 or 2 cutlets, they can be dipped in mixture of 1 egg and 2 tablespoons milk; however, if cooking 5 to 8 cutlets, use 2 eggs and ¼ cup milk, and for 9 to 12 cutlets, use 3 eggs and 6 tablespoons milk.

CUTS OF MEAT

BEEF

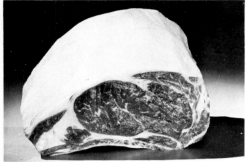

Rib Roast

Standing Rump

Arm Pot Roast (Chuck)

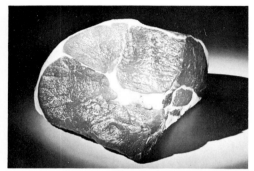

Heel of Round

Blade Pot Roast

Sirloin Tip

Flank Steak

Porterhouse Steak

Sirloin Steak

T-Bone Steak

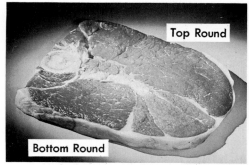

Top Round

Bottom Round

Round Steak (Full Cut)

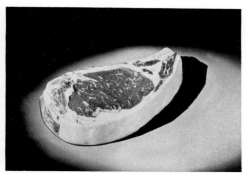

Club Steak

Plate Boiling Beef

Rib Steak

Shank Cross Cuts

LAMB

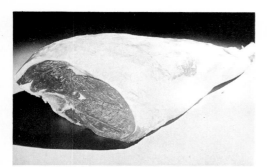

Leg of Lamb

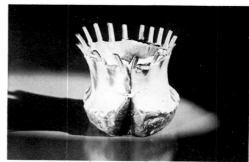

Crown Roast

Square Cut Shoulder

Rolled Shoulder

Loin Chops

Rib Chops

Lamb Shanks

Lamb Patties

PORK

Loin Roasts

Ham

Picnic Shoulder

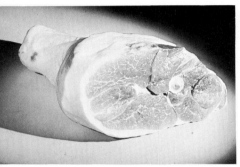
Boston Butt Shoulder

Rib Chops

Loin Chops

Spareribs

VEAL and CALF

Leg (Center Cut)

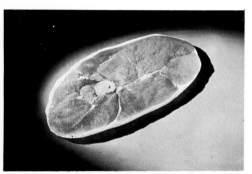

Round Steak

Loin Chop

Rib Chop

Foreshank

Photographs courtesy of the National Live Stock and Meat Board

For each serving: ⅓ to ½ pound.

Sprinkle both sides of cutlets with salt and, if desired, with pepper. Flatten veal by pounding on each side with mallet, back of heavy, large spoon, or a rolling pin. Beat egg(s), in bowl large enough to hold meat, 60 strokes with fork or wire whip, stir in milk and beat only long enough to blend. Place crumbs on several thicknesses of paper or aluminum foil. Dip cutlets in egg mixture; turn each one several times so that it is thoroughly coated; then dip in crumbs—if necessary more crumbs may be added, but cutlets must be completely covered. Heat butter or margarine until it bubbles (360° F.). Add cutlets and brown on both sides (8 to 10 minutes per side). If you do not have thermostat control, watch carefully so that heat can be adjusted if needed to prevent fat from overheating. Add just enough of liquid of your choice to cover bottom of frying pan and stir until blended with fat. Lower heat to simmer (220° F.). Cover pan and cook 20 to 25 minutes until meat can be easily pierced with fork.

VARIATIONS

Wiener Schnitzel—Sprinkle *Breaded Veal Cutlets** with lemon juice to taste or place 1 slice lemon on each cutlet. Garnish with grated hard-cooked eggs, allowing 1 for each 2 cutlets, chopped capers, and, if desired, sardellen or green olives wrapped in anchovy fillets.

Eggs à la Holstein: Substitute 1 fried egg for each ½ hard-cooked egg in *Wiener Schnitzel**.

SWISS STEAK

⅓ cup flour seasoned with ½ teaspoon salt and, if desired, ⅛ teaspoon pepper

1½- to 2-pound beef round or flank steak, approximately 1½ inches thick

Melted butter, margarine, or vegetable shortening or cooking oil to fill frying pan to depth of ⅛ inch (approximately ¼ cup for 9-inch pan)

Any or all of following, if desired:

⅓ cup coarsely chopped onion

⅓ cup coarsely chopped celery

⅓ cup coarsely chopped green pepper

1 clove garlic, peeled, finely minced

⅓ cup drained canned mushroom pieces

1¾ cups boiling canned or fresh stewed tomatoes

¼ cup water or red or white wine

¼ cup ketchup or chili sauce, if desired

1 teaspoon vinegar, if desired

Salt to taste (approximately ½ teaspoon)

Tabasco sauce or cayenne pepper, to taste, if desired

For each serving: ⅓ to ½ pound steak.

Pound seasoned flour into both sides of meat with mallet, back of large, heavy spoon, or a rolling pin until steak is flattened. Heat fat until bubbling (360° F.), but not browned. Place meat in hot fat and brown on both sides (8 to 10 minutes for each side). Approximately 4 minutes before meat finishes browning on second side, add, if you desire: onion; celery; green pepper; garlic; and/or mushrooms.

Combine boiling tomatoes and water or wine. If desired, add ketchup or chili sauce and/or vinegar. Add mixture to browned meat and stir until blended with fat and drippings. Add salt and, if you wish, Tabasco or cayenne pepper to taste. Bring to a boil; reduce heat to slow simmer (220° F.) and securely cover pan. Cook until meat can be easily pierced with fork—1⅔ to 2 hours.

VARIATIONS

Grillades—Substitute ½-inch thick veal round or grillade steaks for beef round or flank steak. If desired, after tomato mixture and fat are blended, add 1 small bay leaf, whole or crumbled, and/or ¼ teaspoon oregano. Veal should be tender and cooked through after simmering 30 to 40 minutes.

BEEF POT ROAST
LAMB POT ROAST
VEAL OR CALF POT ROAST

Beef: 4- to 5-pound top or bottom round or sirloin tip,
  OR
3½- to 4-pound round bone or blade chuck
  OR
3- to 4-pound rolled roast, cut from plate or brisket
  OR
Lamb: 3- to 4-pound boned and rolled shoulder
  OR
Veal or Calf: 3- to 4-pound boned and rolled shoulder
Either of following:
  ⅓ to ½ teaspoon salt and, if desired, ⅛ teaspoon pepper per
  pound meat
  OR
  1 cup sifted flour mixed with 1½ to 1¾ teaspoons salt,
  according to taste, and, if desired, ⅙ to ¼ teaspoon pepper
Melted butter, margarine, or vegetable shortening or cooking
  oil to fill frying pan to depth of ⅛ inch (approximately ¼ cup
  for 9-inch pan)
Any or all of following, if desired:
  ¼ cup minced onion
  1 tablespoon minced parsley
  ⅓ cup chopped celery
Any of following liquids to fill pan to depth of ⅓ to ½ inch:
  water; stock; bouillon; equal parts dry white wine and water,
  stock, or bouillon; 1 part red wine and 4 parts water, stock,

or bouillon; 1 part *White Sauce**, or desired variation, to 3
parts water; stock, or bouillon; equal parts tomato juice and
water or dry white wine, plus, if desired, for each cup of
mixture, 2 tablespoons ketchup or chili sauce
Any or all of following, if desired:
⅓ cup canned mushroom pieces
¼ teaspoon thyme
1 bay leaf (whole or crumbled)
Salt and/or pepper to taste

For each serving: ½ to ⅔ pound meat with bone; ⅓ to ½
pound boneless meat.

Remove meat from refrigerator 15 to 20 minutes before cooking.
Sprinkle whole roast lightly with salt and, if desired, with pepper
OR combine flour with salt and, if desired, with pepper and
roll meat in mixture. Heat fat until bubbling (360° F.); place
meat in it and brown on all but one side. Before browning last
side, if desired, add onion, parsley, and/or celery; complete the
browning of the meat. Temperature of fat should be kept constant during browning period; if fat gets too hot, reduce heat.
If frying pan is large and deep enough so that meat may be
covered, cooking may be completed in it. If not, as soon as meat
is browned on all sides and onion, if used, is clear, transfer to
large heavy pan equipped with cover. Heat liquid of choice to
boiling point and add just enough to meat to fill pan to depth of
⅓ to ½ inch. If mushroom pieces are used, add to liquid and
then cover pan securely. Reduce heat to low simmer (220° F.).
Estimated simmering times after meat is browned are as follows:

	POUNDS	HOURS
Beef	3 to 4	2½ to 3
	4 to 5	3 to 3½
Lamb	3 to 4	1¾ to 2⅓
Veal or Calf	3 to 4	2

If needed during cooking period, additional hot liquid may be
added. If you wish, 40 minutes before estimated cooking time

expires, add thyme and bay leaf. When meat is easily pierced with fork, remove from heat. Check gravy and, if desired, add salt and/or pepper to taste.

VARIATIONS

With Vegetables—Add any or all of the following for each serving 30 to 40 minutes before estimated simmering time expires —and meat appears to be nearly tender when tested with fork:

2 small whole peeled onions or 1 large peeled onion cut in thick slices

1 large or 2 tiny scraped carrot(s), cut in ¾-inch chunks

2 small peeled whole potatoes or 1 large peeled potato cut into eighths

2 or 3 canned whole mushrooms

Bring liquid to boil (if using electric frying pan, set at 320° F.), and then reduce heat to slow simmer (220° F.) to complete cooking. Check vegetables as well as meat by piercing with fork shortly before estimated simmering time for meat expires, and when both can be easily pierced with fork, roast is ready to serve.

With Artichoke Garnish—Serve garnished with heated fresh simmered artichoke bottoms or canned artichoke hearts.

BEEF STEW—LAMB STEW—VEAL STEW
STEWED CHICKEN (CHICKEN FRICASSEE)

1¾-inch chunks beef, cut from plate, brisket, chuck, neck, or
round
OR
1¼- to 1½-inch cubes lamb, cut from brisket, shoulder, neck,
or shank
OR
¾- to 1¼-inch chunks veal, cut from round, plate, brisket, or
chuck
OR
Disjointed fat hen or large fryer
Either of following:
   ¼ to ⅓ teaspoon salt and ⅛ teaspoon pepper per pound
   for chicken; ⅓ to ½ teaspoon salt and ⅛ teaspoon pepper
   per pound for meat.
   OR
   1 cup sifted flour mixed with 1¼ to 1¾ teaspoons salt and, if
   desired, ⅙ to ¼ teaspoon pepper
Melted butter, margarine, or vegetable shortening or cooking
   oil to fill frying pan to depth of ⅛ inch (approximately ¼ cup
   for 9-inch pan)
Any or all of following, if desired: ¼ cup minced onion; 1
   tablespoon minced parsley; ⅓ cup chopped celery
Any of following liquids to cover meat or chicken: water;
   stock; bouillon; equal parts of dry white wine and water,
   stock, or bouillon; 1 part red wine and 4 parts water,
   stock, or bouillon; 1 part *White Sauce**, or desired variation,
   to 3 parts water, stock, or bouillon; equal parts tomato
   juice and water or dry white wine, plus, if desired, for each
   cup of mixture, 2 tablespoons ketchup or chili sauce.
Any or all of following, if desired: ⅓ cup canned mushroom
   pieces; ¼ teaspoon thyme; 1 bay leaf (crumbled or whole);
   salt and/or pepper to taste

For each serving: ½ to ⅔ pound meat with bone or chicken; ⅓
to ½ pound boneless meat.
Remove meat or chicken from retrigerator 15 to 20 minutes be-

fore cooking. Sprinkle lightly with salt, and, if desired, with pepper OR roll meat or chicken in flour mixture. Heat fat until bubbling and place meat or chicken in it. Don't crowd pan. Brown meat or chicken, turning pieces from time to time to brown evenly. If necessary to keep frying pan filled to depth of ⅛ inch, additional fat may be added when needed. Just before last sides of meat or chicken pieces are browned, if desired, add onion, parsley, and/or celery. If frying pan is large enough, cooking may be completed in it. If not, as soon as meat or chicken pieces are browned on all sides and onion, if used, is clear, transfer entire contents of frying pan to large, heavy pan with cover. Heat liquid of choice to boiling point. Add a small amount to meat or chicken and stir until this liquid and fat in which chicken or meat was browned are blended. Add additional liquid to cover meat or chicken pieces, stirring as liquid is added. Bring to a boil; then immediately reduce heat to slow simmer (220° F.).

Estimated simmering times after meat or chicken is browned are

HOURS

Beef	2
Lamb	1¾ to 2
Veal	1½ to 1⅔
Hen	2 to 3 (depending on size and quality)
Fryer pieces	¾ to 1

After half of estimated simmering time has expired, if desired, add mushrooms, thyme, and/or bay leaf. Check seasoning 10 to 15 minutes before estimated simmering time expires, and, if needed, add salt and/or pepper to taste. When meat or chicken can be easily pierced with fork, remove from heat. Serve piping hot.

VARIATIONS

With Thickened Gravy—To brown flour, sift thin layer of flour into frying pan. Cook over medium heat, stirring constantly until rich brown. Remove from frying pan, cool, and store, until ready to use, in covered container.

Combine, for each 1½ cups estimated liquid[2] in stew, the following 20 to 25 minutes before estimated cooking time for stew expires:

   1 to 2 tablespoons browned flour (quantity depending on how
      thick a gravy you want)
   2 tablespoons cool tap water

Beat flour paste until smooth. Add ½ cup hot stew gravy and stir vigorously until blended. Pour mixture into stew and stir well. Continue cooking over low heat, stirring from time to time—for at least 15 minutes so that there will be no floury taste—until meat or chicken is tender.

With Vegetables—Add, for each serving, any or all of following 30 to 40 minutes before estimated simmering time expires:

   2 small whole or 1 large sliced, peeled white onion(s)
   1 medium-sized scraped carrot, cut in ¾-inch chunks
   2 small whole or 1 medium-sized halved peeled potato(es)
   1 tablespoon raw fresh or frozen green peas and/or 1
      tablespoon green beans

[2] To make *rough estimate of quantity of liquid* in pot, deduct from original quantity of liquid added to meat or chicken:

For each approximate ½ inch, liquid has been reduced When Using Pot with Diameter of:

INCHES	REDUCTION IN CUPS (APPROXIMATE)
5½	¾
8	1½
9	2
11	2½

Bring to boil; reduce temperature to low simmer (220° F.). Complete cooking. When vegetables, as well as meat, can be easily pierced with fork, stew is ready to serve.

Brunswick Stew (Brought Up to Date)—Substitute for half of beef in *Beef Stew** an equal quantity of 1½-inch chunks pork cut from Boston Butt. Use water as liquid; omit mushrooms, thyme, and bay leaf. For each serving, 30 to 40 minutes before estimated simmering time (2 hours) expires, add:

    2 tablespoons finely chopped cabbage
    2 tablespoons canned or stewed tomatoes
    2 tablespoons canned or fresh corn niblets
    2 tablespoons fresh or frozen (defrosted) okra slices

Bring to boil; reduce to low simmer (220° F.) to complete cooking. When vegetables, as well as meat, can be easily pierced with fork, stew is ready to serve.

Ragout of Beef; Ragout of Lamb; Ragout of Veal—Prepare *Beef Stew*, *Lamb Stew**, or *Veal Stew**, using white or red wine mixture for liquid. Use onion, parsley, celery, thyme, and bay leaf (optional in basic recipe). When bay leaf is added, also add ¼ teaspoon of desired 2 or 3 of following: basil; chives; fines herbes; marjoram; oregano; savory.

MEAT SAUCE (QUICK)

    Ground beef
    ⅓ teaspoon salt and, if desired, ⅛ teaspoon pepper per pound
        ground beef
    Melted butter, margarine, vegetable shortening, bacon grease,
        or cooking oil to fill frying pan to depth of ⅛ inch[3]
    ⅓ cup *Tomato Sauce** for each ¼ pound beef
    ⅓ cup water or red or white wine (approximate) for each
        ¼ pound beef
    Salt and pepper, if needed, to taste

[3] If using only ¼ or ½ pound ground beef to serve 1 or 2, brown meat in small frying pan.

For each serving: ¼ pound ground beef.

Remove ground beef from refrigerator 15 to 20 minutes before cooking. Sprinkle with salt and, if desired, with pepper. Heat fat until it bubbles (360° F.). Add meat and cook, stirring constantly, until particles separate and are a light brown. Combine *Tomato Sauce** and water or wine. Bring to a boil. Add liquid to meat and stir until well mixed. Reduce heat to slow simmer (220° F.). Cover pan securely and cook over low heat 25 to 30 minutes. Check from time to time and, if needed, add additional water or wine. Before serving, if needed, add salt and pepper to taste. Serve piping hot.

SHRIMP STEW (SHRIMP CREOLE)

Raw, shelled, deveined shrimp
⅓ to ½ teaspoon salt per pound shrimp
⅛ teaspoon white pepper per pound shrimp
Melted butter or margarine to fill frying pan to depth of ⅛
   inch (approximately ¼ cup for 9-inch pan)
For each ½ cup raw shrimp:
   ½ cup tomato juice
   ½ cup water or red or dry white wine
Any or all of following, if desired, for each ½ cup shrimp:
   2 tablespoons ketchup or chili sauce
   1 tablespoon finely minced or dehydrated pieces onion
   1 tablespoon minced celery
   1 tablespoon coarsely chopped green pepper
   1 teaspoon finely minced parsley
   1 tablespoon mushroom pieces
   ⅛ teaspoon thyme
   Tabasco, cayenne pepper, or dehydrated red pepper pieces
   Salt and white pepper to taste

For each serving: ½ cup shrimp.

Remove shrimp from refrigerator 15 to 20 minutes before cooking. Sprinkle with salt and *white pepper*. Heat fat until it bubbles (360° F.). Place shrimp in hot fat; cook until lightly browned (about 2 minutes on each side). Bring remaining ingredients, excepting salt and pepper, to a boil while shrimp are browning. Pour over shrimp and stir until blended with fat in frying pan. Reduce heat to slow simmer (220° F.); cover pan; cook 20 minutes. Check seasoning and add salt and pepper to taste. Serve piping hot.

BROWN RICE

¼ cup butter or margarine
1 cup long grain rice (uncooked)
⅓ cup finely minced onion, if desired
1 tablespoon minced or dehydrated parsley, if desired
1 cup boiling undiluted canned bouillon, plus ¼ cup
    Worcestershire sauce, or 1¼ cups boiling undiluted canned
    bouillon
1⅜ cups boiling water
¼ teaspoon salt
Any or all of the following, if desired:
    ⅓ cup canned mushrooms (pieces or slices)
    ¼ teaspoon dehydrated red pepper pieces, or ⅛ teaspoon
    cayenne pepper or 4 drops Tabasco sauce
    ¼ teaspoon thyme
Salt and pepper to taste, if desired

Heat fat to 380° F. (bubbling rapidly and turning brown). Add rice. Stir from time to time until a light straw color. If desired, add onion and parsley and cook until onion is clear. Stir in boiling liquids and ¼ teaspoon salt. If you wish, add mushrooms, pepper pieces, cayenne or Tabasco, and/or thyme. Blend liquid with fat and rice in pan. Reduce to simmer just below boiling point. Cover pan securely and cook until rice is almost dry (about 40 minutes). Or, should you prefer, after rice has been browned and onion, if used, cooked until clear, spoon rice into baking-serving dish and add boiling liquids combined with the ¼ teaspoon salt and remaining ingredients, as desired, except salt and pepper. Bake for

50 minutes in 350° F. oven. Before serving, if needed, add salt and pepper to taste. *Serves 6.*

NOTE: To reheat, place in colander over boiling water and steam until piping hot.

STEWED OKRA, ONION, AND TOMATOES

¼ cup butter, margarine, or bacon grease
1½ cups sliced fresh, or canned or 10-ounce package defrosted,
　　drained frozen okra
¼ cup coarsely chopped onion
⅓ cup coarsely chopped celery, if desired
1½ cups tomato juice or canned or stewed tomatoes
¼ cup water, dry white or red wine
½ teaspoon salt
Any or all of following, if desired:
　¼ cup ketchup or chili sauce
　1 small green pepper, coarsely chopped
　1 tablespoon minced parsley
　1 bay leaf (crumbled or whole)
　¼ teaspoon thyme
　¼ teaspoon Tabasco sauce or dehydrated red pepper pieces
　or cayenne pepper
　Salt and pepper to taste

Heat butter, margarine, or bacon grease until it bubbles (360° F.). Add okra and cook, stirring from time to time, for 8 minutes. Add onion, and if desired, celery and cook until onion is clear. Stir in tomato juice or canned or stewed tomatoes, water or wine, and ½ teaspoon salt. Add, if desired, ketchup or chili sauce, green pepper, parsley, bay leaf, thyme, and/or Tabasco, red pepper pieces, or cayenne pepper. Bring to boil; reduce heat to slow simmer (220° F.). Cover pan. Cook 20 minutes. Increase heat to 300° F. and stirring constantly but gently cook until okra is tender and most of tomato has cooked into okra. Check seasoning, and if needed, add salt and pepper to taste. *Serves 6.*

VARIATION

Stewed Okra One Platter Meal—*To steam rice,* combine in top of double boiler, 1 cup raw long grain rice, 1½ cups boiling water and 1 teaspoon salt. Cover securely and cook over boiling water 50 minutes. While rice is cooking prepare *Stewed Okra, Onion, and Tomatoes** and from 10 to 15 minutes before rice is ready, prepare 3 cups *Oven Broiled Shrimp**, or 8 to 12 minutes before rice is done, prepare 2 to 3 pounds (depending on appetites) of *Oven Broiled Chicken Livers**. Spread hot rice on platter, top with piping hot okra mixture, which in turn is topped with hot shrimp or chicken livers. *Serves 6.*

10

Simmered or Poached Food

It's said there's a wrong way and a right way to do just about everything. Usually we don't completely reverse our thinking as to what is wrong and what is right, but when I first learned to cook, what we thought was the right way of cooking vegetables is now regarded as all wrong.

I was taught to follow religiously the rule that if a vegetable grew in the dark (the root ones), you started cooking it in cold water, but regardless of how you started, "boiled" as applied to vegetables was certainly no misnomer. Furthermore, you used so much water that even if you forgot for a time that you had something on the stove, there really wasn't too much danger of its burning. And how much emphasis we did place on getting those vegetables tender—actually, more often than not they were so tender they were almost mushy! I remember using soda to "preserve" the color of peas and beans, and I didn't have the slightest notion that soda was a vitamin and mineral thief, which, additionally, robbed the food of some of its taste and sight appeal.

The most popular way of cooking vegetables is to simmer or poach them, and if you learn how to simmer or poach one vegetable, you are well on the way to being able to cook just about any vegetable. Also, you won't have a bit of trouble with simmered or poached fruit, eggs, chicken, or fish.

GENERAL RULES FOR SIMMERING OR POACHING VEGETABLES

1. Prepare vegetables for the pot according to directions in Section 5, *Simmered or Poached Vegetable Chart**.

2. Pour quantity of cold tap water needed for proper cooking into pan:

(a) For chicory, dandelion greens, kale, and spinach, use water that clings to leaves after last washing, plus ¼ inch of water[1] in bottom of pan.

(b) For young beet, collard, mustard, and turnip greens, use water that clings to leaves after last washing, plus, if cooking *Greens Southern Style*, 1 inch water[1] in pot; otherwise, use only ¼ inch water[1] in bottom of pot.

(c) For small mild-flavored vegetables or large mild-flavored ones that have been pared and cut in pieces, use ¼ inch water[1] in a very heavy pan and 1 inch water[1] in pan of lighter weight.

(d) For strong-flavored vegetables, as well as large whole ones, use enough water to cover.

[1] I don't recall ever seeing a pot, though there may be some, with inch markings, and since water is usually measured by cupfuls in order that the proper amount of salt may be added, the following, though only a rough estimate, may eliminate some of the guesswork:

NUMBER OF CUPFULS WATER TO INCH (FRACTIONS OF AN INCH MAY BE ESTIMATED FROM THESE FIGURES)

Diameter of Pan (at top) in inches	Capacity		Number of cupfuls required to fill pan to depth of 1 inch
5½	1	quart	1½
8	3	quarts	3
9	2	gallons	4
11	2½	gallons	5

(e) Tomatoes are simmered in their own juice and no water is added.

3. With the exception of corn on the cob, which is a bit more tender when cooked without salt and seasoned at table, and of young *Beet, Collard, Mustard,* or *Turnip Greens* or *Cabbage Southern Style** (cooked with ham bone or piece of salted or pickled pork), which should be seasoned with salt when ⅔ done, at this point, add salt to taste to water. If you wish to measure, use ½ rounded teaspoon salt for each cup water and stir salt into water until completely dissolved.

4. Bring salt water to rolling boil and add vegetables.

SIMMERED OR POACHED VEGETABLE CHART

VEGETABLE	HOW TO PREPARE FOR COOKING	FOR EACH SERVING	ESTIMATED SIMMERING TIME IN MINUTES
ARTICHOKES, GLOBE OR FRENCH Use barely enough water to cover. After heat is lowered, cover pan securely.	Trim stem to ½ to ¾ inch. Wash, and if desired, tie string around vegetable to hold leaves in place.	1	45 to 60
ARTICHOKES, JERUSALEM Use 1 inch water.[2] After heat is lowered, cover pan securely.	Wash, scrape, or pare with vegetable parer. Soak 20 minutes in cold water to which ½ tablespoon vinegar has been added. Drain. Slice or cook whole, as you wish.	¼ pound	14 to 33

[2] With very heavy pot, ¼ inch water may be used where 1 inch is specified.

VEGETABLE	HOW TO PREPARE FOR COOKING	FOR EACH SERVING	ESTIMATED SIMMERING TIME IN MINUTES
ASPARAGUS Use 1 inch water.[2] After heat is lowered, cover pan securely.	Discard part of stalk that can be easily snapped off. Remove scales with knife. Wash. Tie in serving-sized bundles.	$\frac{1}{3}$ to $\frac{1}{2}$ pound	Tips: 11 to 14 Whole: 15 to 20
BEANS, BUTTER OR LIMA Use 1 inch water.[2] After heat is lowered, cover pan securely.	If possible, just before cooking cut off rounded side of pod rim, cutting as close to edge as you can. Release beans from pod. Wash. If beans must be shelled in advance, store in plastic bag in refrigerator.	In Pod: $\frac{1}{2}$ to $\frac{2}{3}$ pound Shelled: $\frac{1}{3}$ to $\frac{1}{2}$ cup	18 to 25
BEANS, GREEN Use 1 inch water.[2] After heat is lowered, cover pan securely.	Chop or break off ends. If there are strings, remove. Cook whole, cut crosswise into 2 or 3 pieces, or lengthwise into thin strips.	$\frac{1}{4}$ pound	Whole: 18 to 28 Cut: 12 to 20
BEETS Use 1 inch of water.[2] After heat is lowered, cover pan securely.	Trim off leaves, but allow at least 1 inch of stalk to remain attached to root to prevent "bleeding." Wash. Do not cut, slice, or pare until cooked. Then blanch by pouring cold water over beets and slipping off skins.	$\frac{1}{4}$ pound	30 to 55

[2] With very heavy pot, $\frac{1}{4}$ inch water may be used where 1 inch is specified.

VEGETABLE	HOW TO PREPARE FOR COOKING	FOR EACH SERVING	ESTIMATED SIMMERING TIME IN MINUTES
BROCCOLI Use enough water to cover. Do not cover pan.	Remove large, tough leaves as well as tough parts of stalk. Wash and soak 15 minutes in cool tap water. Split stalks lengthwise in halves or quarters.	½ to ⅔ pound	15 to 25
BRUSSELS SPROUTS Use barely enough water to cover. Do not cover pan.	Wash. Remove outer leaves. Soak in cool tap water 15 minutes.	¼ pound	12 to 25
CABBAGE (*COOKBOOK STYLE*) Use barely enough water to cover. Do not cover pan.	Remove wilted outer leaves. Wash. Shred or quarter.	¼ to ⅓ pound	Shredded: 7 to 9 Quartered: 15 to 20
(*SOUTHERN STYLE*) Use barely enough water to cover. To cool, unsalted water, add ham bone, salt, or pickled pork. Bring to a boil. Add cabbage and again bring to a boil. Reduce heat. Do not cover pan. When ⅔ of estimated cooking time has expired, check "pot likker" and season to taste with salt and, if desired, with pepper.	SAME AS FOR COOKBOOK STYLE		

VEGETABLE	HOW TO PREPARE FOR COOKING	FOR EACH SERVING	ESTIMATED SIMMERING TIME IN MINUTES
CABBAGE, CELERY OR CHINESE Use barely enough water to cover. Do not cover pan.	Wash. Soak 15 minutes. Shred.	¼ to ⅓ pound	4 to 5
CARROTS Use 1 inch water.[2] After heat is lowered, cover pan securely.	Wash and scrape or pare with vegetable parer. Cook whole, sliced, or cubed.	¼ pound	Whole: 20 to 35 Sliced or Cubed: 6 to 20
CAULIFLOWER Use barely enough water to cover. Do not cover pan.	Remove outer leaves and stalk. If cooked whole, center core may be removed, if you desire. Cook whole, preferably tied in cheesecloth, or separated into flowerets.	⅓ to ½ pound	Whole: 17 to 22 Flowerets: 8 to 14
CELERY Use 1 inch water.[2] After heat is lowered, cover pan securely.	Wash. Cut off leaves and scrape. Remove all tough strings. Cut in 1- to 3-inch pieces, as you wish.	2 to 3 stalks	13 to 22

[2] With very heavy pot, ¼ inch water may be used where 1 inch is specified.

VEGETABLE	HOW TO PREPARE FOR COOKING	FOR EACH SERVING	ESTIMATED SIMMERING TIME IN MINUTES
CORN ON COB Use barely enough water (no salt) to cover. After heat is lowered, cover pan. Butter, salt, and pepper at table.	Husk and remove silk immediately before cooking. Wash.	1 to 2 ears	5 to 12
EGGPLANT If cooking whole, use barely enough water to cover. If cooking small cubes or pieces, use 1 inch water.[2] After heat is lowered, cover pan.	Wash. Do not pare if cooking whole. If you wish to cut into slices, or cubes, first pare.	½ small ⅓ medium ¼ large	Cubed or Sliced: 12 to 15 Whole: 20 to 45
GREENS: YOUNG BEET; CHARD; CHICORY; COLLARD; KALE; MUSTARD; SPINACH; TURNIP			
(COOKBOOK STYLE) Any of Above Greens Use ¼ inch water, plus water that clings to leaves after last washing. After heat is lowered, cover pan securely. If desired, drain and chop after simmering.	Remove roots and wilted leaves. Wash twice in lukewarm water and twice in cool water, lifting greens up and out of water after each washing so that sand will settle to bottom of pan.	⅓ to ½ pound	Young: 9 to 16 Not So Young: 20 to 32

[2] With very heavy pot, ¼ inch water may be used where 1 inch is specified.

VEGETABLE	HOW TO PREPARE FOR COOKING	FOR EACH SERVING	ESTIMATED SIMMERING TIME IN MINUTES
(*SOUTHERN STYLE*) Young Beet, Collard, Mustard, or Turnip Greens	SAME AS FOR COOKBOOK STYLE		

(*SOUTHERN STYLE*)
Young Beet, Collard, Mustard, or Turnip Greens
Use 1 inch water. To unsalted water, add ham bone, salt, or pickled pork. Bring to boil. Add greens. Again bring to boil; reduce heat. Cover pan securely. When ⅔ of estimated simmering time has expired, check "pot likker" and season to taste with salt and, if desired, with pepper.

TURNIP GREENS WITH ROOTS— SOUTHERN STYLE
Add turnip roots, pared and cut in 1-inch chunks, with greens to boiling water and ham bone, salt, or pickled pork. Cook your "mess of greens" until both root and greens are tender.

KOHLRABI
Use barely enough water to cover. Cook uncovered.   Cut off leaves. Pare and cut into slices or quarters.   1 to 1½   25 to 45

VEGETABLE	HOW TO PREPARE FOR COOKING	FOR EACH SERVING	ESTIMATED SIMMERING TIME IN MINUTES
OKRA Use 1 inch water.[2] After heat is lowered, cover pan securely.	Cut off stem end. Wash; cook whole.	6 to 8 pods	15 to 25
ONIONS Use barely enough water to cover. Do not cover pan.	Wash. Peel and cook whole, sliced, or quartered.	¼ to ⅓ pound	12 to 40
PARSNIPS Use 1 inch water.[2] After heat is lowered, cover pan securely.	Pare and if core is tough, remove it. Cut in ½-inch slices, quarters, or halves.	⅓ pound	8 to 15
PEAS, GREEN Use 1 inch water.[2] After heat is lowered, cover pan securely.	If possible, shell and wash just before cooking. If peas must be shelled in advance, store in plastic bag in refrigerator.	⅓ to ½ pound	12 to 22
POTATOES, SWEET Use barely enough water to cover. After heat is lowered, cover pan securely.	Wash and cook whole in jackets.	1 to 2	33 to 40
POTATOES, WHITE (IRISH) Use barely enough water to cover whole potatoes. Use 1 inch water for potatoes that have been cut in eighths, quarters, or halves or sliced. After heat is lowered, cover pan securely.	Wash. Cook in jackets or pare, with vegetable parer, and cook whole, or in eighths, quarters, halves or in thick slices.	⅓ to ½ pound	Whole: 30 to 45 Cut: 15 to 28

[2] With very heavy pot, ¼ inch water may be used where 1 inch is specified.

VEGETABLE	HOW TO PREPARE FOR COOKING	FOR EACH SERVING	ESTIMATED SIMMERING TIME IN MINUTES
SQUASH, SUMMER For whole squash, use barely enough water to cover. For slices or cubes, use 1 inch water.[2] After heat is reduced, cover pot securely.	Wash, but do not pare. Cook whole or cut in ½-inch slices or 1- to 1½-inch cubes.	½ to ⅔ pound	Sliced or Cubed: 10 to 15 Whole: 25 to 55
SQUASH, WINTER (HUBBARD) Use 1 inch water.[2] After heat is lowered, cover pan securely.	Wash, pare, if desired, and remove seeds and fibers. Cut into small pieces.	½ to ⅔ pound	23 to 33
TOMATOES Use no water, but cook in own juice, seasoned to taste with salt and pepper.	Wash, peel if desired. Slice or quarter.	¼ to ⅓ pound	8 to 10
TURNIPS Use barely enough water to cover. Do not cover pan.	Wash, pare, cut in thin slices or 1-inch cubes.	¼ pound	White: 18 to 22 Yellow: 22 to 24

6. If you want vegetables herb-flavored, see section on Vegetables under *Matching the Herb and/or Spice to the Food** for recommendations on which herbs to use with which vegetables. Add herbs when vegetables are added to boiling water.

7. When vegetables are added to boiling water, the temperature of the water will drop. Bring it back to boiling point and then reduce to low simmer. Securely cover greens or mild-flavored vegetables, but let those with strong flavor remain uncovered.

[2] With very heavy pot, ¼ inch water may be used where 1 inch is specified.

8. Several times during estimated cooking time, carefully stir contents in your pot, so that what was on top is moved to the bottom and vice versa, but do this so gently that nothing gets mashed.

9. After approximately ⅔ of estimated cooking time has expired, check salt, and if needed, add to taste. It should be gently stirred in so that it is evenly distributed.

10. The estimated simmering times shown in the *Simmered or Poached Vegetable Chart**, like the estimated cooking times for meat dishes, are only educated guesses. Many factors such as size, amount cooked, and just how tender the vegetable was when the cooking process started will govern the length of the simmering time; however, the estimate will at least give you some idea of what to expect. Shortly before the estimated cooking time expires, check either by piercing vegetable with a thin wire cake tester or, in the case of small vegetables, by tasting to see if tender. If the vegetable is not tender, and it cannot be reiterated too often, this means tender but still crisp, keep checking at frequent intervals to avoid overcooking.

11. And here are a few suggestions for serving:

(a) In the liquid in which vegetables were cooked. If it's "pot likker," this is a must. Also, if you can find some, and your doctor has no objections, the greens or cabbage in the "pot likker" should be accompanied with a jar or bottle of red pepper vinegar. And don't forget the *Cornbread**.

(b) Drain vegetables and serve hot with *White Sauce** or *Hollandaise Sauce** or any variation of either you choose, since most of them marry very happily with a vast majority of simmered vegetables. To make *CREAMED SPINACH*, add just enough hot *White Sauce**, *White Wine Sauce**, or *Cream Sauce** to the heated, drained, finely chopped simmered spinach to hold it together. Also, for variety, occasionally add ⅛ teaspoon cinnamon, nutmeg, or curry for each cup of drained, chopped spinach.

(c) Drain vegetables and serve with butter or margarine, either cut in thin slices and placed on top of the very hot vegetables, or melted. Should you wish, a small amount of minced chives, leeks, onion, or shallot may be cooked in the melted fat over low heat just until tender and then poured over the hot vegetable.

(d) Drain piping hot simmered artichoke bottoms, asparagus, broccoli, Brussels sprouts, green or lima beans, cauliflower, or white onions. Serve with sour cream or mayonnaise, which has been warmed over hot, but not boiling water, in the top of a double boiler, and to which, according to your taste, any of the following have been added: minced chives, parsley, and/or cayenne pepper. Also, just enough warmed mayonnaise as is needed to hold the vegetable together may be added to hot, finely chopped, well-drained simmered spinach. And a dash of curry lends a superb flavor to the spinach and mayonnaise (about ⅛ teaspoon of curry for each cup of the vegetable).

(e) Drain vegetables, chill and serve with salad dressing of your choice. Simmered artichokes, asparagus, beets, cauliflower, green beans, green peas, okra, and white potatoes are excellent when used as a salad.

(f) Drain and mash vegetables such as carrots, white or sweet potatoes, squash, and turnip roots. To the sweet potato, add, to taste, melted butter or margarine and brown or white sugar. If desired, stir in, also to taste, vanilla, sherry, or rum. Add onion juice or powder to taste to melted butter or margarine and whip into carrots, squash, or turnip roots. As for the white potato, a properly mashed and *CREAMED POTATO* is a work of art and just about as rare, even though it's quite simple to achieve, if you will only:

(*1*) Simmer potato just to point where pared pieces are tender enough to mash easily, but not in the least mushy.

(*2*) Drain well and then, to make doubly sure, shake (in pan in which they were cooked) over medium heat until dry.

(*3*) If desired, quickly pass through a coarse sieve.

(*4*) Add 1½ teaspoons butter or margarine for each medium-sized potato. Potato should be hot enough to melt fat.

(*5*) Mix butter or margarine with potato, mashing the vegetable as this is done, if it has not already been put through a sieve. The potato must be lump free.

(6) Gradually pour in hot milk, approximately 1 tablespoon for each medium-sized potato, beating constantly while pouring. Continue beating with fork or electric mixer until potato is light and fluffy. Milk must be added slowly, so as not to overdo a good thing, since, even though it's quite common, a slightly soupy mashed potato is a most unappetizing sight.

(7) When potato is light and fluffy, check seasoning and add salt to taste, beating it in so that it is evenly distributed.

(8) Serve without delay.

(g) Stuffed—see *Stuffed Eggplant** or *Stuffed Squash**

(h) Sprinkle asparagus, broccoli, or green beans liberally with toasted pecans or almonds.

12. Brief Recipe for Simmering or Poaching Vegetables: Measure water needed for particular vegetable being cooked—for recommended quantity see foregoing Section 5. Prepare vegetable for cooking, also as directed in Section 5. Add ½ rounded teaspoon salt for each cup water except for corn on cob or when smoked, salted, or pickled pork is used. Bring to boil. Add vegetable. Reduce heat to simmer. Cover pan when cooking mild-flavored vegetables. When ⅔ of estimated simmering time expires—also shown in Section 5, check salt and add to taste if needed. Check doneness by piercing with thin wire cake tester.

APPLES SIMMERED OR POACHED IN
SUGAR SYRUP
PEARS SIMMERED OR POACHED IN
SUGAR SYRUP

For each serving:

  1 large cooking apple
     OR
  1 large cooking pear
  Simple syrup enough to cover fruit (2 parts sugar to 1 part
     water or equal parts water and sauterne)
  4 whole cloves and/or ½ inch stick cinnamon, if desired

Peel and core fruit. Cut in half or quarter. Dissolve sugar in water and bring to a boil. Add fruit and again bring to a boil. Add spice, if desired. Reduce heat to slow simmer. Cover pan. Cook until fruit can be easily pierced with thin wire cake tester. Estimated cooking time 12 to 20 minutes.

VARIATIONS

Simmered or Poached Peaches—For each serving, substitute 2 large or 3 whole medium peaches for each apple or pear. Do not peel or stone fruit. When fruit is tender, if desired, skins may be slipped off and stones removed.

Simmered or Poached Carrots (Also known as **Candied Carrots)** —For each serving, substitute 2 medium-sized scraped carrots, cut in ½ - to ¾ -inch slices, for the apple or pear. If desired, when spice is added, 1 teaspoon grated orange or lemon peel may be added for each serving.

POACHED OR SIMMERED EGGS

    2 eggs for each serving
    Tap water to ⅔ fill shallow pan
    ¼ teaspoon salt for each cup of water
    Additional salt and, if desired, pepper to taste

Gently break each egg into a shallow saucer. Pour water into a pan with a 2¼ - to 2¾ -inch rim until pan is ⅔ filled. Add ¼ teaspoon salt for each cup water used. Bring to a boil. Add eggs, one at a time, slipping them very carefully to the sides of the pan. Reduce heat so eggs may simmer. Cover pan and cook 3 to 4 minutes (estimated). The eggs will come to top of water. Don't overcook as the yolks should be runny. Lift each egg with slotted spoon or pancake turner and hold above pan so water will drain off. Sprinkle with salt and, if desired, with pepper to taste. Serve without delay.

SUGGESTIONS FOR SERVING: Serve with spinach as a Florentine[3] or with toast or with *White Sauce** or *Hollandaise Sauce** or any desired variation of either.

POACHED OR SIMMERED CHICKEN
POACHED OR SIMMERED FISH

Quarters or halves of cleaned dressed broilers (between 1½ and 2¼ pounds)
OR
Breasts of fryers (from chickens weighing 2½ to 3½ pounds)
OR
Small whole fish (1¾ pounds or less) from which entrails have been removed
OR
½- to ¾-inch thick fish fillets or steaks
Water or equal parts water and dry white wine to cover
½ rounded teaspoon salt for each cup of water
⅛ teaspoon white pepper, if desired, for each cup of water
1 onion, peeled and cut in thin slices, if desired
1 tablespoon minced parsley, if desired

For each serving: ½ to ⅔ pound chicken, 1 to 1¼ pounds whole fish, as it comes from water, ½ to ⅔ pound dressed fish, or ⅓ to ½ pound fish fillets or steaks

Remove chicken or fish from refrigerator 10 to 15 minutes before cooking. Place in pan in which it is to be cooked—the pieces should not overlap—and measure amount of water needed to cover. Remove food from pan; pour off water and measure same quantity cool tap water or water and wine into pan. Add salt and, if desired, pepper. Bring to a boil. Add chicken or fish and, if desired, onion and/or parsley. Again bring to a boil. Reduce heat to

[3] See *Eggs Florentine**.

slow simmer and cover pan securely. Cook chicken until it can be easily pierced with fork or cook fish until when a small amount is pulled away, it will flake easily, although it is firm.

Estimated simmering times after heat is lowered are:

Chicken	40 to 50 minutes
Fish	7 to 12 minutes per pound (Estimate by weight of each piece and not total weight of all fish in pan.)

SUGGESTIONS FOR SERVING: Top either chicken or fish with *White Sauce** or *Hollandaise Sauce** or any of their variations.

POACHED OYSTERS

Sprinkle oysters lightly with salt and white pepper. Place in their own liquid in a saucepan and bring just to boiling point. Reduce heat and let oysters simmer until they puff and edges curl (3 to 5 minutes). Few people will just poach an oyster and serve it. It is actually an ingredient and not a dish.

11

Stuffings (or Dressings)

If you started your life during the first 20 years of this century, in a middle-class American family, then your upbringing undoubtedly included "chicken and dressing"—maybe in your part of the country it was "chicken and stuffing"—every Sunday and "turkey and dressing" (or "stuffing") on Thanksgiving and Christmas. Actually, many people prefer the stuffing to whatever it accompanies, and since it does a quite important basting job from the inside, it is a common and popular part of our diet.

The bread stuffings, be they crumbly or moist, are far and away the most popular of all the combinations that are used to fill the cavity in bird, fish, vegetable, or meat.

The methods for making crumbly and moist dressings are nearly the same. The big difference is that with a crumbly stuffing, you start by crumbling stale bread or *Cornbread** and with the moist one, you soak bread in water, stock, bouillon, or white wine and then squeeze it nearly dry.

GENERAL RULES FOR PREPARING STUFFING
(OR DRESSING)

1. Adjust recipe to make amount adequate for requirements. Unfortunately, there is no way to come up with a master recipe that will make exactly the amount of dressing for the particular size bird you are cooking, inasmuch as cavities are not made on an assembly line and so they differ; however, extra stuffing need not be wasted. Bake in a greased casserole or put in a carton or plastic bag and store in freezer for later use. The recipes for stuffings in this book are designed for an average 8- to 10-pound fowl, but they can be adjusted to meet almost any requirements as shown below:

ADJUSTING STUFFING RECIPES TO REQUIREMENTS

FOR	NUMBER OF EGGS	AMOUNT OF EACH OF OTHER INGREDIENTS
1½ to 2¼ pounds meat that is to be rolled	1	½ quantity specified in recipe
4- to 6½-pound chicken, capon, duck, or fish	2	⅔ to ¾ quantity specified in recipe
8- to 10-pound goose or turkey		Recipes as Given
11- to 13-pound goose or turkey	4	Full recipe plus ½ specified quantity of each ingredient
14- to 16-pound turkey	5	Full recipe plus ⅔ to ¾ specified quantity each ingredient
17- to 18-pound turkey		Double all quantities specified
19- to 20-pound turkey	7	Double recipe plus ½ specified quantity each ingredient

2. Hen, goose, duck, capon, or turkey may be stuffed on day previous to that on which it is to be baked and stored in refrigerator, or dressing may be prepared shortly before bird is to be cooked and stuffed into fowl as soon as stuffing is cool enough to handle. Also, dressing may be made a day ahead and stored in covered container in refrigerator or a week or so ahead and stored in freezer.

3. For a crumbly dressing, crumble bread or cornbread into large coarse crumbs; for a moist dressing, cut bread into large cubes. Measure crumbs or cubes.

4. If preparing moist dressing, put bread in shallow pan and add water, stock, bouillon, or an inexpensive dry white wine. Let stand 30 minutes. Squeeze as dry as possible. If wine, stock, or bouillon is used, reserve "squeezings."

5. Melt butter, margarine, vegetable shortening, or bacon drippings and heat to bubbling (360° F.).

6. Add onion and celery. Cook, stirring from time to time, until onion is clear.

7. Add crumbs or squeezed bread. Stir—the crumbs of course require more gentle handling—until fat is absorbed and onion and celery are well distributed throughout bread pieces or crumbs.

8. If desired, stir in parsley.

9. Stir in or sprinkle with stock, bouillon, or dry white wine. (The strained squeezings from the bread, and, if needed, additional liquid to make required amount, may be used.)

10. Beat eggs 60 strokes. Add a small amount of stuffing to eggs and when well blended, combine egg mixture with remainder of stuffing.

11. Add salt, and, if desired, pepper to taste. Stir into mixture so that seasoning is evenly distributed.

12. If using chestnuts, chopped giblets, herbs, nuts, poached oysters, or sage, add to stuffing and stir until evenly mixed throughout stuffing.

13. Cool and, at your convenience, stuff into bird, fish, meat pocket, or vegetable or spread on meat and roll. Do not pack stuffing as it expands; therefore, it should be loosely stuffed into a cavity.

CRUMBLY BREAD STUFFING
CRUMBLY CORNBREAD* STUFFING

For 8- to 10-pound bird[1]:

> Stale bread or *Cornbread** to make 4 cups very coarse
> crumbs
> 6 tablespoons (approximately ⅓ cup) butter, margarine,
> vegetable shortening, or bacon grease
> 12 tablespoons (¾ cup) minced onion
> 1½ cups (1 cup, plus 8 tablespoons) coarsely chopped scraped
> celery
> 4½ teaspoons (1½ tablespoons) minced parsley, if desired
> 4 tablespoons (¼ cup) stock, bouillon, or dry white wine
> 3 whole eggs
> Salt and pepper, if desired, to taste

Crumble bread or *Cornbread**. Measure. Melt fat and heat until
bubbling (360° F.). Add onion and celery and cook, stirring from
time to time, just until onion is clear. Add crumbs and stir gently
until fat is absorbed and onion and celery are mixed throughout
crumbs. Stir in parsley, if desired. Sprinkle liquid over mixture.
Beat eggs 60 strokes. Add small amount of hot stuffing to eggs
and when thoroughly mixed, stir into remainder of stuffing. Add
salt and, if desired, pepper to taste, stirring so that seasoning is
evenly distributed. Cool, and at your convenience, stuff into bird,
fish, or vegetable, or spread on meat and roll.

VARIATIONS

Moist Bread Stuffing—Cut bread in small cubes and substitute
for crumbs. Place in shallow pan and for each 4 cups bread cubes
add 1⅓ cups water, stock, bouillon, dry white wine. Let stand
30 minutes. Squeeze as dry as possible. If desired, "squeezings"

[1] Refer to Section 1 under *General Rules for Preparing Stuffing (or Dress-ing)** for suggestions on how to adjust recipe for differing requirements.
Measurements are shown both by spoon and cup so that it will be easier to
figure adjustments in recipe when either more or less dressing is required.

may be reserved and strained for use as liquid specified in basic recipe. If needed to make up required quantity, additional liquid may be added.

Chestnut Stuffing—After salt and, if desired, pepper are added to crumbly or moist stuffing, mix 1 cup chopped boiled chestnuts throughout dressing.

Chopped Giblet Stuffing—After salt and, if desired, pepper are added to crumbly or moist stuffing, add simmered chopped giblets and, if desired, coarsely chopped simmered neck meat from 1 or more birds.

Ground Giblet Stuffing—Put simmered giblets and, if available, the neck meat through fine blade of meat grinder. Combine with ¼ cup stock. Add to moist dressing before adding salt and, if desired, pepper. For a really luscious stuffing, for each 4 cups cubed bread, broil ½ pound young chicken livers. Cut half of livers into bite-sized pieces and mash remainder. When ground giblets are added to moist stuffing, add liver.

Herb Stuffing—For each 4 cups crumbs or bread cubes, add any or all of following with salt: ¼ teaspoon basil; ¼ teaspoon thyme; ⅛ teaspoon marjoram; ⅛ teaspoon cumin; 1 teaspoon monosodium glutamate. Also see *Sage Stuffing**.

Mushroom Stuffing—After salt and, if desired, pepper are added to crumbly or moist stuffing, mix throughout dressing ⅓ cup canned mushrooms (whole or in pieces).

Nut Stuffing—After salt and, if desired, pepper are added to crumbly or moist stuffing, mix throughout dressing any of following: 1 cup pecans, broken in pieces; 1 cup lightly toasted blanched almond slivers; 1 cup chopped filberts.

Oyster Stuffing—For each 4 cups crumbs or cubes of bread, use 12 medium-sized or 16 small *Poached Oysters**. Drain oysters and, after adding salt to stuffing, gently stir in oysters until they are evenly distributed throughout dressing.

Sage Stuffing—After adding salt and, if desired, pepper to dressing stir in ¾ teaspoon sage and ¼ teaspoon thyme for each 4 cups crumbs or bread cubes.

Sausage Stuffing—Before adding salt and, if desired, pepper to stuffing, stir in for each 4 cups crumbs or bread cubes ½ pound fresh pork sausage.

SEAFOOD STUFFING

For stuffing 4- to 5-pound fish or as main course to serve 4 or 5 people.

> *Moist Bread Stuffing**, made with 2 eggs and ⅔ of each of other ingredients specified in basic recipe, excepting salt and pepper
> 2½ cups cooked crab meat and/or cooked, shelled, deveined shrimp cut in ½-inch segments
> OR
> 2 cups cooked crab meat and shrimp with 16 small drained *Poached Oysters**
> Any or all of following:
> ¼ teaspoon cumin
> ¼ teaspoon basil
> 1 teaspoon monosodium glutamate
> ¼ teaspoon turmeric
> 1 tablespoon Worcestershire sauce
> ¼ teaspoon Tabasco sauce
> Salt and, if desired, pepper to taste

Prepare stuffing up to point where salt is added. Add seafood and any or all of following, as desired: cumin, basil, monosodium glutamate, turmeric, Worcestershire sauce, and Tabasco sauce. Season to taste with salt and if desired with pepper. Stuff into fish or if using as main course, spoon into shallow 9-inch baking dish and bake in 350° F. oven for approximately 22 minutes.

NOTE: If using as main course, if you wish, before baking, sprinkle with ⅓ cup fine toast or cereal crumbs, combined, if you like, with 2 tablespoons grated Parmesan cheese and dotted with small dabs of butter or margarine.

STUFFED EGGPLANT
STUFFED SQUASH

For each 2 servings:

2 tablespoons margarine or butter
2 tablespoons minced onion
4 tablespoons celery, chopped fine
⅔ cup loosely packed bread crumbs
1 teaspoon parsley, if desired
1 cup simmered eggplant[2] or white or creamy white summer
  squash pulp,[2] drained and well mashed
⅛ teaspoon thyme, if desired
⅛ teaspoon basil, if desired
1 egg
Salt and, if desired, pepper to taste
2 tablespoons bread or cereal crumbs
1½ teaspoons butter or margarine

Melt 2 tablespoons margarine or butter until it bubbles (360° F.).
Add onion and celery and cook, stirring from time to time until
onion is clear. Add crumbs and, if desired, parsley. Cook over
medium heat, stirring until fat is absorbed and onion and celery
are evenly distributed throughout crumbs. Stir in vegetable pulp,
and, if desired, thyme, and/or basil. Beat egg slightly; add small
amount of hot vegetable mixture to egg and stir until blended.
Combine with remainder of stuffing and season to taste with salt,
and, if desired, with pepper. Spoon mixture into 6-ounce baking
cups or very small vegetable shell. For larger quantities use vegetable shells, individual baking cups, or large casserole. Sprinkle
crumbs over top; dot with butter or margarine. Bake 20 to 25
minutes in 350° F. oven (depending on depth of mixture in baking dish) until crumbs are a rich brown.

[2] See *Simmered or Poached Vegetable Chart**.

VARIATION

Stuffed Eggplant with Seafood; Stuffed Squash with Seafood
—Just before adding salt, for each 2 servings, stir in 1 cup cooked crab meat and/or shelled, deveined, cooked shrimp, cut in 1-inch segments. If desired, also add 6 medium-sized *Poached Oysters**.

NOTE: This is almost a *One Dish Meal* and need only be accompanied by a green salad to provide a delicious dinner.

STUFFED TOMATOES

For each serving:

> 1 firm tomato (approximately ½ pound)
> Salt
> 2 tablespoons butter, margarine, or bacon grease
> 2 tablespoons finely chopped onion
> 1 tablespoon finely chopped celery
> ⅔ cup loosely packed stale bread crumbs
> 1 teaspoon minced parsley, if desired
> ⅛ teaspoon thyme, if desired
> ¼ egg[3]
> Salt and pepper to taste
> ½ tablespoon fine bread or cereal crumbs
> ½ teaspoon butter or margarine

Cut slice from stem end of tomato. Scoop out pulp with small spoon, being careful not to break tomato shell. Sprinkle inside of shell lightly with salt and turn upside down on rack. Let stand for 20 to 30 minutes, as convenient. Cut pulp in small pieces. Heat 2 tablespoons fat until it bubbles (360° F.). Add onion and celery and cook, stirring from time to time, until onion is clear. Add crumbs, and if desired, parsley and thyme. Stir while cook-

---

[3] Beat whole egg 60 strokes. Measure out needed quantity. If desired, remainder may be put in jar, securely covered, and stored in refrigerator for a couple of days until needed for something else.

ing over medium heat until fat is absorbed. If tomato pieces have not drawn much liquid, mash part of pulp and then add pulp and liquid to crumb mixture. Stir until blended. Combine a small amount of stuffing with slightly beaten egg, and then add to remainder of mixture. Season to taste with salt and pepper. Spoon into tomato shell. Top with crumbs and dot with butter or margarine. Bake in 350° F. oven 20 to 25 minutes until tomato shell is tender, but still firm enough to hold shape.

VARIATIONS

If desired, add any one of the following for each tomato, just before spooning stuffing into shell—1 tablespoon crisp, crumbled bacon; 1 tablespoon cooked, shelled, deveined shrimp, cut in small segments; 1 tablespoon cooked crab meat; 1 tablespoon grated cheese.

12

The Biscuit, Dumpling, Shortcake, and Pie Dough Family

I have met a lot of people who don't like ice cream and even more who can't stand caviar, but I have never met a man who didn't like biscuits—especially homemade ones.

It's a fortunate coincidence, therefore, that jokes and legends to the contrary, biscuits are quite easy to make and can be mixed and baked in a hurry.

GENERAL RULES FOR PREPARING BISCUITS

1. Preheat oven 10 minutes to 450° F. for large soft biscuits and to 475° F. for *Small Flaky Southern-type Biscuits**.

2. Sift plain all purpose flour and then place sifter in a fairly large bowl, preferably with a flat bottom—the big bowl of the electric mixer is ideal. Measure sifted flour specified in recipe and put it in sifter.

3. Add a scant ¼ to a rounded ¼ teaspoon (according to taste) salt and 1½ teaspoons baking powder for each cup of flour and sift.

4. If making herb-flavored biscuits, add herbs to flour mixture.

5. Measure shortening, which should be room temperature and soft, but not runny. Lard may be used, but a vegetable shortening or one made of a mixture of vegetable oil and animal fat is preferable. For the large soft biscuits use 2 tablespoons shortening for each cup of sifted flour; for the flaky, small biscuits that are typical of the South, use 3 tablespoons shortening for each cup of flour. As each tablespoon of shortening is measured, place it on the flour, keeping the 2 (or 3, as the case may be) tablespoons shortening separated. Actually, it could be added in a lump, but it's easier and quicker to cut in if each tablespoon is put in a different part of the bowl.

6. Use a pastry blender or 1 or 2 small sharp knives to cut the shortening into the flour until you have a mixture that resembles coarse meal with a few particles the sizes of peas and beans in the "meal."

(a) If using a pastry blender, bring it down through 1 tablespoon of fat and into flour. With the bottom of the blender just touching the bottom of the bowl, quickly and lightly push blender back and forth from one side of bowl to the other, but never in exactly the same path, so that your blender will "travel" through all the flour and shortening in the bowl. At least 5 or 6 times during the short period it takes to cut in shortening, using the pastry blender, bring the flour and fat from the sides of the bowl to the center. Continue cutting through flour and fat until there are hundreds of tiny particles and a few larger ones as mentioned above.

(b) If using 1 small sharp knife, continue cutting down through the shortening into the flour, holding your knife at just the angle it would be held if you were cutting a piece of meat on a dinner plate—until you get a mixture that has the desired meal-like consistency.

(c) If using 2 knives, handle them just as you would if you were cutting meat into shreds with the paths of the 2 knives crossing each other during this cutting-in process. Continue cutting until mixture has a meal-like consistency, with a few pea- and bean-sized particles in it. If for some reason you find you have a "lump" of flour and shortening, or several "lumps," use 1 small sharp knife to cut the "lump(s)" into particles.

7. If making cheese- or bacon-flavored biscuits, the cheese or bacon should be mixed with shortening and flour particles before liquid is added.

8. Add milk by sprinkling it by the tablespoon over the particles. For the large soft biscuits, use approximately ⅓ cup for each cup sifted flour and for the Southern-style biscuit use approximately ¼ cup. If you make a mistake and dump all the milk into the dry ingredients at one time, there'll be no dire consequences—in fact, many excellent cooks do just this. As milk is added, stir particles together with a table fork. It is probable that by the time the quantity of milk specified in the recipe is stirred in you will have a single mass of dough. If not, gently pat it into a ball with your fingers. Incidentally, if there are some "dry" particles remaining in the bowl, very, very gradually—a teaspoonful at a time—sprinkle them with milk so that they will be slightly dampened and will adhere to and become part of the ball.

9. Rub sifted flour into pastry cloth, or if you don't have a pastry cloth, use a piece of wax paper and cover it evenly and lightly with sifted flour. It is best to sift flour onto paper and it takes approximately ¼ cup to cover a piece of paper 12×14 inches. If you are going to use a rolling pin (this is a matter of choice), if you have a stockinette cover, rub sifted flour into cover; if you don't have a cover, sift flour over pin until it is lightly covered with a film of the flour. When you roll any dough you must watch (a) that you have enough flour on cloth, or paper, and on pin so that the dough does not stick to any of them, (b) that you don't use so much flour on cloth, paper, or pin so that it gets into the dough and toughens it.

10. Large soft biscuits should be kneaded, but since an excellent small flaky biscuit can be made without kneading, it is a matter of personal preference in the latter case. Whether you knead or not, shape the dough with lightly floured hands into a ball and place the ball on the floured pastry cloth or wax paper. Flatten the ball by pressing it down gently with the palm of the hand. To knead, fold dough toward yourself so that it forms 2 layers; press down on folded dough with heel of hand and then give a quarter turn; again fold, press with heel of hand, and turn again. Repeat folding, pressing, and turning operations 12 to 14 times until the dough feels springy and elastic for the soft large biscuits, and repeat, if you wish to knead the small flaky ones, 4 or 5 times.

11. Either pat dough or lightly roll it away from yourself with a rolling pin until you have a rectangle approximately ½-inch thick for the large biscuits and ¼-inch thick for the small flaky ones. If using a rolling pin, do not roll it back and forth over the dough. You may have to go over the same area of dough several times to get it to the desired thickness, but if you do, raise your rolling pin above the dough to bring it back to the starting point or to the beginning of the area that is too thick and then lightly roll it away from yourself just as you did the first time.

12. Cut biscuits to desired size—1¾ to 2 inches in diameter for the large ones and 1¼ to 1½ inches for the small ones. When making square biscuits, either use a floured sharp knife and cut dough into squares or use a lightly floured ice cube divider from your freezer tray. In any case, when squares are made there are no leftover pieces of dough to fit together. If making rounds, use a round biscuit cutter, a small glass with a thin edge, a metal jigger measure, or the large end of a metal tube from an icing decorator set. Lightly dip the rim of whatever you are using as a cutter to a depth that is equal or just a little more than the thickness to which dough has been rolled in sifted flour. Rounds should be cut as close together as possible to keep leftover dough to a minimum. When the rounds have been placed on a baking sheet, gently push the leftover pieces together, then pinch cracks together and pat or, if desired, roll to desired thickness. Do not reknead your dough. While reworking the dough into a ball before patting or rolling it is not generally accepted practice, I have done this, handling the dough lightly and with care, many times, and I've never had a complaint about any of the biscuits. After dough has been patted or rolled out, cut rounds very close together.

13. Place biscuits on a heavy or a shiny ungreased baking sheet without a rim. If your baking sheet has a rim, turn it over and place biscuits on top of the bottom of the pan. The large soft biscuits should be placed close together; the small flaky ones should be baked 1 to 1½ inches apart so their sides will be crusty.

14. If you are cooking 1 tray of biscuits, place in center of oven; if you are cooking 2 trays of biscuits, place one in center and put second tray on a rack approximately 2 inches above center rack.

15. Biscuit dough may be made either just before baking or the dough may be prepared in advance. If it is made in advance, wrap ball of dough in plastic wrap or aluminum foil, store in refrigerator and take it out of refrigerator about 5 minutes before rolling or patting it out and cutting out the biscuits, *or* first roll and cut biscuits, place on baking tray, and store in refrigerator until just a few minutes before baking. Biscuit dough also keeps very well in the freezer. If the dough is stored in a freezer, let it stand at room temperature just until it softens before rolling, as while this won't improve or harm the dough, it will make the job of rolling and cutting easier.

16. Bake large, soft biscuits in a 450° F. oven 10 to 12 minutes; *Small Flaky (Southern-type) Biscuits** in a 475° F. oven 6 to 7 minutes.

17. If at the end of estimated baking time, biscuits are fully risen and as brown as desirable on bottoms, but not brown enough on top, place them so that top surface is approximately 4 inches under broiler unit and cook just until tops are golden brown. Watch closely as this should only take a couple of minutes.

BISCUITS—LARGE AND SOFT TYPE

1 cup sifted all purpose flour
¼ scant to rounded teaspoon salt, according to taste
1½ teaspoons double acting baking powder
2 tablespoons vegetable or combined animal fat and vegetable
  oil shortening
⅓ cup (approximate) milk

Yield: 6 2-inch diameter biscuits or 10 1¾-inch diameter biscuits.

NOTE: Double quantity of each ingredient to make 12 2-inch diameter biscuits and triple each quantity for 18 2-inch diameter biscuits.

Preheat oven to 450° F. Measure sifted flour, salt, and baking powder into sifter and sift into a large bowl. Add shortening. Cut through shortening and dry ingredients until mixture has consistency of coarse meal, with a few particles the sizes of peas and beans mixed through the "meal." Add milk by tablespoons —when making 12 or 18 biscuits, use ¼ of milk for each addition—and stir with fork as milk is added until there is a mass of dough. If there are some dry particles remaining in the bowl, very, very gradually—a teaspoonful at a time—sprinkle them with additional milk so that they will be slightly dampened and will adhere to and become a part of the mass. Knead dough a total of 12 to 14 times; roll or pat to ½-inch thickness; cut out biscuits; place rounds or squares close together on baking sheet; and bake in 450° F. oven 10 to 12 minutes. If desired, tops may be browned under broiler unit.

VARIATIONS

Small Flaky (Southern-type) Biscuits—For each cup of sifted flour, increase shortening to 3 tablespoons and decrease milk to ¼ cup (approximate). If you desire, knead dough 4 or 5 times.

Roll or pat to ¼-inch thickness and for each cup of flour, cut out twelve 1½- or sixteen 1¼-inch diameter biscuits. Place biscuits 1 to 1½ inches apart on baking sheet and bake in 475° F. oven 6 to 7 minutes.

Bacon Biscuits—For each cup of sifted flour used, add 3 tablespoons crisply cooked and crumbled bacon just before adding milk.

Caraway Seed Biscuits—For each cup of sifted flour, add, just before cutting in shortening: ¾ teaspoon caraway seed and, if desired, ¼ teaspoon dry mustard and/or ⅛ teaspoon sage.

Cheese Biscuits—For each cup of sifted flour, add 3 tablespoons grated Cheddar cheese before adding milk.

Chive Biscuits—For each cup of sifted flour used, add, just before cutting in shortening, 1½ tablespoons minced chives.

DUMPLINGS

For dumplings, use a little more milk and a little less baking powder than for biscuits. The dumplings are dropped by teaspoonfuls and steamed instead of being rolled, cut, and baked.

PLAIN DUMPLINGS

1 cup sifted all purpose flour
¼ rounded teaspoon salt
1¼ teaspoons double acting baking powder
3 tablespoons vegetable or combined animal fat and vegetable oil shortening
½ cup milk

Yield: Approximately 20 dumplings.

Measure sifted flour and place in sifter. Add salt and baking powder and sift into large bowl. Cut in shortening until mixture resembles coarse meal with a few pea- and bean-sized particles mixed throughout. Add milk gradually and stir mixture only until smooth. Drop dough by teaspoonfuls into pot of stewing chicken or meat that has been brought to a boil. Drop dumplings so that they rest on chicken or meat and are not in the liquid. Cook 10 minutes in uncovered pot; cover pan securely and cook 10 minutes more. Serve at once.

VARIATION

Herb and/or Cheese Dumplings—Add any or all of following to sifted flour, baking powder, and salt before cutting in shortening: ¼ teaspoon cumin; 1 tablespoon minced parsley or dehydrated parsley flakes; 2 tablespoons grated Parmesan or Cheddar cheese (or 1 tablespoon of each); 1 tablespoon chives.

SHORTCAKES

For the shortcake, cut shortening into flour mixture in 2 separate operations (while it can actually be done in 1 operation, the dough won't be as flaky). Roll dough, dot half of it with butter or margarine and then fold second (and undotted) half over first half to make 2 layers from which rounds or rectangles are cut.

SHORTCAKES FOR CREAMED FOOD

1 cup sifted all purpose flour
¼ rounded teaspoon salt
1½ teaspoons double acting baking powder
3 tablespoons vegetable or combined animal fat and vegetable oil shortening
¼ cup milk
1½ teaspoons firm but not hard butter or margarine

Yield: 4 2-inch or 3 3-inch shortcakes. To make 8 2-inch or 6 3-inch shortcakes, double quantity of each ingredient.

Preheat oven to 450° F. Measure sifted flour, salt, and baking powder into sifter and sift into large bowl. Add half of shortening and cut into dry ingredients until mixture resembles coarse meal; cut in remaining shortening until it appears to be made up of hundreds of particles the sizes of small peas and beans. Add milk by tablespoons (when recipe is doubled use ¼ of milk for each addition), stirring with a fork until there is a single mass of dough. If by the time all milk has been stirred into dry ingredients this mass has not formed, help it along by lightly shaping dough with floured fingers into a ball. If desired, knead dough 5 or 6 times on floured pastry cloth or wax paper. Flatten dough and shape into a rectangle. Roll or pat until the rectangle is ⅜-inch thick and approximately 4×6 inches. Dot surface of half of rectangle nearest yourself with tiny pieces of butter or margarine. Fold other half of rectangle over "dotted" half, making 2 layers of dough. Very lightly press edges of the 2 layers together. Cut into rectangles or rounds and place about 1½ to 2 inches apart on heavy or shiny ungreased baking sheet without rim. Bake in 450° F. oven 10 to 12 minutes. If necessary, tops may be browned under broiler unit. Split shortcakes in two; cover lower half of each with *Creamed Meat or Poultry**, *Creamed Eggs**, or *Creamed Seafood**.

Dessert Shortcakes—Add 1½ tablespoons granulated sugar to the cup of sifted flour. Instead of creamed food, spoon sweetened, room-temperature, fresh, defrosted, frozen, or drained canned fruit slices or berries of your choice over lower half of each shortcake. Cover with top layer and pour thick cream or spoon whipped cream, slightly sweetened to taste, if you so desire, over it. If you wish, decorate with berries and/or fruit.

PIE DOUGH

Pie dough is the shortest member of the family, so it contains more shortening, less liquid (the liquid used is water and I like mine iced, but regular tap water may be used), and the baking powder may be omitted entirely or just a small quantity used.

1 cup sifted all purpose flour
¼ rounded teaspoon salt
⅛ teaspoon double acting baking powder, if desired
5 tablespoons vegetable or combined animal fat and vegetable oil shortening
2 tablespoons (approximate) water—iced preferred, but regular tap water may be used

Yield: 1 9-inch pie shell. For 2 shells or double crust pie, double quantity of each ingredient.

Measure sifted flour, salt, and, if desired, baking powder into sifter, and sift into large bowl. Add 3 tablespoons of shortening and cut into dry ingredients until mixture resembles coarse meal. (If making 2 shells or double crust pie, add 5 tablespoons shortening at this time, since a total of 10 tablespoons will be required). Add remaining shortening and cut in fat until mixture appears to be made up of hundreds of particles the sizes of small peas and beans. Sprinkle 1 tablespoon water over mixture, stirring with fork as liquid is added, and then sprinkle second tablespoon of water over it, continuing to stir with fork. If making 2 shells or double crust, sprinkle water by tablespoons and stir after each addition until 4 tablespoons of liquid are used. After the water has been stirred into flour and shortening, handling with care (I treat pie dough and gin the same way; I don't bruise either), with your fingers, gather the dough into a mass and gently pat into a ball. If there are some dry particles remaining in the bowl, very, very gradually—a teaspoonful at a time—add water so that they will be slightly dampened in order that they may also be gathered into the mass of dough. Pinch together any "cracks" in the ball until it is entirely smooth. If making 2 *Pie Shells** make 2 balls of equal size, and if making a *Double Crust Pie**, make 2 balls with the one for the bottom crust just slightly larger than the other.

Rolling Out Pie Dough

Put ball of dough on center of lightly floured pastry cloth or wax paper, placed if possible on a small table around which you can move or at least get around a couple of sides, since pastry should be kept in a circle and this is much easier to do if when rolling the pastry you can get at it from different angles; however, if this can't be arranged, you can, of course, stand in one spot and move the pin so as to roll the dough out in a circle. Flatten the ball of dough into a small "perfect" circle. If there are any breaks in the dough during this flattening process, mend by pinching dough together and then pat the "mend" smooth.

Use rolling pin with stockinette cover and rub flour into cover so it won't stick, or sift flour over rolling pin so that it is lightly covered with a film (and whenever it gives any indication of sticking, sift a little more flour over it). Lightly and quickly roll dough, doing everything possible to keep it in a circle. Don't roll pin back and forth over dough, although to keep it circular you are going to have to start the "rolls" of the pin from different spots inside the circle. Inasmuch as the dough is short, there will undoubtedly be breaks around the circumference when you roll, but whenever there is such a break, stop rolling, pinch the edges of the broken dough together and mend the circle.

For a 9-inch pie shell, roll dough until it is approximately ⅛-inch thick and until the circle has a diameter of 12½ to 13 inches.

Pie Shell

Fold the rolled out pastry across center into 2 equal parts. Place pie pan next to the "fold" so that rim almost touches pastry. Lightly moisten rim of pan with a very small amount of water. Working as fast, but most of all, as carefully as possible, lift and transfer pastry to pan, placing pastry so that fold in dough bisects pie pan. Gently lift top layer of dough, so as to unfold pastry, and arrange it loosely so that entire pie pan is covered. Don't stretch the dough. Pat it gently into place so that it is a "good (though not tight) fit" for the pie pan. If the dough should break at any spot while this is being done, gently pinch edges of break together and then lightly pat the "mend" until dough in this spot is smooth. A small amount of iced water can be used on the finger for this "mending" job. Trim dough with scissors from around the rim so that about 1 inch of pastry hangs over edge. Since accidents happen to the best of us, if your "edge of dough" is not even, patch the spots where dough is needed by pinching some of dough that was trimmed from pie onto the part of the shell that is a little "shy" of dough. If necessary, these patches may also be sealed by dipping a finger in ice water and then passing it around the edges of the patch.

Fold the extra inch of dough that overhangs the rim of the pie pan under the dough that covers the rim. Seal these layers of dough that make up the rim together: (1) for a **Ridged Pie Rim,** place a dinner fork diagonally across the rim and press down so that the layers of dough are sealed together (but not cut through) and the rim of the pie is decorated by the ridges left by the tines of the fork. Continue doing this until entire rim is covered with ridges made by tines of the fork; or (2) for a **Fluted Pie Rim,** place ends of thumb and the index finger diagonally across the dough on the pie pan rim. The thumb and finger should be about ⅙ inch apart. Pinch dough between thumb and finger together. Move thumb to where index finger was and place end of index finger diagonally across dough about ⅙ inch from thumb. Again pinch dough between 2 digits together. Repeat until whole rim is fluted.

DRIED PIE SHELL

(One culmination of *Pie Dough**, *Rolling Out Pie Dough**, and *Pie Shell**)

If mixture not much thicker than milk[1] is to be poured into shell, place slice of bread in center of *Pie Shell** and arrange pieces of bread around center slice until bottom of shell and part of sides are protected by bread. Place in oven that has been pre-heated to 475° F. for 10 minutes. Loosely arrange sheet of aluminum foil over shell, including rim. Bake 4 minutes. Remove from oven. Cool and remove bread. If there are any crumbs left in shell, either lightly brush or blow them out.

BAKED PIE SHELL

(Another possible culmination of *Pie Dough**, *Rolling Out Pie Dough**, and *Pie Shell**)

If a thick custard[2] is to be placed in *Pie Shell**, the shell may be baked before filling is added. Prick entire inner surface, sides as well as bottom, with a fork. Place in 475° F. oven and bake 8 minutes. Should pastry puff while baking, immediately prick in several places.

[1] See *Baked Custard Pies**, *Baked Vanilla Custard Pie**, *Baked Caramel Custard Pie**, *Baked Butterscotch Custard Pie**, *Baked Chocolate Custard Pie**, *Baked Lemon Custard Pie**, *Baked Sour Cream Custard Pie**, and *Coconut Custard Pie**.
[2] See *Refrigerator Custard Pies**, Vanilla—Butterscotch—Caramel—Chocolate—Coconut—Eggnog—Fruit and/or Nut—Lemon—Sour Cream. See also *Top of the Stove Custard Pies**, Custard—Butterscotch—Chocolate—Coconut ⚬1 or ⚬2—Coffee—Lemon—Mocha.

DOUBLE CRUST PIE

Double *Pie Dough** recipe and from the slightly larger ball roll
out circle of dough with a diameter of 11½ to 12¼ inches and
prepare *Pie Shell**. Trim dough even with the outer edge of the
rim of the pie pan. Roll smaller ball of dough, also keeping it
circular, until it is just slightly thinner than dough for the shell.
This circle should have a diameter of between 10½ and 11 inches.
Fold the rolled out pastry exactly in half. Make 8 or 10 slits in
and around what will be the center of the top crust when the
pastry is unfolded on top of pie, so as to permit steam to escape
(otherwise, top crust will puff up, leaving hollows between it
and the filling). Quickly fill shell with any of the *Fruit Fillings
for Pies**. Working quickly, but also as carefully as you can, lift
and transfer folded pastry to top of pie, so that fold bisects middle
of pie. Gently unfold pastry. Trim dough of top "crust" with a
scissors so that about ¾ inch of pastry hangs over edge of rim.
Fold this edge under the pastry of the shell that covers the rim of
the pie pan. Press dough together all around edge of the rim of
pan. Either make a *Ridged Pie Rim** or a *Fluted Pie Rim**.

OR

If you prefer a LATTICE CRUST, roll out pastry reserved for top
crust until it is ⅛-inch thick. Cut into ⅜-inch wide strips. Place
a 12×12-inch square of wax paper on a flat surface. Weave the
strips of dough into a lattice by crisscrossing them. Chill thoroughly.
Quickly turn lattice over filling, immediately after lightly brushing
rim of shell with iced water. Trim off dough from lattice that
overhangs rim of pan. Seal lattice top to shell rim by pressing end
of each strip firmly down on that part of the rim on which the
strip rests.

FRUIT FILLINGS FOR PIES

See *Double Crust Pie**.

BLACKBERRY PIE

4 cups fresh, washed, drained, and dried blackberries
⅓ cup all purpose flour, measured, then sifted
1 cup sugar
1½ tablespoons butter, if desired

Combine berries with flour and sugar. Spoon into 9-inch pie shell. If desired, dot with small pieces of butter. Cover with top crust (*Lattice Crust** may be used, if you wish). Bake in 425° F. oven 35 to 40 minutes until light golden brown.

VARIATIONS

Blueberry Pie—Substitute 4 cups fresh, washed, drained, and dried blueberries for blackberries.

Boysenberry Pie—Substitute 4 cups fresh, washed, drained, and dried boysenberries for blackberries.

Loganberry Pie—Substitute 4 cups fresh, washed, drained, and dried loganberries for blackberries.

Raspberry Pie—Substitute 4 cups fresh, washed, drained, and dried raspberries for blackberries.

Cherry Pie—Substitute 4 cups pitted, washed, drained, and dried fresh cherries for blackberries.

Canned Cherry and Fresh Apple Pie; Canned Cherry and Fresh Peach Pie—Several hours before baking pie, drain 1¼ cups pitted red canned pie cherries and mix well with 1 teaspoon red vegetable coloring. Add just enough water to cover cherries and place in refrigerator. Stir from time to time. Shortly before baking pie, again drain cherries and combine with 2¾ cups peeled, sliced peaches or cored, peeled, and sliced tart apples. Substitute this fruit mixture for blackberries.

Sliced Peach Pie—Substitute 4 cups peeled, sliced peaches for blackberries.

Sliced Apricot Pie—Substitute 4 cups sliced, peeled apricots for blackberries.

Apple Pie ⚹1—Substitute 6½ cups peeled, cored, and thinly sliced pie apples for blackberries. Omit flour. After fruit and sugar are combined, mix in ½ teaspoon cinnamon, ¼ teaspoon nutmeg or cardamon, ¾ teaspoon grated lemon peel, and 1½ teaspoons lemon juice.

Apple Pie ⚹2—Substitute 3¾ cups cooked, sweetened, drained, and well-mashed apples for blackberries. Omit flour, sugar, and butter.

Mince Pie—Substitute 3¾ cups mincemeat for blackberries and omit flour, sugar, and butter. If desired, 3¼ cups of mincemeat and ½ cup finely chopped, peeled and cored apples may be used instead of the 3¾ cups mincemeat. Also, if you like, before placing mincemeat or mincemeat and apples in shell, sprinkle filling lightly with cognac, Napoleon brandy, rum, or applejack.

13

Baked Custards
and Gelatin Custards

If you have never done any cooking, but would like to have the very pleasant sensation of succeeding in the kitchen without really trying (even at the very start of your career as a cook), begin with a baked cup custard. It's easy to make; it's a favorite with young and old, sick and well, the epicure and the man of the simplest tastes. Furthermore, if you can make a *Vanilla Custard**, you are just a step or maybe two from making:

1. *Baked Cup Custards**, in many flavors, including the perennial favorite chocolate.
2. *Custard Gelatin Desserts**, also in numerous flavors.
3. Refrigerator Freezer Custard Ice Creams (*Country Custard Ice Cream**), as smooth and lip-smacking good as the old-fashioned, crank-freezer kind of mama's day.
4. *Baked Custard Pies** and *Refrigerator Custard Pies**.
5. *Baked Bread Puddings** and something equally delicious, but brand new, *Refrigerator Bread Puddings**.

GENERAL RULES FOR BAKED CUSTARDS

1. Preheat oven for 10 minutes to 350° F.

2. Bring water in bottom of double boiler to a rapid boil.

3. If custards are to be unmolded, grease cups thoroughly with butter or margarine.

4. If using either the *Cooked Butterscotch Topping** or the *Caramel Topping**, prepare and divide equally between custard cups. Let stand until solidified enough to stay in place—this will only take a few minutes—before pouring or spooning in custard mixture.

5. Except for *Sour Cream Custard**, measure milk or milk and caramel mixture into top of double boiler. If using chocolate, add premelted type or cooking type, broken in small pieces, to milk. When making the *Sour Cream Custard**, let cream and ¼ cup milk stand until room temperature.

6. Scald milk over boiling water. If using either caramel or chocolate, before removing from over hot water, beat with rotary egg beater until smooth.

7. When milk is scalded or in the case of the *Sour Cream Custard** when milk and cream are room temperature, beat eggs 60 strokes with fork or wire whip—just enough to combine yolks and whites without overbeating.

8. Add sugar (or sugar substitute), salt, and vanilla or other flavoring, and lemon rind, if specified in recipe, to eggs. Stir only until well blended.

9. Pour milk through a sieve into egg mixture or stir in sour cream and ¼ cup milk into egg mixture. Beat only long enough to mix ingredients completely—the sugar should be completely dissolved.

10. Place custard cups in large pan with 1½- to 2-inch rim and pour or spoon custard mixture into cups, dividing it equally.

11. Pull out center rack of oven so that it extends 2 or 3 inches beyond open door and place pan holding custard cups on rack gently.

12. Pour very hot water—it's all right to use water from bottom of double boiler—into pan holding cups, filling it to a depth of approximately ¾ inch. Try not to get any water on the custards, but a drop or two won't ruin them.

13. Bake until a small table knife inserted in center of one of the cup custards will come out "clean." In the case of the baked custard pie or the bread pudding, insert knife in side of pie or pudding instead of in center. The center will set after pie or pudding is removed from oven. Don't overcook custards; this results in their being watery. Baking time will vary, depending on size of baking cups, whether they are completely or only partially filled, temperature of water in pan in which cups are placed, etc. If the 6-ounce cup is used, as suggested for following recipes, custards should bake in approximately 40 to 50 minutes. Since this estimated cooking time is one of those educated guesses, it would be advisable to make first check (inserting knife into custard) after custard has cooked 35 minutes. If custard is not done—and it probably won't be—watch carefully from that time on and test at frequent intervals (after you have baked custard a few times, you will have a good idea of approximate additional time needed after you make the first test), letting cup custards stay in oven until the knife inserted in center comes out clean. If you use a smaller baking cup, make first check after about 20 or 25 minutes, depending on size of cup.

14. When knife comes out clean, remove from oven and place cup custards or bread pudding in a pan filled to a depth of ½ to ¾ inch with ice water. If you wish, a few small pieces of ice may also be placed in pan.

15. When cool, place in refrigerator until ready to use.

16. If custard is to be unmolded, do this just before serving. To unmold cup custard, run small knife around the sides. After custard is loosened from cup, place a small serving dish over top of cup. Support bottom of dish with palm of one hand and bottom of custard cup with palm of other hand. Invert custard cup and dish. Place dish on table and lift off cup.

BAKED CUP CUSTARDS

VANILLA CUSTARD

2¼ cups milk
3 large eggs
⅔ cup white granulated sugar
¼ teaspoon salt (recommended, but may be omitted)
1 teaspoon vanilla[1]
Ground or grated nutmeg, if desired

Yield: 5 6-ounce custards.

Preheat oven for 10 minutes to 350° F. Scald milk over rapidly boiling water in top of double boiler. Beat eggs 60 strokes with wire whip or fork. Add sugar, salt, and flavoring to eggs. Stir only until well mixed. Pour in scalded milk (through strainer) and beat with spoon or whip just long enough to blend ingredients. Pour custard into cups. If desired, sprinkle with nutmeg. Place cups in pan with 1½- to 2-inch rim and carefully place on oven rack. Pour very hot water to a depth of approximately ¾ inch into pan. Gently push rack into oven and close door. Bake approximately 40 to 50 minutes until small table knife inserted in center of custard comes out clean. Remove from oven and place cups in pan filled to depth of ½ to ¾ inch with ice water. When cool, refrigerate.

VARIATIONS

Yield for each of these recipes is the same as for *Vanilla Custard** unless otherwise specified.

Butterscotch Custard—Substitute firmly packed granulated brown sugar for white sugar. Use either vanilla or rum flavoring.

[1] The flavoring of your choice, such as banana, rum, etc., may be substituted.

Caramel Custard—Prepare **Caramel Sauce**[2] by melting 30 small caramels (approximately 10 ounces) over boiling water. Stir in ½ cup scalded milk and continue cooking over hot water, stirring constantly until blended and smooth. Cool slightly. Combine sauce with just enough milk to make 2¼ cups and use mixture as substitute for 2¼ cups milk. When scalded, beat with rotary egg beater until smooth and strain into egg mixture.

Chocolate Custard—Cut or break 2 ounces cooking chocolate into small pieces or use 2 ounces premelted chocolate. Add to 2¼ cups milk and scald. Beat with rotary egg beater until smooth; strain into egg mixture. *Yield: 6 6-ounce cups.*

Lemon Custard—Substitute 1½ teaspoons lemon extract for 1 teaspoon vanilla and, when added, also stir in 2 teaspoons grated lemon rind. It is possible that the lemon custard will require more time for baking than basic recipe.

Sour Cream Custard—Let 2 cups commercial sour cream and ¼ cup milk stand until room temperature. Use as substitute for scalded milk. Stir cream and milk into egg mixture. Add 1 teaspoon grated lemon rind, if desired.

Weight Watcher's Custard—Substitute skimmed milk for milk and ⅔ cup Sweetness and Light or any equal sugar substitute (powdered form) for the ⅔ cup white granulated sugar.

TOPPINGS FOR CUSTARD

Easy Butterscotch Topping: Grease custard cups with butter or margarine, using fat quite liberally when greasing bottoms of cups. Cover bottom of each cup with 2 teaspoons dark brown sugar and press sugar into bottoms of the cups with fingers.

[2] *Caramel Sauce** can be used as dessert sauce. For the ½ cup milk, ½ cup boiling water or equal parts water and brandy, rum, or sherry may be substituted.

Carefully spoon desired custard mixture over topping and bake. Just before serving, unmold.

Cooked Butterscotch Topping: Evenly distribute ⅓ cup firmly packed brown sugar over bottom of heavy skillet. Cook over low heat until sugar melts, stirring constantly. Add ⅓ cup hot water, being careful not to burn hands with steam.[3] Continue cooking and stirring until water and sugar are blended and mixture is smooth. Cover bottoms of well-greased cups with topping and allow to harden before spooning or pouring in custard mixture. Bake. Unmold just before serving.

Caramel Topping: Grease custard cups well. Place ½ cup granulated white sugar in skillet. Cook over low heat, stirring constantly[3] until sugar melts and turns golden brown. Cover bottom of cups with topping and allow to harden before spooning or pouring in custard. Bake. Unmold just before serving.

BAKED CUSTARD PIES

VANILLA — CARAMEL — LEMON
BUTTERSCOTCH — CHOCOLATE — SOUR CREAM

Any of following *Baked Cup Custard* * mixtures, just at point where all ingredients have been mixed: *Vanilla Custard* *; *Butterscotch Custard* *; *Caramel Custard* *; *Chocolate Custard* *; *Lemon Custard* *; *Sour Cream Custard* *
9-inch *Dried Pie Shell* * OR *Graham Cracker Crumb Pie Shell* * OR *Vanilla Wafer Crumb Pie Shell* *
Graham Cracker Crumb Topping * OR *Vanilla Wafer Crumb Topping* * OR whipped cream, sweetened to taste or *Pie Meringue* *

Prepare desired custard mixture and instead of pouring into cups, pour or spoon into pie shell. The filling should come to just slightly below the rim of the shell and as egg sizes vary, it may be necessary to be extravagant occasionally and waste a spoonful

[3] Wear padded gloves and use a long-handled spoon, if at all possible.

or two of filling, but don't fill shell so full that filling runs over rim. If using crumb topping, sprinkle it over filling. Place pie on center rack of 425° F. oven and bake 15 minutes; reduce heat to 350° F. Pie will require approximately 20 minutes baking at the latter temperature. Lemon pie may take slightly more time. To guard against overcooking, after pie has cooked 12 to 15 minutes at 350° F., test by inserting blade of small table knife into side of filling. If pie is done, knife will be "clean" when withdrawn from custard. If additional cooking time is required, continue baking and test for doneness at frequent intervals. If at any time during entire baking period rim of crust appears to be browning too quickly, arrange aluminum foil to cover both filling and crust rim loosely. Don't let foil rest on filling. When custard tests "done," remove pie from oven. If crumb topping has been used, or if whipped cream topping is to be used, cool and then store in refrigerator. If meringue is to be used, top hot filling with meringue, being sure entire top surface of filling is completely and evenly covered and that at least ½ of width of entire rim of pie shell is covered with meringue, so that between shell and meringue, the filling is completely encased. Place pie in middle of center rack of 500° F. oven and cook until it is a light golden brown (about 3 minutes). Cool, and if pie is not to be used as soon as removed from oven, store in refrigerator. When whipped cream topping is used, cover chilled pie with whipped cream, sweetened to taste, if desired. In the event that only part of pie is to be served at one time, it is suggested that cream be spread on individual wedges as pie is cut. *Serves 8.*

VARIATION

Coconut Custard Pie—Prepare filling for *Baked Vanilla Custard Pie** and stir in 1 cup grated coconut. Pour into shell and bake. If meringue is used, it may be lightly sprinkled with grated coconut before meringue-covered pie is placed in oven.

BAKED BREAD PUDDINGS

VANILLA — BUTTERSCOTCH — CARAMEL
CHOCOLATE — LEMON

3 cups white or raisin bread
⅓ cup rum, sherry, brandy, or Almond Marsala, if desired
Same egg, sugar, and milk mixture that is used to make up
    any of following *Baked Cup Custards**: *Vanilla Custard**;
    Butterscotch Custard*; *Caramel Custard**; *Chocolate Custard**;
    Lemon Custard*

Cut bread into ¾-inch cubes. If desired, sprinkle with rum, sherry, brandy, or almond Marsala, very gently stirring cubes while doing this, so that they will be evenly sprinkled. Place cubes in 8×8×2-inch baking dish or in 1½- to 2-quart round or oval baking dish. Prepare desired custard mixture and after milk has been blended with other ingredients, pour mixture over cubes. Allow to stand 15 minutes. While cubes are soaking in custard, preheat oven for 10 minutes to 350° F. Place pan with 1- to 1½-inch rim in oven. The pan should be large enough to hold baking dish containing pudding with room to spare on all sides. Fill pan with very hot water to depth of ½ to ¾ inch. Place baking dish in center of pan. Bake until a small table knife inserted slightly to one side of center of pudding comes out "clean"—approximately 50 to 60 minutes. As soon as baking dish is removed from oven, place it in pan holding ice water to a depth of ½ to ¾ inch. Cool and then refrigerate. *Serves 8 (approximately)*.

VARIATIONS

Cake Pudding—Substitute 3 cups cake cubes (fresh or stale, sponge or butter) or 4 cups small whole vanilla wafers or 3 cups vanilla wafers and 1 cup cake cubes for bread.

Fruit and/or Nut Pudding—Mix any or all of following with bread or cake cubes before placing cubes in baking dish. A 2- to 2½-quart dish should be used, size depending on the quantity of fruit and nuts used: ⅔ cup raisins; ⅔ cup pitted dates; ½ cup drained, quartered or halved Maraschino cherries; ½ cup candied fruit, cut into pieces approximately ⅓ × ⅓ × ¼ inch; ½ cup small pecan pieces or toasted blanched almonds.

Upside Down Bread Pudding, Upside Down Cake Pudding, Upside Down Fruit and/or Nut Pudding—Melt ¼ cup butter or margarine in the 8×8×2-inch baking dish. Tilt pan so some of melted fat will run over sides. Spread evenly on sides with paper napkin, leaving, however, greater portion of butter or margarine on bottom of pan. Sprinkle, as evenly as possible, ½ cup brown sugar over melted fat in bottom of pan. Cover sugar with any of the following well-drained canned fruit: 1 No. 1 can sliced peaches; 8 pineapple rings; 8 small peach or pear halves; 12 apricot halves. If desired, fruit may be decorated with drained green and/or red Maraschino cherries.

Place cubes of bread or cake (with fruit and nuts, if used) on top of fruit. Pour hot custard mixture over cubes and proceed as directed in recipe for *Baked Bread Puddings** up to point where pudding is removed from oven. Let stand 5 minutes. Loosen pudding by running knife around sides of pan. Place large serving dish on top of baking dish and place palm over bottom of serving dish. Place other hand (protected with padded glove), palm up, under baking dish. Invert baking and serving dishes. Gently but quickly slide serving dish onto table, easing hand from underneath as this is done. Let stand 3 minutes to allow "syrup" to run down sides of pudding. Lift baking dish off pudding. Cool and, if desired, store in refrigerator.

SERVING NOTE: If desired, serve individual squares of pudding, topped with ice cream.[4]

[4] See *Country Custard Ice Cream** and *Top of the Stove Custard—Frozen**.

GENERAL RULES FOR MAKING CUSTARD
GELATIN (CONGEALED) DESSERTS

1. Line mold(s) with plastic wrap, allowing a fraction of an inch to overhang mold(s) to facilitate unmolding when time comes.

OR Oil mold(s) with vegetable oil by pouring a small amount of oil into bottom of mold and then spreading it over remainder of bottom and over sides with paper towel or napkin. Every part of mold should be lightly coated and any excess oil should be poured off. For the recipes in this book, five 6-ounce molds or a 1-quart mold are suggested, except for the chocolate custard gelatin for which six 6-ounce molds or a 1½-quart mold are suggested or for the *Fruit and/or Nut Custard Gelatin** or for the puddings, for which 8×2×2-inch or 1½- to 2½-quart molds are recommended, depending on quantity of fruit and/or nuts used.

2. Let ½ cup milk, or, if making *Sour Cream Custard Gelatin** ¼ cup milk and the sour cream stand until room temperature.

3. Pour milk in 1-quart pot, Teflon preferred, and sprinkle— and I do mean sprinkle—gelatin over milk. Let stand at least 5 minutes.

4. Measure 1¾ cups milk or milk and caramel mixture into top of double boiler. If using chocolate, add premelted chocolate or cooking chocolate, broken in small pieces.

5. Scald milk over boiling water. If using chocolate or caramel and milk mixture, beat with rotary egg beater until smooth before removing from stove.

6. While milk is scalding, beat eggs 60 strokes with fork or wire whip—just enough to combine yolks and whites, without overbeating.

7. Add sugar or sugar substitute, salt, and flavoring, including lemon rind if specified in recipe and stir only until well blended.

8. When milk is scalded, place gelatin mixture on stove, and cook over low heat for 1 minute, stirring constantly while cooking.

9. Except for the *Sour Cream Custard Gelatin**, stir in scalded milk, continue stirring until completely blended, and then strain into egg mixture. Beat just long enough to mix thoroughly all ingredients. In the case of the *Sour Cream Custard Gelatin**, add hot milk and gelatin mixture to egg mixture. Stir until blended and fold in room-temperature sour cream.

10. If fruit and/or nuts are to be used, except for the uncooked bread or cake puddings, place custard mixture (in the bowl in which it was mixed) into refrigerator. If in a hurry, pour mixture into a large shallow pan or dish before placing it in refrigerator, as the thinner it is, the quicker it will thicken. When mixture is thickened, but not set, fold in fruit and/or nuts.

11. Spoon custard mixture into mold(s). Place in refrigerator and let stand until firm. It is suggested that 6 to 8 hours be allowed for making this dessert when a large mold is used, as it should be completely congealed before it is used, particularly if it is to be unmolded. If dessert is to be stored for more than a day, it is suggested that once it is congealed, plastic wrap be used to cover top.

Unmolding Gelatin

If a plastic wrap lined mold was employed, using the fraction of an inch of wrap that overhangs rim, gently pull plastic lining slightly away from mold to let air between lining and mold escape. Place dish over top of mold, invert, holding dish with palm of one hand and bottom of mold with palm of other. Slide onto table, pulling hand from under dish as this is done. Lift mold off gelatin and carefully pull off plastic. Refrigerate until serving time. If gelatin is to be refrigerated for more than an hour, cover it with fresh plastic wrap to prevent its drying out.

OR

If oiled mold was used, and it can be arranged, remove gelatin from mold 30 to 40 minutes before serving. Select spot on one side of gelatin and insert blade of table knife between gelatin and mold until knife touches bottom of mold. Run knife around the gelatin. Place mold in pan filled with hot water to depth of 1 to 2 inches depending on depth of mold. Let stand several minutes. Working as fast as possible, wipe all water from outside of mold and put serving dish on top of it. Place one palm over bottom of dish and place other palm under mold so that both mold and dish are well supported. Invert dish. Gently but quickly slide dish and mold onto table, easing hand from underneath as this is done. Lift mold from gelatin and return gelatin to refrigerator. Store in refrigerator until ready to use, but if gelatin is to be stored more than an hour, protect by covering with plastic wrap.

VANILLA CUSTARD GELATIN

1 tablespoon, plus 1 rounded teaspoon unflavored gelatin
½ cup milk, at room temperature
1¾ cups milk
3 large eggs
⅔ cup white granulated sugar
¼ teaspoon salt
1 teaspoon vanilla

Yield: 5 6-ounce cups or 1 quart gelatin dessert.

Oil mold(s) or line with plastic wrap. Let ½ cup milk stand until room temperature. Pour this milk into 1-quart pot, sprinkle with gelatin, and let stand at least 5 minutes. Measure remaining milk into top of double boiler. Scald and while milk is scalding, beat eggs 60 strokes with wire whip or fork. Add sugar, salt, and vanilla and stir only until blended. When milk is scalded, cook milk and gelatin mixture 1 minute over low heat, stirring constantly. Add scalding milk to gelatin mixture and continue to stir until smooth and blended. Pour hot mixture through strainer into egg mixture and beat just long enough to blend completely all ingredients. Spoon into mold(s). Store in refrigerator until gelatin is thoroughly congealed. If desired, unmold 30 to 40 minutes before serving.

VARIATIONS

Yield for each of these recipes is the same as for *Vanilla Custard Gelatin** unless otherwise specified.

Butterscotch Custard Gelatin—Substitute ⅔ cup firmly packed brown granulated sugar for white sugar. Rum flavoring may be substituted for vanilla, if desired.

Caramel Custard Gelatin—Prepare *Caramel Sauce**. Cool slightly. Combine sauce with just enough milk to make 1¾ cups of mixture and use this mixture as substitute for 1¾ cups milk. When mixture is scalded, beat for several minutes with rotary egg beater.

Chocolate Custard Gelatin—Cut or break 2 ounces (squares) cooking chocolate into small pieces or use 2 ounces premelted chocolate. Add to the 1¾ cups milk and scald. Beat with rotary egg beater until smooth before adding chocolate mixture to gelatin mixture.   *Yield: 6 6-ounce "custards."*

Coconut Custard Gelatin—Prepare *Vanilla Custard Gelatin** and place in refrigerator. When thick, but not set, fold in 1 cup grated canned or fresh coconut. Spoon into mold(s).

Eggnog Custard Gelatin—Substitute ½ cup room-temperature whisky, rum, brandy, or sherry for the ½ cup milk in which gelatin is soaked. Omit vanilla or other flavoring.

Fruit and/or Nut Custard Gelatin—Prepare *Vanilla Custard Gelatin**. When thick, but not set, fold in any or all of following: ¼ cup drained, sliced, candied or Maraschino cherries; ¼ cup candied fruit cut into pieces ⅓ × ⅓ × ¼ inch; ¼ cup nuts cut in small pieces. Spoon into mold(s). Size or number of molds required depends on quantity of fruit and/or nuts.

Lemon Custard Gelatin—Substitute 1½ teaspoons lemon extract for 1 teaspoon vanilla. When flavoring is added, also stir in 2 teaspoons grated lemon rind.

Sour Cream Custard Gelatin—Reduce total quantity of milk to ¼ cup and substitute for other 2 cups milk, 2 cups commercial sour cream. Let milk and cream stand until room temperature. Sprinkle ¼ cup milk with gelatin. When eggs, sugar, salt, and vanilla are combined, add 1 teaspoon grated lemon rind. Cook milk and gelatin 1 minute over low heat, stirring constantly. Stir into egg mixture and then fold in sour cream.

Weight Watcher's Custard Gelatin—Substitute skimmed milk for whole milk and ⅔ cup Sweetness and Light or any equal sugar substitute (powdered form) for the ⅔ cup white granulated sugar. Salt may be omitted.

REFRIGERATOR CUSTARD PIES

VANILLA — BUTTERSCOTCH — CARAMEL
CHOCOLATE — COCONUT — EGGNOG
FRUIT AND/OR NUT — LEMON — SOUR CREAM

Any of following custard gelatins, prepared and then stored in
  refrigerator until thick, but not set: *Vanilla Custard Gelatin**;
  *Butterscotch Custard Gelatin**; *Caramel Custard Gelatin**;
  *Chocolate Custard Gelatin**; *Coconut Custard Gelatin**; *Eggnog
  Custard Gelatin**; *Fruit and/or Nut Custard Gelatin**; *Lemon
  Custard Gelatin**; *Sour Cream Custard Gelatin**
Any one of following 9-inch pie shells: *Baked Pie Shell**;
  *Graham Cracker Crumb Pie Shell**; *Vanilla Wafer Crumb Pie
  Shell**
Any of following toppings: *Graham Cracker Crumb Topping**;
  *Vanilla Wafer Crumb Topping**; whipped cream sweetened
  to taste, if desired

Prepare desired custard gelatin and store in refrigerator in bowl in which it was made until custard mixture is thick, but not set. If making a coconut or fruit and/or nut refrigerator pie, fold in coconut or fruit and/or nuts. Spoon into pie shell. If desired, sprinkle with either of crumb toppings. Place in refrigerator and let stand until filling is very firm (6 to 8 hours, if possible). When ready to serve, if crumb topping was not used, remove pie from refrigerator, and top with whipped cream, sweetened, if desired. The whipped cream may be used to cover entire top or individual wedges if pie is served from kitchen. *Serves 8.*

REFRIGERATOR BREAD PUDDINGS

VANILLA — BUTTERSCOTCH — CARAMEL
CHOCOLATE — EGGNOG — LEMON

3 cups white or raisin bread
⅓ cup rum, sherry, brandy, whisky, or almond Marsala, if
    desired (Do not use spirit if *Eggnog Bread Pudding** is
    being made.)
Any of following custard gelatin, prepared up to point where
    scalding milk and gelatin mixture has been combined with
    egg mixture: *Vanilla Custard Gelatin**; *Butterscotch Custard
    Gelatin**; *Caramel Custard Gelatin**; *Chocolate Custard
    Gelatin; Eggnog Custard Gelatin**; *Lemon Custard Gelatin**
*Caramel Syrup Topping**, if desired

Cut bread into ¾-inch cubes. If desired, sprinkle with any of above listed spirits, gently stirring cubes while doing this so that they will be evenly sprinkled. If pudding is to be unmolded, oil or line with plastic wrap 8×8×2-inch baking dish or 1½- to 2-quart round or oval mold. Place bread cubes in baking dish or mold. Prepare desired custard gelatin and, while hot, pour over bread. Let stand 15 minutes. Place in refrigerator, and store there for 6 to 8 hours until quite firm. If pudding is unmolded, if you wish, cover with:

Caramel Syrup Topping

½ cup granulated white sugar
½ cup water or ¼ cup rum or Cointreau and ¼ cup water
Drained, canned, sliced peaches or pineapple rings or ⅓ cup
  chopped pecans or toasted almond slivers and/or drained,
  halved Maraschino cherries, if desired

Melt sugar over low heat in very heavy skillet, stirring constantly until it is a deep golden brown. Quickly bring water or water and rum to a boil (in pan with long handle, since steam can burn when liquid and sugar are mixed). With hand(s) protected with padded glove(s), carefully pour liquid into melted and browned sugar, continuing to cook over low heat and also continuing to stir constantly, until any of sugar that may have hardened when liquid was added is melted and syrup reduced to approximately ¼ cup. Let cool slightly. Unmold pudding and spread syrup over top. Decorate, if desired, by embedding canned fruits or nuts and/or Maraschino cherries in syrup. *Serves 8.*

VARIATIONS

Refrigerator Cake Pudding—Substitute for bread, 3 cups cake cubes (fresh or stale, sponge or butter) or 4 cups small whole vanilla wafers or 3 cups vanilla wafers and 1 cup cake cubes.

Refrigerator Fruit and/or Nut Pudding—Mix any or all of following with bread or cake cubes before placing mixture in 2- to 2½-quart mold—size depending on quantity of fruit and/or nuts used: ⅔ cup raisins; ⅔ cup pitted dates; ½ cup drained, quartered, or halved Maraschino cherries; ½ cup candied fruit, cut into pieces approximately ⅓ × ⅓ × ¼ inch; ½ cup small pecan pieces or toasted blanched almonds.

COUNTRY CUSTARD ICE CREAM

(Made in Home Freezer or Refrigerator Freezer)

VANILLA

Firm *Vanilla Custard Gelatin**
1 quart cold whipping cream
1¾ cups confectioners' sugar, measured then sifted
⅓ cup all purpose flour, measured then sifted
1 tablespoon vanilla

When custard gelatin is completely congealed, whip cream, in cold bowl with cold beaters, until stiff. Beat in sugar, flour, and vanilla. Gradually add gelatin by heaping tablespoons and beat with rotary egg beater or on creaming speed of food mixer until mixture is blended and smooth—about 4 minutes of beating after last of gelatin has been added to cream.

Line a ¾-gallon or gallon plastic freezer carton (whichever you have) with large-size extra-heavy plastic bag. Spoon custard and cream mixture into bag. With a scissors, cut down at each of the 4 corners to the top of the ice cream mixture, thus creating 4 plastic flaps. Fold flaps one at a time over top surface of dessert so that it is completely covered and so that plastic flaps are in contact with the dessert. Securely cover freezer container with its lid. Place in home freezer or refrigerator freezer. Let stand until completely frozen (overnight to 16 hours). Remove from freezer and allow to soften slightly. Spoon into large bowl and whip with rotary egg beater or on low speed of food mixer until smooth. Then beat rapidly with rotary egg beater or on creaming speed of mixer for 4 minutes. Spoon back into plastic bag lining of plastic freezer carton. Again fold flaps one at a time over top surface of dessert so that they touch the entire top of the ice cream. Cover carton with its lid. Return to freezer. When firmly frozen, serve as desired. *Yield: Slightly less than ⅝ gallon.*

VARIATIONS

Butterscotch—Substitute firm *Butterscotch Custard Gelatin** for the *Vanilla Custard Gelatin**. If desired, 1 tablespoon rum flavoring may be substituted for 1 tablespoon vanilla.

Caramel—Substitute firm *Caramel Custard Gelatin** for the *Vanilla Custard Gelatin**.

Chocolate—Substitute firm *Chocolate Custard Gelatin** for *Vanilla Custard Gelatin** and substitute ⅓ cup cocoa, first measured and then sifted, for flour.

Lemon—Substitute firm *Lemon Custard Gelatin** for *Vanilla Custard Gelatin**, 2 teaspoons lemon extract for 1 tablespoon vanilla, and when flavoring is added to whipped cream, also add 2 teaspoons grated lemon rind.

Sour Cream—Make these substitutions in ingredients: *Sour Cream Custard Gelatin** for *Vanilla Custard Gelatin** and 1 quart commercial sour cream for 1 quart whipping cream. Break gelatin into small pieces and beat with rotary egg beater or on creaming speed of mixer just until smooth. With wooden spoon, fold sugar, flour, and vanilla into sour cream and then fold cream mixture into gelatin (also with spoon). Proceed as directed in *Vanilla Country Custard Ice Cream**.

14

Top of the Stove Custards

There is just 1 recipe in this chapter—the *Top of the Stove Custard**, but there are so many variations in flavor possible and so many different ways of serving this custard that by using this recipe you could serve a different dessert every day for at least a year.

For example: Cook the ingredients 2 to 3 minutes and you have a sauce; cook them 4 to 5 minutes and you have a soft custard; cook them 7 to 10 minutes and you have a filling.

You can cook a *Top of the Stove Custard** over low direct heat or over boiling water. I prefer to cook mine over the boiling water, as I think those done in this manner are smoother and less prone to "lump," as well as less apt to burn if your attention is diverted for a minute or so; however, custards cooked over direct heat do take just a little less time to make.

GENERAL RULES FOR TOP OF THE STOVE CUSTARDS

1. Place water in bottom of double boiler and bring to a boil.

2. Place milk or mixture of milk and cream in top of double boiler.

3. If using chocolate, break or cut squares into small pieces or use premelted type. Add to milk or to milk and cream mixture.

4. Scald milk or milk mixture over boiling water. For lemon- or coffee-flavored custards, bring tap water or coffee to boiling point over direct heat.

5. While milk or milk mixture or water or coffee is being heated, beat egg yolks 60 strokes with wire whip or fork.

6. Stir sugar, flour, and salt into yolks, but stir only long enough to blend ingredients.

7. Add heated liquid—if chocolate has been used, beat mixture with rotary egg beater until completely blended before adding —to yolk mixture and stir until all ingredients are well mixed and sugar is entirely dissolved.

8. Pour into top of double boiler and cook over rapidly boiling water, stirring constantly, preferably with long-handled spoon— it's also a good idea to shield the hand that stirs with padded glove or mitten—until desired consistency is reached. Custards in which milk or milk and cream are used will take a little less time to cook than custards made with water or coffee.

9. When custard reaches desired consistency, remove from over boiling water. If for any reason it is lumpy—maybe you had to stop stirring while it was cooking—beat with a rotary egg beater and then put through a fine sieve—no great harm done.

10. Add extract of your choice, or lemon rind and pulp, or alcoholic spirit.

TOP OF THE STOVE CUSTARD SAUCE
TOP OF THE STOVE SOFT CUSTARD
TOP OF THE STOVE CUSTARD FILLING

VANILLA FLAVORED

1½ cups milk or ¾ cup milk and ¾ cup breakfast cream
4 yolks from large eggs
1 cup granulated sugar
⅛ teaspoon salt
¼ cup flour, measured and then sifted
1 teaspoon vanilla

Scald milk or milk and cream over boiling water. Beat yolks 60 strokes with fork or wire whip. Add sugar, salt, and sifted flour and stir only long enough to mix ingredients thoroughly. Add scalded milk and beat with spoon just until ingredients are blended and sugar is completely dissolved. Pour mixture into top of double boiler and cook over rapidly boiling water, stirring constantly with long-handled wooden spoon until desired consistency is reached.

Cook *Custard Sauces* until slightly thickened (2 to 3 minutes); *Soft Custards* until they coat silver or stainless steel spoon (4 to 5 minutes); *Custard Fillings* until very thick (7 to 10 minutes). Remove from heat and stir in vanilla.

Yield: Custard Sauce—approximately 2 cups; Soft Custard— 4 servings; Custard Filling—one 9-inch pie, filling for Angel Food Roll* *or* Chocolate Angel Food Roll*, *or use ½ quantity of each of ingredients to make filling for two 9-inch layers of* 1–2–3–4 Cakes*.

FLAVOR VARIATIONS

1. Substitute 1 teaspoon almond, banana, lemon, maple, peppermint, pineapple, or rum extract for 1 teaspoon vanilla.

2. Butterscotch Custard Sauce; Butterscotch Soft Custard; Butterscotch Custard Filling—Substitute 1 cup firmly packed brown sugar (dark preferred, and don't use granulated brown) for 1 cup white sugar and add any or all of following when extract is added: ½ teaspoon cinnamon; ¼ teaspoon ground nutmeg; 1 teaspoon grated lemon rind; 1 teaspoon grated orange rind.

3. Chocolate Custard Sauce; Chocolate Soft Custard; Chocolate Custard Filling—Add 2 ounces cooking chocolate to cold milk or milk and cream. Squares should be broken or cut into pieces before being added. After mixture is scalded, beat vigorously with rotary egg beater so that chocolate and milk will be completely blended before being added to egg yolk mixture.

4. Coconut Custard Sauce; Coconut Soft Custard; Coconut Custard Filling

(✕1) Combine in bowl 1 cup grated coconut and ¾ cup milk and ¾ cup breakfast cream. Store in refrigerator for at least 2 hours and substitute for milk or milk and cream. OR

(✕2) After vanilla is added, fold 1 cup grated coconut into cooked custard.

5. Coffee Custard Sauce; Coffee Soft Custard; Coffee Custard Filling—Substitute 1½ cups strong black coffee for milk or milk and cream, and bring to a boil over direct heat instead of scalding. Use, if desired, any one or all of following: ½ teaspoon cinnamon; ¼ teaspoon nutmeg; ¼ teaspoon cardamon; 1 teaspoon grated lemon rind; 1 teaspoon grated orange rind.

6. Lemon Custard Sauce; Lemon Soft Custard; Lemon Custard Filling—Substitute 1½ cups water for milk or milk and cream and bring to a boil over direct heat instead of scalding. Omit vanilla and substitute grated rind, pulp, and juice of 2 large lemons. *Grating a whole lemon* is a bit tricky, since the thick white membrane found between the yellow rind and the pulp is bitter and just as little of it as possible should be used. After all yellow rind is grated from lemon, with a small sharp knife or vegetable parer cut 2 or 3 thin strips from the thick white membrane. This will enable you to get a finger under part of remaining membrane so that it can be pulled from the lemon, leaving pulp covered by a thin skin. Very gently grate the pulp; rough handling will result in all juice and no pulp. From time to time, inspect surface being grated to see if any seeds can be lifted out, and if so, remove them. If you miss some of the seeds and if you are handling the grating gently, the seeds will fall into the grated pulp and juice mixture and can be removed if you will run your fingers through mixture at frequent intervals. Discard small piece of white membrane left when most of pulp is grated.

7. Mocha Custard Sauce; Mocha Soft Custard; Mocha Custard Filling—Substitute 1¼ cups strong black coffee that has been completely blended with ¼ cup commercial chocolate syrup for milk or milk and cream. If desired, any or all of following may be used: ½ teaspoon cinnamon; ¼ teaspoon nutmeg; ¼ teaspoon cardamon; 1 teaspoon grated lemon rind; ¼ teaspoon grated orange rind.

8. Spirit Custard Sauce; Spirit Soft Custard; Spirit Custard Filling —Prepare custard, making sauce, soft custard, or filling just a little thicker than usual by cooking just a little longer. Remove from heat and when slightly cooled, stir in, according to taste, ¼ to ⅓ cup of rum, whisky, or the brandy, cordial, or dessert wine of your choice. Omit vanilla.

SUGGESTIONS FOR SERVING TOP OF THE STOVE CUSTARD SAUCE

Fruit and Custard Sauce: Prepare *Top of the Stove Custard Sauce** in desired flavor and chill. Shortly before serving time, prepare 3 cups chilled fresh or canned berries or fruit of your choice, draining the canned fruit, and where necessary, pitting, peeling, coring, slicing, or halving fresh fruit. Place fruit in shallow serving dish or put ½ cup fruit in each of 6 individual serving dishes or cups. Top fruit with sauce, using about ⅓ cup sauce for each individual serving. Garnish, if you desire, with ½ cup small pecan pieces, toasted almond slivers, or Maraschino cherries. *Serves 6.*

Cake and Custard Sauce: 1. Prepare *Top of the Stove Custard Sauce** in desired flavor and chill. On each of 6 individual dessert plates place a square or a thick slice of cake or 2 small cupcakes—butter or sponge (see *1–2–3–4 Cakes** and *Angel Food**). Spoon sauce over cake. Garnish, if you wish, with nuts or Maraschino cherries. *Serves 6.*

2. Prepare *Top of the Stove Custard Sauce** in desired flavor and chill. Break butter or sponge cake (see *1–2–3–4 Cakes** and *Angel Food**) into bite-size pieces. Approximately 2½ cups of cake pieces will be needed. Using sherbet cups or parfait glasses, alternate layers of cake and custard, starting with cake and ending with custard. Garnish if you wish with any one or any desired combination of the following: chopped nuts; Maraschino cherries; marrons; chocolate "trims," or colored sugar crystals. *Serves 6.*

Cake, Custard Sauce, and Fruit: 1. Prepare *Top of the Stove Custard Sauce** in desired flavor and chill. On each of 8 individual dessert plates, place a square or a thick slice of cake—butter or sponge (see *1–2–3–4 Cakes** and *Angel Food**). Spoon ¼ cup sauce over each square or slice of cake and arrange chilled fresh or canned berries or fruit of your choice on top of custard, allowing ¼ cup fruit or berries for each serving. *Serves 8.*

2. Prepare *Top of the Stove Custard Sauce** in desired flavor and chill. Break into small pieces 16 double ladyfingers or enough butter or sponge cake (see *1–2–3–4 Cakes** and *Angel Food**) to fill 2½ cups. Using sherbet cups or parfait glasses, alternate layers of cake, custard sauce, and chilled fruit or berries, starting with cake and ending with fruit or berries. *Serves 8.*

3. Arrange 2½ cups ladyfingers, butter or sponge cake (see *1–2–3–4 Cakes** and *Angel Food**), broken into bite-size pieces, on serving platter. Cover with chilled *Top of the Stove Custard Sauce** of your choice and top with chilled fruit or berries. *Serves 8.*

SUGGESTIONS FOR SERVING TOP OF THE STOVE SOFT CUSTARD*

1. Floating Island: Prepare soft custard in desired flavor and chill. Also prepare *Meringues for Floating Island** or *Spirit Meringues for Floating Island**. Spoon custard into shallow bowl and dot with meringues, or using parfait glasses, alternate layers of custard and meringues and top with meringues (over which a small amount of custard should be dribbled). *Serves 4.*

2. Floating Island with Berries or Cherries: Prepare soft custard in desired flavor and chill. Also prepare *Meringues for Floating*

Island* or *Spirit Meringues for Floating Island**. Prepare 1½ cups chilled fresh or (thawed) frozen strawberries or raspberries or pitted canned or fresh dessert cherries. If desired, sprinkle lightly with Cointreau, cognac, or kirsch. Place berries or cherries in bottom of shallow serving bowl, cover with soft custard and dot with meringues or place ¼ cup of berries or cherries in bottom of parfait glass and fill glass with alternate layers of custard and meringues. *Serves 6.*

3. Custard and Marshmallows: Prepare soft custard in desired flavor and chill. Fold in 1 cup midget marshmallows and return to refrigerator until ready to serve. *Serves 6.*

SUGGESTIONS FOR SERVING TOP OF THE STOVE CUSTARD FILLING*

1. Custard Fluff: Prepare custard filling in desired flavor and chill. Beat 4 egg whites—those left after yolks were used to make filling—until stiff, but not dry. Fold into custard filling and spoon into 6 parfait or sherbet glasses. Chill thoroughly before serving. Garnish, if desired, with Maraschino cherries, whole or chopped nuts, or whole marrons. *Serves 6.*

2. Custard Fluff Parfait (for large dinner parties): Prepare any 3 desired flavors of *Custard Fluffs**. Divide one of fluffs equally between 18 parfait glasses. If desired, sprinkle with chopped, drained Maraschino cherries or marrons or other nuts. Spoon second fluff into glasses, also dividing it equally between them. Sprinkle, if desired, with the chopped cherries or marrons or nuts. Top parfaits with third *Custard Fluff** and garnish each with whole green or red drained Maraschino cherry. If you wish, sprinkle chopped nuts and/or chocolate "trims" and/or colored sugar crystals around cherry.

3. Custard Filling for Cakes: Prepare full recipe of *Top of the Stove Custard Filling** in desired flavor for *Angel Food Roll** or

Chocolate Angel Food Roll*, but halve quantity of each ingredient when filling is to be used between two 9-inch cake layers (see *1–2–3–4 Cakes**).

4. TOP OF THE STOVE CUSTARD PIES

CUSTARD VANILLA — BUTTERSCOTCH — CHOCOLATE COCONUT ✳1 OR ✳2 — COFFEE LEMON — MOCHA

Top of the Stove Custard Filling* or any of the following
variations: *Butterscotch Custard Filling**; *Chocolate Custard
Filling**; *Coconut Custard Filling ✳1** or *✳2** *Coffee
Custard Filling**; *Lemon Custard Filling**; *Mocha Custard
Filling**
Baked Pie Shell* (9 inches)
Pie Meringue*

Prepare desired *Top of the Stove Custard Filling** and *Baked Pie Shell**. Let both cool, but don't chill. Spoon meringue onto filling, being sure entire top surface of filling is completely and evenly covered and that at least ½ of width of entire rim of pie shell is covered with meringue, so that between shell and meringue, the filling is completely encased. Place pie in middle of center rack in 325° F. oven and cook until it is a light golden brown (about 20 minutes). Let pie stand until cool. As it is a custard pie, if it is not to be eaten as soon as it has cooled, store in refrigerator until serving time. *Serves 8.*

TOP OF THE STOVE CUSTARD—FROZEN

For many years I have sought to find a way to make a perfectly smooth refrigerator-freezer custard ice cream that did not require cream—a fattening and expensive ingredient, to say the least— and which did not have to be beaten either during the freezing process or after the cream was frozen (and then returned to the freezer for refreezing). The following is just that, and, as you will see, it introduces a simple way to make custard ice cream in the home, without too much expense. In addition to being velvet smooth and fluffy, this ice cream can be made in many flavors. Furthermore, unless the temperature of your home freezer or refrigerator freezer is very low, it can be served immediately after it is removed from the freezer.

FRUIT-FLAVORED FROZEN CUSTARD

**RASPBERRY — BLACK RASPBERRY — STRAWBERRY
STRAWBERRY-BANANA — ORANGE — ORANGE-PINEAPPLE
PINEAPPLE — LEMON — LIME
GRAPE — CHERRY — BLACK CHERRY
BLACKBERRY — SPICED PEAR — PEACH
PINK GRAPEFRUIT — MIXED FRUIT — TROPICAL FRUIT**

Follow recipe for *Top of the Stove Custard Filling** with these changes:

1. Reserve the 4 egg whites when eggs are separated.
2. Omit vanilla.
3. Cook custard over boiling water just 6 minutes.
4. Set custard aside to cool.
5. When cool, blend in ¼ cup milk or rum, brandy, whisky, or cordial.
6. Then stir in 3 tablespoons Jell-O or Royal fruit-flavored gelatin dessert powder.
7. Beat egg whites until stiff and fold them into the custard mixture.
8. Line a 1½-quart plastic freezer carton with an extra-heavy plastic bag.

Spoon custard and cream mixture into bag. With a scissors, cut down at each of the four corners to the top of the ice cream mixture, thus creating 4 plastic flaps. Fold flaps one at a time over top surface of custard so that it is completely covered and so that plastic flaps are in contact with the dessert. Securely cover freezer container with lid. Place carton in freezer. Let stand until completely frozen (8 to 10 hours), or as long as you desire. If using only part of ice cream at any one time, be sure that the plastic bag flaps are rearranged over the top surface of the custard so that it is completely covered. *Yield: Approximately 1 quart.*

VARIATIONS

Peach Frozen Custard ⚹2—Add ¾ cup mellow peeled peach pieces (approximately ¼ ×¼ ×⅙ inches) to custard just before folding in egg whites.

Vanilla Frozen Custard—Follow recipe for *Top of the Stove Custard Filling** with these changes:
1. Reserve the 4 egg whites when eggs are separated.
2. Cook custard over boiling water just 6 minutes.
3. As soon as custard is removed from boiling water, beat 1 tablespoon unflavored gelatin or 1 package Knox gelatine into it; put custard mixture through sieve.
4. Increase vanilla to 2 teaspoons.
5. Set custard aside to cool.
6. When cool, stir in ¼ cup of milk.
7. Beat egg whites until stiff and fold into custard mixture.
Prepare for freezing and then freeze in same way as directed in recipe for *Fruit-Flavored Frozen Custard**.

Spirit-flavored Frozen Custard—Follow directions for the *Vanilla Frozen Custard**, but omit vanilla and substitute ¼ cup whisky, brandy, rum, or cordial for the ¼ cup of milk.

Chocolate Frozen Custard—Prepare *Vanilla Frozen Custard** and make this addition: Before scalding milk, add 2 ounces unsweetened cooking chocolate cut into small pieces or 2 ounces (⅓ cup) semi-sweet chocolate chips to the milk. Scald, beating while milk is scalding from time to time with rotary egg beater so that the milk-chocolate mixture will be completely blended and smooth. (Adults usually prefer the ice cream made from the unsweetened cooking chocolate, while children prefer the sweeter version made with the chips.)

15

Meringue

My dictionary defines a "meringue" as the beaten whites of eggs sweetened and used to garnish pastry; also, pastry so garnished, but this doesn't begin to tell the story, for a meringue is far more than an afterthought for a pie. It's the elegant *Schaum Torte**; it makes the fabulous *Baked Alaska** possible; then there are the delicious cookies and the delicate *Angel Food**, as well as the newest member of an old family, the *Angel Food Roll**.

If, insofar as making them is concerned, you have a "meringue phobia," let me hasten to reassure you. The really big secret of a successful meringue lies in knowing when to stop beating the egg whites[1]. There are, of course, a few other small secrets, but they are all revealed in the next few pages.

GENERAL RULES FOR MAKING MERINGUES

1. Separate whites from yolks of cold eggs. If making a *Pie Meringue**, *Meringue for Baked Alaska**, *Meringues for Floating Island**, *Individual Meringues**, *Schaum Torte**, or *Meringue Cookies**, use cold egg whites or wait until they are room temperature, whichever is more convenient, but if making an *Angel Food**, after whites are separated from yolks, they should stand until room temperature.

2. Add salt to egg whites and beat until frothy on creaming speed of mixer or with rotary egg beater. The single exception is

[1] See *Whipping Stages of Egg Whites**.

Angel Food*, for which whites must be beaten with mixer or with wire whip.

3. If you are using cream of tartar, and I for one like the results when it is used with egg whites, add when eggs are frothy. After it is added, lift beater(s) up through whites and then return to normal position in bowl, from time to time.

4. Continue beating until egg whites will stand in soft peaks (when beater(s) are lifted up through eggs, a peak whose tip will bend just slightly is formed on surface).

5. Start to add sugar gradually, still on creaming speed of mixer or using rotary egg beater or wire whip. Sugar should be added by heaping tablespoons. Continue to lift beaters through whites from time to time. The sugar and whites should be completely blended after each addition. When meringues are being made for pies, there may be "weeping" if sugar and whites are not well blended; therefore, when using a mixer, 2 or 3 times while sugar is being added, assist mixer by gently scraping meringue from side of bowl opposite the revolving beaters into the path of the beaters.

6. Except for an *Angel Food**, to which extract should be added as soon as sugar has been blended with whites when using mixer or to unbeaten whites when using wire whip, beat meringue until stiff, but not dry before adding extract or vinegar. If bowl is reversed, whites will cling to it, but they will still be glossy. Be sure to stop beating before egg whites become dry and have a dull appearance.

7. Add extract, vinegar, or spirit. If spirit is used, add gradually, continuing to beat while it is being added.

8. If nuts, fruit, cornflakes for cookies, or flour and sugar for *Angel Food** are to be added, the addition should be made after the extract, vinegar, or spirit is added. The flour and sugar mixture that makes a meringue into an *Angel Food** should be folded in on the lowest possible mixer speed or with wire whip and the nuts, fruit, and/or cornflakes should be gently folded into the *Meringue Cookies** with a wooden spoon.

9. This is a MUST if you are to successfully top *Baked Alaska** or pie with meringue.

For the Alaska:

Completely cover top and sides of dessert with meringue, being sure there are no air pockets between meringue and the surface of the ice cream and cake portions of the Alaska. Most important of all, bring the meringue all the way down the sides so that it touches the aluminum foil covered board, on which the bottom layer of cake rests, at every point surrounding cake.

For the Pie:

The meringue should be piled on the filling and then spread carefully so that each and every bit of the surface of the filling is in contact with meringue. There should be no air pockets between filling and meringue. Then the meringue must be brought out over at least ½ of the width of the entire rim of crust. If the crust is ridged or fluted, care should be taken that the "valleys" between these ridges or the fluting are filled with meringue for as far as the meringue extends out over the crust.

10. If desired, surface of *Pie Meringue** or *Meringue for Baked Alaska**, may be swirled with back of spoon or lightly ridged with tines of fork.

11. Meringues are cooked at different temperatures:

For Pies:

(a) If custard was not precooked, but was poured into *Dried Pie Shell** and baked, after it is baked, it may be immediately topped with meringue, and placed in 500° F. oven to be cooked 3 to 4 minutes.

(b) When a cool precooked custard is spooned into a cool

*Baked Pie Shell** and topped with meringue, cook 20 minutes at 325° F.

(c) When a hot precooked custard is spooned into *Baked Pie Shell** and topped with meringue, cook at 400° F. for 8 to 10 minutes.

*For Baked Alaska**:

Cook meringue 3 to 5 minutes at 500° F.

*For Small Meringues for Floating Island**:

Cook 16 to 20 minutes at 325° F.

*For Meringue Shells or Schaum Torte**:

(a) Cook shells from 40 to 60 minutes, depending on size, at 275° F.

(b) Cook torte 1 hour at 275° F.

For Cookies:

Cook 18 to 20 minutes at 375° F.

For Angel Food:

I cast my vote for the *Angel Food** that is baked at 3 different temperatures, starting with 15 minutes at 250° F.; then 15 minutes at 300° F., and finally 30 minutes at 325° F.; however, many people bake Angel Food at 250° F. for approximately 1 hour and others bake these cakes for only 30 to 35 minutes at 375° F.

For Angel Food Roll:

Cook at 375° F. 16 to 20 minutes.

PIE MERINGUE

4 whites from large eggs
⅛ teaspoon salt
¼ teaspoon cream of tartar
½ cup white granulated sugar
1 teaspoon vanilla or extract of your choice

Put egg whites in 1½-quart size or slightly larger bowl. Add salt. Beat on creaming speed of mixer or with rotary egg beater until frothy. Add cream of tartar and beat until soft peak stage is reached. Add sugar gradually by heaping tablespoons and beat until meringue is stiff and glossy. Add vanilla or other extract and continue beating only long enough to blend flavoring with meringue. Spoon meringue over filling, being sure that the filling is completely sealed in between pie shell and meringue. If desired, swirl or ridge surface of meringue.

Bake meringue-topped pie:

3 to 4 minutes at 500° F. if filling was baked in *Dried Pie Shell** before meringue was added.

20 minutes at 325° F. when filling is cooled precooked custard, which has been spooned into *Baked Pie Shell**, and topped with meringue.

8 to 10 minutes at 400° F. when a hot precooked custard has been spooned into a *Baked Pie Shell** and topped with meringue.

Yield: Meringue for 9-inch pie.

VARIATIONS

Meringues for Floating Island: Halve quantity of each ingredient specified in *Pie Meringue**, using 2 whites, ¹⁄₁₆ teaspoon salt, ⅛ teaspoon cream of tartar, ¼ cup sugar, and ½ teaspoon flavoring. Prepare the same way as meringue for pie, but instead of spooning meringue on filling, drop by heaping teaspoons on cooky sheet covered with paper. Bake in 325° F. oven. Remove from oven and let stand until cool in draft-free spot. Cut paper with scissors so that meringues are separated and gently remove paper from bottoms. Meringues may be stored in freezer or refrigerator before paper is removed from bottoms, but since they are sticky, they should be stored in single layer and nothing should be put on top. *Yield: 16 meringues for* Floating Island*.

Individual Meringues: (These are larger and more crusty than *Meringues for Floating Island*.)

Use:

    4 whites from large eggs
    ⅛ teaspoon salt
    ¼ teaspoon cream of tartar
    1⅓ cups of white granulated sugar
    1 teaspoon vinegar (distilled white preferred)

Prepare same way as meringue for pie, but instead of vanilla, use vinegar, and instead of spooning meringue on filling, drop by heaping tablespoons on cooky sheet covered with paper in 6 mounds about 2 inches apart. With back of spoon make hollow in top of each about ½ inch deep and about 2 inches in diameter. Place sheet on center rack of 275° F. oven. Bake until meringues are crusty and just beginning to brown—45 to 55 minutes. Remove from oven and let stand in draft-free spot until cool. Cut paper with scissors so that meringues are separated and gently remove paper from bottoms. *Yield: 6 meringues.*

SUGGESTIONS FOR SERVING:

1. Fill meringues with slightly sweetened or sliced or halved canned or fresh fruit or berries and, if desired, top with *Top of the Stove Custard Filling** or *Custard Fluff** or fill with custard and top with fruit.

2. Place tablespoon of chocolate syrup (brandy to taste may be added, if desired) in bottom of meringue, cover with ice cream (see *Country Custard Ice Cream** or *Top of the Stove Custard —Frozen**) and dribble green crème de menthe over ice cream.

3. Fill meringue with ice cream (see *Country Custard Ice Cream** or *Top of the Stove Custard—Frozen**), and top each serving with 1 tablespoon chopped Maraschino cherries, chopped nuts, or crushed drained pineapple.

Schaum Torte: Double quantity[2] of each ingredient specified for *Individual Meringues**, and prepare in large bowl, but in all other ways prepare just as for pie, substituting vinegar for vanilla, up to point where meringue is spooned on filling. Instead, spoon it into 2 9-inch layer cake pans, lined, bottom and sides, with paper—a tuck or two will have to be taken in paper covering sides, and in 2 spots as nearly opposite each other as possible on each pan allow a little paper to hang over rim, as this will make it easier to remove torte from pans. Even top of meringue with back of spoon. When doing this, it is advisable when the spoon comes close to the side to hold paper in place with tip of finger at top of rim of pan. Place pans in opposite corners, but not touching walls, of 275° F. oven. Keep small space between pans. Bake until torte is a beautiful delicate brown—about 1 hour. Remove from oven and let stand in draft-free spot until cool. Lift meringues from pans and gently remove paper. *Serves 8.*

SUGGESTIONS FOR SERVING:

1. Use crushed, slightly sweetened strawberries, raspberries, or sliced peaches between layers. If desired, top of torte may be decorated with berries or fruit.

2. Use ice cream or whipped cream, covered with berries or fruit, if desired, between layers. If you wish, decorate top layer with whipped cream and/or fruit or berries.

3. Use *Top of the Stove Custard Filling** or *Custard Fluff**

---

[2] If softer *Schaum Torte** is desired, double quantity of all ingredients specified for *Individual Meringues** except sugar. Use 2 cups sugar.

between layers and as topping. If desired, fruit or berries may be used with custard.

Brown Sugar and Nut Individual Meringues; Brown Sugar and Nut Schaum Torte: Make *Individual Meringues**, using ⅔ cup white granulated sugar and ⅔ cup firmly packed dark brown sugar in place of 1⅓ cups white sugar, or make *Schaum Torte** using 1⅓ cups white sugar and 1⅓ cups dark brown sugar. After meringue is beaten until stiff and glossy, fold in 1 cup chopped nuts of your choice.

Meringue for Baked Alaska: Double quantity of each ingredient specified in *Pie Meringue**, using 8 whites, ¼ teaspoon salt, ½ teaspoon cream of tartar, 1 cup sugar, and 2 teaspoons flavoring. Prepare in large bowl the same way as for pie, but instead of spooning meringue on filling, completely cover: (1) ice cream sandwich, made of 2 layers of cake with a layer of ice cream between; (2) cake purposely baked with hollow in center of top and filled with ice cream; or, (3) loaf cake from which center has been hollowed out and then filled with ice cream. The cake and ice cream should rest on a large foil wrapped breadboard or cutting board and the meringue should be brought all the way down the sides so that it touches the aluminum foil covered board at every point surrounding the cake. The meringue touching foil should be just as thick as the rest of the meringue covering the sides of the Alaska. Also, make sure there are no air pockets between the meringue and the surface of the ice cream and cake portion of the Alaska. Place board holding *Baked Alaska** in 500° F. oven and cook 3 to 5 minutes until meringue is light golden brown. And just in case you don't have a recipe for making a *BAKED ALASKA* the easy way, here's one I highly recommend:

1 quart very firm bought or homemade ice cream, such as
   *Country Custard Ice Cream**
2 round 9-inch layers of cake (see *1–2–3–4 Cakes**)
*Meringue for Baked Alaska**

Several days before Alaska is to be served, let ice cream soften slightly and then spoon into 8-inch layer cake pan lined with aluminum foil. Place in freezer. When firm, remove ice cream and foil that will cling to it from pan. Use additional foil to cover completely the ice cream and return to freezer until ready to use. Buy or make 2 round 9-inch layers of cake the day Alaska is to be baked. At least 45 minutes before serving time, take ice cream from freezer and remove foil (peeling it off, if necessary). Place cake layer on center of very large piece of aluminum foil. Cover layer with the 8-inch layer of ice cream and top with second layer of cake. Bring aluminum foil on which bottom layer is resting up around ice cream sandwich so that it is completely covered. If needed, use additional foil to do this. Place wrapped dessert in freezer to set. Wrap a breadboard or cutting board large enough to hold Alaska (10½ to 11 inches) with 3 or 4 thicknesses of foil. When ready to serve, remove dessert from freezer. Remove foil from Alaska and place the dessert on the aluminum foil covered board. Cover with meringue and bake as directed in *Meringue for Baked Alaska**. *Serves 10 to 12.*

SPIRIT MERINGUES

In recipe for *Meringues for Floating Island**, substitute for ½ teaspoon vanilla or other flavoring 1½ tablespoons rum, brandy, Marsala, sherry, or desired cordial, adding spirit gradually and beating after each addition, to create *SPIRIT MERINGUES FOR FLOATING ISLAND.*

In recipe for *Pie Meringue**, substitute for teaspoon vanilla or other flavoring, 2 tablespoons rum, brandy, Marsala, sherry, or desired cordial, adding spirit gradually and beating after each addition to create *SPIRIT PIE MERINGUE.*

In recipe for *Meringue for Baked Alaska**, substitute for 2 teaspoons flavoring, ¼ cup rum, brandy, Marsala, sherry, or desired cordial, adding spirit gradually and beating after each addition to create *SPIRIT MERINGUE FOR BAKED ALASKA.*

MERINGUE COOKIES

DATE AND NUT MERINGUE COOKIES

4 whites from large eggs
¼ teaspoon salt
½ teaspoon cream of tartar
1 cup white granulated sugar
1 teaspoon vanilla
1 pound pitted dates—cut each date in about 5 pieces
2 cups small pecan pieces or slivered blanched almonds

Advance Preparation: Grease cooky sheets with vegetable shortening and wipe away excess. Preheat oven for 10 minutes to 375° F.

Put egg whites in 1½-quart size or slightly larger bowl. Add salt. Beat on creaming speed of mixer or with rotary egg beater until frothy. Add cream of tartar and beat until soft peak stage is reached. Add sugar gradually by heaping tablespoons and beat until meringue is stiff and glossy. Add vanilla, and beat until blended. Transfer meringue to larger bowl, and using spatula or wooden spoon, fold in dates a few at a time, separating pieces as they are added to meringue, as they have a tendency to stick together. Fold in nuts. Drop meringue mixture by heaping teaspoons about 1½ inches apart on cooky sheets. Place one sheet on center rack and second sheet on rack above it. Bake 18 to 20 minutes until cookies are light golden brown. Remove from oven; loosen from tray with spatula (cookies when warm may be slightly sticky, so keep spatula clean even if it's necessary to wash it several times while loosening cookies). Place cookies on trays or plates to cool. *Yield: 48 cookies.*

VARIATIONS

Date and Nut Meringue Cookies for Christmas—Insert candied cherry or piece of candied pineapple, about thumbnail size, in middle of top of each cooky before baking. If available, use both the red and green candied fruit.

Nut, Coconut, and Cornflake Meringue Cookies—Substitute 1 cup shredded canned coconut and 4 cups cornflakes for dates. Use only 1 cup nuts instead of 2 cups specified for *Date and Nut Meringue Cookies**. After cookies are dropped by heaping teaspoons on greased sheets, using fingertips, very gently round each cooky. At this time as well as when cornflakes are folded into meringue, care must be taken not to crush the flakes. While these cookies like the date and nut cookies are baked 18 to 20 minutes in a 375° F. oven, they should be a rich golden brown instead of light golden brown. *Yield: 48 cookies.*

ANGEL FOOD

Starting with egg whites, ingredients are listed in order in which they are added when using mixer. When mixing with wire whip, vanilla is added at same time as salt and cream of tartar.

   1½ cups egg whites, plus 1 additional white[3]
   ½ teaspoon salt
   1½ teaspoons cream of tartar
   1 cup granulated sugar
   1¼ teaspoons vanilla and 1 teaspoon almond extract (2¼
      teaspoons vanilla may be used and almond extract
      omitted)
   1⅛ cups (1 cup plus 2 tablespoons) sifted cake flour
   ¾ cup granulated sugar
   Any of *Double Boiler Mallow Frostings** or any other fluffy
      frosting, if desired

[3] In view of the fact that most 10-inch angel food cakes specify 1½ cups egg whites, there may be a lifted eyebrow or two over the 1½ cups plus 1

Preparation

Separate whites from yolks of cold eggs. Let whites stand until room temperature. If there are lumps in white granulated sugar, sift. Measure 1 cup sugar. Sift cake flour, measure and add ¾ cup of sugar. Sift flour and sugar mixture 5 more times. Place sifter in pan or bowl and spoon flour mixture into it. Preheat oven to 250° F. for 10 minutes.

Mixing with Food Mixer

1. Place egg whites in large mixer bowl and add salt.

2. Beat until frothy on creaming speed of mixer.

3. Add cream of tartar and continue beating until whites form soft peaks when beaters are lifted through them. While the whites are being beaten, the beaters should be lifted up and down through whites from time to time during at least 4 or 5 (not consecutive) revolutions of beaters around bowl.

4. Add cup of sugar by heaping tablespoons, being sure that each addition is blended with meringue before adding more sugar, but don't beat 1 second more than necessary. Continue lifting beaters up and down through meringue at intervals during period sugar is added.

5. When sugar is blended with egg whites, immediately cut mixer speed as low as possible (this is folding-in speed) and add extract. Beat on this low speed for ½ minute.

6. Sift flour and sugar mixture and add to meringue by heaping kitchen tablespoons, still on lowest possible mixer speed.

egg white in this recipe. For many years I used the 1½ cups of egg whites and then my "Why not?" side got the best of me. I started wondering what would happen if I added just a little more of the egg white, since I have never been able to believe that the most convenient measurement always produces the best results. Each time I made an angel food after that, I "cheated" by continuing to increase slightly the measurement until finally I found that with 1 additional egg white, I had everything I could ever want in an angel food.

After each addition, assist mixer by running plastic or rubber spatula over side of bowl that is opposite the beaters in order to sweep any unmixed flour into path of beaters. Just as quickly as each addition of the flour and sugar mixture is blended into batter, add next tablespoon of mixture.

Mixing with Wire Whip

1. Place egg whites in large bowl and add salt, cream of tartar, and extract.

2. Using wire whip, beat until soft peak stage. Add cup of sugar by heaping tablespoons, continuing to beat and being sure that each addition is blended with meringue before more sugar is added. Continue beating until meringue is stiff but not dry.

3. Sift flour and sugar mixture by heaping tablespoons over meringue, and after each addition fold the dry ingredients into the egg whites.

Getting Batter Ready for Baking

When all of mixture has been folded into batter—and don't forget overbeating at this point won't improve anything and could very well ruin a good cake—spoon batter into a 10-inch ungreased tube pan—for true perfection, use a pan that has never been greased. With back of spoon level surface of batter. Then, using a small dinner knife, gently cut through batter, going around the tube 5 or 6 times in ever widening circles so as to let large air bubbles escape. If any of batter has been splattered over sides or tube of pan, carefully wipe clean with paper napkin or towel.

Baking

Place pan in middle of center rack of a 250°F. oven. Bake 15 minutes and increase temperature to 300°F. At end of 15 minutes, raise temperature to 325°F. and bake 30 minutes. Test with finger—cake should spring back leaving no indentation when surface is gently touched with finger. The cake should be done after baking for 1 hour, but if not, let it remain in oven until it tests "done," which should only be a few minutes more. Don't overbake. Remove from oven.

The Finishing Touches

Gently invert pan and let cake hang at least 1 hour, but preferably 2, so cells will expand. Loosen cake from pan by running a small dinner knife—nylon knife if cake was baked in Teflon pan—around sides and tube. Tap edge of pan sharply on counter or tabletop. Turn out onto serving tray or on cardboard cut to fit and then covered with aluminum foil. Gently brush crumbs from sides of cake, and if desired, ice with a fluffy frosting. *Yield: 1 10-inch cake.*

VARIATIONS

Angel Food in Gold—Use 1¼ teaspoons lemon extract and 1 teaspoon vanilla instead of vanilla and/or almond. After flour and sugar mixture has been added to meringue, fold in (on lowest mixer speed or with wire whip) 8 egg yolks that have been beaten until thick and lemon-colored. Bake 15 minutes at 250° F., 15 minutes at 300° F., and approximately 45 minutes at 325° F. until when center of cake is lightly pressed with finger, no indentation is left.

Angel Food with Semi-sweet Chocolate Morsels—After flour and sugar mixture has been added, with a wooden spoon, very, very gently fold in ⅔ cup semi-sweet chocolate morsels.

Chocolate Angel Food—Substitute for the 1⅛ cups sifted cake flour, ¾ cup plus 1 tablespoon sifted cake flour and 5 tablespoons (¼ cup plus 1 tablespoon) cocoa that has been first measured and then sifted.

Angel Food Roll—Preparation and mixing are the same; however, the quantity of each ingredient is changed and confectioners' sugar must be used for rolling cake. Also, *Top of the Stove Custard Filling** or *Custard Fluff** is used in place of the frosting, and since custard is used, the roll must be stored in the refrigerator.

Use:

1 cup egg whites
⅜ teaspoon salt
1 teaspoon cream of tartar
¾ cup white granulated sugar
1 teaspoon vanilla
½ teaspoon almond extract
⅔ cup plus 1 tablespoon sifted cake flour
⅓ cup granulated sugar
Confectioners' sugar
Top of the Stove Custard Filling* or *Custard Fluff**

Liberally oil 10½ ×15½ -inch cooky tray with 1-inch rim (Teflon preferred) with vegetable oil. Cover bottom of pan with wax paper, allowing 1½ inches of paper to hang over each of the 2 ends of pan. Paper should be cut so that while the entire bottom of pan is covered there is no paper on the 2 long sides. Brush paper thoroughly with oil, but if there is any excess, wipe it away. When batter has been mixed, spoon into prepared cooky tray. Level off batter with back of small spoon and then, going from one end to the other and starting at one side and going to opposite side, gently cut through the batter with a small knife (nylon, if Teflon pan is being used), so that the large air bubbles can escape. Wipe away any batter that has splattered on sides of pan with paper napkin.

Baking

Place pan in middle of center rack of 375° F. oven. Bake 16 to 20 minutes until indentation springs back when center of cake is lightly pressed with finger.

The Finishing Touches

While cake is baking, sift confectioners' sugar liberally over a small (smooth fabric) towel. Towel must be large enough for cake to fit on it. When cake is removed from oven, immediately loosen sides with sharp knife—Teflon pan would require nylon knife—and turn cake out on sugar-covered towel. Loosen paper from edges of cake (with small sharp knife, if necessary), and then make hole in the middle of the paper with knife. Very gently —rough handling will tear cake—remove paper by starting at hole in center and pulling off strips in direction of cake's outer edge. The larger the strips that can be pulled off without damaging the cake the better. Spread half of filling or fluff over cake and then, starting with the 10½-inch side, roll up[4] to make a short thick roll. Wrap roll in sugared towel and let stand 15 or 20 minutes. Place in refrigerator until cold. When chilled, unwrap and put roll on serving platter. Cover cake with remaining custard and return to refrigerator. *Serves 10.*

Chocolate Angel Food Roll—Substitute ⅔ cup sifted cake flour, plus 2½ tablespoons cocoa, which was first measured and then sifted, for the ⅔ cup plus 1 tablespoon sifted cake flour specified in *Angel Food Roll**.

[4] Because the *Angel Food Roll** is a little thicker and lighter than most cake rolls, several large cracks may appear while cake is being rolled. If so, you need not be bothered by this as the custard (filling or fluff) will completely fill in and cover these cracks.

16

Butter Cakes—
Featuring the
1-2-3-4 Cakes in Many Guises

I am told the Washingtons served their guests at Mount Vernon with *1-2-3-4 Cake**. It was then, as it is now, a cake worthy of any gathering and any occasion, and yet one so easy to make there is no reason why any family can't have it often. Besides, it comes in 17 different flavors and 4 different shapes (round layer, small cupcakes, loaf, or oblong), not to mention the cookies.

GENERAL RULES FOR MAKING BUTTER CAKES

ADVANCE PREPARATION

1. Prepare Pan(s):

(a) *For Layer Cakes:* (Use 2 9-inch round, 1½-inch deep layer pans for following recipes.) If shiny aluminum pans are used, they do not have to be greased; instead cut wax paper into rounds just a fraction of an inch smaller than the bottom of each pan and fit paper into pans. If pans are not shiny and must be greased, use vegetable shortening. After greasing sides and bottoms, cover bottoms with wax or brown paper cut to fit, and then grease paper with vegetable shortening.

(b) *For Cupcakes:* (The tea size are recommended for a more attractive platter.) Grease cups of muffin pans with vegetable shortening, or to save time, dishwashing, and greasing, use paper baking cups to line muffin pan cups, being sure to use the size paper cup that fits your particular size muffin pan.

(c) *For Loaf Cakes:* (Use 2 9×5×3-inch loaf pans for following recipes.) Grease pans thoroughly and line with brown or wax paper cut to fit bottom of each pan. Grease paper well.

(d) *For Oblong Cake:* (A 13×9×2-inch pan is suggested for following recipes.) Cut brown or wax paper to fit bottom of pan. Grease sides and bottom thoroughly with vegetable shortening. Cover with paper cut to fit. Grease paper well.

(e) *For Fruit Cake:* (Use 10-inch tube pan.) Grease pan well. Cover bottom with brown paper cut to fit and grease paper thoroughly with vegetable shortening.

2. Separate whites from yolks of cold eggs. In cold or cool weather, let yolks and whites stand until room temperature. If weather is hot, use cold yolks and whites.

3. Measure milk and in cold or cool weather, let stand until room temperature. If weather is hot, use cold milk.

4. Measure butter or margarine, and let stand until slightly soft. This does not mean, by any stretch of the imagination, melted or runny.

5. Measure sugar.

6. Sift flour—unless recipe specifies otherwise, use cake flour. Place sifter in pan or bowl and measure sifted flour into it. Add baking powder, and if used, cocoa, spice, and/or salt.

7. Preheat oven for 10 minutes:
    To 300° F. for Fruit Cake
    To 325° F. for Loaf Cake
    To 350° F. for Layer Cake or Oblong Cake
    To 400° F. for Cupcakes

MIXING BATTER WITH FOOD MIXER

NOTE: Don't let length of following directions frighten you. Even a beginner should take no more than 15 minutes for mixing a batter and when mixer is used, since it does all the hard labor, there is very little work entailed for the cake maker. The directions are long, since step by step, the things that must be done, and in some instances the things that must not be done—and it's taken me over 25 years to learn all these things—have been included, so that from this day forth, you too can make a "perfect" cake. *It is important that you remember when using a mixer to avoid overbeating* so your cakes won't be tough. The exception to the rule is pound cake (see *1–2–3–4 Pound Cake**), which is beaten 7 minutes while sugar is being added and 3 minutes after it is all added, before eggs are added. It is also important that you remember—and there are no exceptions on this point—to use lowest speed when adding flour and baking powder mixture, as overbeating would liberate carbon dioxide gas from the baking powder and result in the cake not rising to the proper height. Butter or margarine, sugar, stewed fruit or preserves, when used, egg yolks or whole eggs are beaten on the "creaming speed," since the high speed has been found to be preferable for dissolving sugar and also since its use results in cakes with lighter and finer texture. The flavoring, flour mixture, and milk—or any other liquid substituted for milk—are added on mixer's lowest speed, which is the "folding" speed. For true perfection, use a wooden spoon to fold in the beaten egg whites.

1. Place butter or margarine in large bowl. Beat on creaming speed until light and fluffy—the consistency of a stiff mayonnaise —from 30 to 45 seconds. Stop mixer and scrape butter or margarine from sides of bowl into the path of the beaters with rubber or plastic spatula.

2. Start mixer up again on creaming speed and gradually add sugar by heaping tablespoons, beating only long enough after each addition to blend sugar and fat. When all of sugar is added, stop mixer, scrape dough from beaters and from sides of bowl into middle of bowl. Again turn mixer on creaming speed and beat 1 minute. During this minute, from time to time, assist mixer by scraping batter from side of bowl opposite revolving beaters with spatula. At end of minute, stop mixer and repeat scraping of beaters and bowl.

3. On creaming speed add egg yolks or whole eggs. If adding yolks, beat 2 minutes, continuing to assist mixer by scraping side of bowl 3 or 4 times during this period. If using whole eggs, add 1 by 1, beating on creaming speed from 30 seconds to 1 minute after each addition or add all together and beat batter 2 minutes, in accordance with recipe being used, and also assist mixer by scraping side of bowl with spatula.

Since no yolks are used for a white cake, skip Step 3 when this type of cake is made.

4. If melted or premelted baking chocolate is used, it should be added with yolks, and, with them, beaten for 2 minutes, or if whole eggs are used, after they have all been added to batter, add chocolate and beat only until blended with other ingredients (about ½ minute).

5. Turn mixer to lowest possible speed and add extract. Continue beating 30 seconds, scraping side of bowl opposite revolving beaters with a motion that sweeps batter from side into path of beaters.

6. Sift flour mixture. If a small quantity of dried fruit and/or nuts is being used, it can now be mixed with flour, so that each piece of fruit or nut is coated.

7. Still on lowest possible speed, alternately add flour mixture and milk or other liquid, using approximately a heaping kitchen tablespoon flour and ⅕ of the liquid for each addition. Start and end with flour and several times while flour and liquid are being "folded" into batter, run spatula over side of bowl opposite beater so as to sweep batter from side of bowl into beater path.

8. Beat egg whites so stiff that they will cling to bowl when it is turned upside down, but will still be a uniform white. With wooden spoon, *fold whites* into batter. This is best done by placing whites on top of batter. Holding spoon so that its bowl is sideways, bring it across bottom of bowl, up the side completely over the stiffly beaten egg whites and then down the opposite side through the batter. Do this 2 or 3 times; turn bowl just slightly—this is done with ease if you put bowl on lazy Susan or on revolving stand of mixer and remove beaters. Repeat folding-in process several times before again turning bowl. Continue folding in, turning bowl slightly from time to time, until whites are blended in with batter and mixture appears satiny smooth. If for any reason it becomes necessary, egg whites may be added on the lowest possible mixer speed, but I certainly don't recommend this.

MIXING BATTER WITH SPOON

1. Place butter or margarine in large bowl. Hold spoon so its bowl is sideways and move it rapidly through butter or margarine from 1 side of mixing bowl to other, then bring spoon up side of bowl and over fat back to spot in bowl from which you started. Continue creaming fat until it has consistency of a stiff mayonnaise. This should require around 60 strokes.

2. Gradually add sugar by heaping tablespoons, creaming after each addition until fat and sugar are blended. After all sugar has been added, beat about 150 strokes, until light and fluffy.

3. If using yolks, add, and beat 120 strokes. If using whole eggs, add 1 at a time, and beat 60 strokes after each addition or add all eggs at one time and beat 2 minutes.

4. If melted or premelted baking chocolate is used, it should be added when yolks are. If whole eggs are used, after they have all been added to batter, add chocolate and beat only until blended with other ingredients.

5. Stir in extract—60 strokes should do this.

6. Sift flour mixture. If a small quantity of dried fruit and/or nuts is being used, it can now be mixed with flour, so that each piece of fruit or nut is coated.

7. Alternately stir in flour and milk or other liquid, using approximately a heaping kitchen tablespoon flour and ⅕ of liquid for each addition. Start and end with flour. Stir only long enough after each addition to blend it completely with batter.

8. Fold stiffly beaten egg whites into batter in accordance with instructions in Section 8, *Mixing Batter with Food Mixer**.

BAKING

1. If using more than 1 pan, divide dough as equally as possible. If using ungreased layer pan, spoon dough into pan very gently; otherwise, you may move wax paper in bottom of pan, and if this is done, it's a little difficult to correct. Also, when ungreased pan is used, don't shake batter to level it, as this will cause paper to move out of place.

If baking cupcakes, fill cups about ⅔ full—never more.

2. When all of dough has been spooned into pan(s), if a greased pan has been used, you may gently "rock" the pan from side to side, holding it in your hand while doing this, to level the dough. For ungreased or greased pan, respectively, level or finish leveling with back of spoon. Wipe away any and all splatters, on inside or outside of pan, with paper napkin or towel. If using 2 pans, place on opposite corners of the preheated oven rack. Keep a small space between pans and don't let them touch oven walls. If cooking only 1 cake, place pan in middle of center rack of preheated oven.

3. When cake is properly baked, a wire cake tester inserted in the center will come out clean or no imprint will remain when you lightly press center of cake with a finger. In the case of the fruit cake only, the cake will start to come away from the pan, but don't wait for this to happen with other cakes, as they would then be on the dry side. There is no need to keep opening and closing the oven door as it is most important that the temperature be kept constant and this is an impossibility if the door is opened and shut at frequent intervals.

TESTING AND ESTIMATED BAKING TIMES FOR CAKES

OVEN TEMPERATURES	TEST AT	ESTIMATED BAKING TIMES
Fruit cakes in 300° F. oven (10-inch tube pan)	2 hours 30 minutes	2 hours and 40 minutes to 3 hours
Loaf cakes in 325° F. oven (2 9×5×3-inch loaf pans)	45 minutes	55 to 65 minutes
Layer cakes in 350° F. oven (2 9-inch layers)	38 minutes	42 to 48 minutes
Oblong cakes in 350° F. oven (1 13×9×2-inch pan)	40 minutes	45 to 55 minutes
Cupcakes in 400° F. oven		
Small	10 minutes	12 to 14 minutes
Large	15 minutes	16 to 20 minutes

If cake is not done at first test, cook fruit cake about 15 minutes more and other cakes 3 to 5 minutes before again testing. Continue testing at these intervals of time until cake tests "done."

4. Remove cakes from oven as soon as they test done. Let them stand in pans for 10 minutes away from drafts. Unless paper baking cups were used, loosen from sides of pan by running a small knife between sides of cakes and sides of pans. Turn cakes out on a wire rack to prevent their becoming slightly soggy while cooling. If you don't have a cake rack large enough for the oblong cake, turn it out on cutting board.

If you want cake bottom-side-up on rack, place rack over top of pan. With palms up, place tips of 4 fingers of each hand on opposite sides of pan, so that they rest immediately under the rim. Place thumbs so that they rest comfortably on top of rack. Press with fingers and thumbs so that pan and rack are held together firmly. Invert. Place rack on table and lift off pan.

If you want cake right-side-up on rack, cover palm and outstretched fingers with a smooth textured towel, which has been folded 3 or 4 times, and place towel supported by hand across top of cake. Slip palm of other hand, with fingers outstretched (if possible, hand should be protected with a padded glove), under cake pan. Quickly but carefully turn pan so that cake rests on towel and hand. Lift off pan. Cover cake with rack. Place other hand with palm down and fingers outstretched over rack. Invert (with care). Remove hand and towel and slide rack onto table. Let cake stand on rack until cool.

GOURMET TOUCH

If desired, as soon as cake(s) is or are turned out of pan(s), brush or sprinkle with rum, brandy, dessert sherry, or cordial of your choice (Cointreau, curaçao, Maraschino, and white crème de menthe are highly recommended).

FROSTING[1] THE CAKE

Frost top and sides of *cupcakes* or only top, as you desire. When only tops are frosted, it is suggested that the small cakes be served in colored paper baking cups.

Cut *oblong cake* when cool into squares or rectangles of desired size. Beat egg white just until frothy and, using a brush, lightly cover cut sides of cake with egg white. Let stand until completely dry and frost.

Place *loaf cake* on serving platter before icing. Platter may be made of cardboard covered with aluminum foil. The platter

[1] See *Double Boiler Mallow Frosting** or *Butter Cream Frosting**.

should be large enough to hold cake after it is frosted, so it is wise to select a platter or make the foil covered one at the very least an inch larger on each side than the uniced cake.

Layer cakes should be put together with frosting or filling so that the two matching sides are together—that is, one layer should be right-side-up and the other layer should be right-side-down or one layer should be bottom-side-up while the other layer is bottom-side-down. Place platter on top of one layer of cake. With palms up, place tips of 4 fingers of each hand under opposite sides of cake rack and place thumbs so that they rest on platter. Holding as steady as possible, invert. Slide platter onto table and lift off rack. After layer on platter is frosted or covered with filling, place rack holding uniced cake next to it. Lift unfrosted layer quickly and gently and put it on top of frosted layer (right-side-up to right-side-down or bottom-side-up to bottom-side-down). Try to keep the top layer from overhanging the bottom layer in one spot while the bottom layer extends out on platter beyond the top layer in another spot. If, however, this happens, remember that frostings cover a lot of sins.

The easiest way *to spread frosting* on cake is to put a heaping tablespoon on top of a large cake and a heaping teaspoon on cupcakes or cut squares or rectangles. Spread as fast and as evenly as possible with side of blade of small dinner knife. Continue adding icing by tablespoon for the larger cakes and spreading until entire top is evenly covered. Place a heaping tablespoon of frosting on rim of iced top of large cake or a heaping teaspoon on rim of cut cake squares or rectangles or cupcakes, if sides are to be iced, and with side of knife bring it down, covering as much of side of cake as possible, but keeping frosting just about the same thickness as that on top. Continue doing this until sides are completely covered. Check carefully to see if you have missed a spot or if you have any thin spots and with a little frosting on the end of the knife, properly cover these spots. If any of icing that was placed on rim of cake for use on sides remains on top, use side of knife to smooth it down. If desired, frosting may be swirled with tip of knife or small spoon.

1–2–3–4 CAKES

For detailed step by step instructions, from preparing the pans to putting on the last bit of frosting, see *General Rules for Making Butter Cakes**.

YELLOW LAYER CAKE — YELLOW OBLONG CAKE
YELLOW CUPCAKES

Starting with butter or margarine, ingredients are listed in order in which they are added.

1 cup butter or margarine
2 cups granulated white sugar
4 unbeaten yolks of large eggs
1½ teaspoons vanilla
3 cups sifted cake flour
2¼ teaspoons double acting baking powder
⅞ cup milk
4 stiffly beaten, but not dry, whites of large eggs
Frosting, if desired

Prepare 2 9-inch layer pans, 1 13×9×2-inch pan, or muffin tins (recipe will make approximately 55 tea-size cupcakes). Separate whites from yolks of cold eggs. Measure milk. In cool or cold weather let eggs and milk stand until room temperature. Use cold eggs and milk when weather is hot. Measure butter or margarine and let stand until slightly softened. Measure sugar. Sift flour and measure into sifter. Add baking powder to flour and let stand.

Preheat oven:

To 350° F. for Layer or Oblong Cake(s)

To 400° F. for Cupcakes

Cream butter or margarine in large bowl until it is consistency of stiff mayonnaise. Gradually add sugar by heaping tablespoons, beating after each addition until sugar and fat are blended, and then after all sugar is added, creaming until light and fluffy. Add egg yolks and beat batter, if using mixer, for 2 minutes or cream, if using spoon, for 120 strokes. If using food mixer, all of foregoing is done on creaming speed and all of following on lowest possible speed. Blend in extract. Sift flour mixture. Alternately stir in, or fold in on mixer, the flour-baking powder mixture and milk, using approximately a heaping kitchen tablespoon flour and ⅕ of milk for each addition. Start and end with flour. Stir or fold only long enough after each addition to blend it completely with batter. Fold stiffly beaten egg whites into batter with wooden spoon.

Spoon dough into prepared pans. Bake until a wire cake tester inserted in the center comes out clean or until no imprint remains when you lightly press center with finger.

Bake 2 9-inch layer cakes 42 to 48 minutes

Bake 1 13×9×2-inch oblong cake 45 to 55 minutes

Bake small cupcakes 12 to 14 minutes (larger ones from 16 to 20 minutes)

When cake tests "done," remove from oven. Let stand 10 minutes. Turn out on cake rack(s) and let stand until cool. Frost with *Double Boiler Mallow Frosting**, *Butter Cream Frosting**, or any other frosting, if desired.

VARIATIONS

I. 1–2–3–4 CAKES MADE WITH YOLKS AND WHITES OF EGGS BEING ADDED SEPARATELY

Apple Spice Layer Cake; Apple Spice Oblong Cake; Apple Spice Cupcakes—Add to flour in sifter: 1 teaspoon each cinnamon, cloves, and nutmeg. Add ¾ cup drained, cooked, mashed unsweetened apple to creamed butter or margarine and sugar mixture. Beat on creaming speed, if using mixer, for 1 minute, or cream with spoon, if mixing with spoon, for 100 strokes before adding egg yolks. Use only ¾ cup milk.

Brown Sugar Spice Layer Cake; Brown Sugar Spice Oblong Cake; Brown Sugar Spice Cupcakes—Add to flour in sifter: 1 teaspoon each cinnamon, cloves, and nutmeg. Substitute 2 cups granulated brown sugar for white sugar.

Chocolate Layer Cake; Chocolate Oblong Cake; Chocolate Cupcakes—Add with yolks 3 ounces melted or premelted baking chocolate.

Chocolate Pecan Layer Cake; Chocolate Pecan Oblong Cake; Chocolate Pecan Cupcakes—Add with yolks 3 ounces melted or premelted baking chocolate. After flour mixture is sifted, add 1 cup pecans, broken in small pieces, and stir gently until pieces are coated with the flour. Then add to batter alternately with milk.

Cocoa Layer Cake; Cocoa Oblong Cake; Cocoa Cupcakes—Substitute 2½ cups sifted cake flour and ½ cup cocoa, first measured then sifted for the 3 cups of sifted cake flour.

Coconut Layer Cake; Coconut Oblong Cake; Coconut Cupcakes—Before folding in egg whites, quickly stir in 1 cup canned, grated coconut.

Dark Marble Cake; Dark Marble Cupcakes—*For 1 large cake:* cut wax paper so that it will cover bottom of 10-inch tube pan with ½ inch of paper extending up the outer sides of pan. Grease pan with vegetable shortening and fit wax paper into it. Grease paper. *For cupcakes:* Grease cups of muffin tins with vegetable shortening. *For both:* After egg whites are folded into batter, measure 1 cup of batter. Combine 1 ounce melted or premelted baking chocolate, ⅛ teaspoon soda, and 1 tablespoon warm water. Stir until blended and then fold chocolate mixture into cup of batter. *For large cake:* Spoon half of vanilla batter into tube pan. Drop spoonfuls of chocolate batter about 1 inch apart on top of batter in pan, using half of chocolate mixture. With a knife, cut through batter several times. Spoon remainder of vanilla batter into pan carefully and top with spoonfuls of chocolate batter about 1 inch apart. Using a knife, cut through batter several times. Bake in 350° F. oven for approximately 1 hour until wire cake tester inserted in center of one of the sides comes out clean. Let stand 10 minutes and then turn out on rack to cool. *For cupcakes:* Half fill the cups of muffin tins with vanilla batter. Place approximately ⅔ teaspoon of chocolate mixture for small cupcakes and 1½ teaspoons for the large ones on top of each cake and with a small knife cut through dough twice, letting path of second cut crisscross path of first cut. Bake in 400° F. oven 12 to 14 minutes for small cupcakes and 16 to 20 minutes for large ones until when wire cake tester is inserted in center of cupcake it comes out clean. Remove from oven. Let stand for 10 minutes and turn out of pans onto rack to cool.

Upside Down Cake—Cut quantity of each ingredient in half (you will use ½ cup butter or margarine, 1 cup sugar, 2 egg yolks, ¾ teaspoon vanilla, 1½ cups sifted cake flour, 1⅛ teaspoons double acting baking powder, 7 tablespoons milk, 2 egg whites). After batter is prepared, make following topping:

¼ cup butter or margarine
½ cup firmly packed brown sugar
8 canned, drained peach or pear halves or pineapple rings or
    12 apricot halves
Drained Maraschino cherries (8 for peach, pear, or pineapple
    topping and 12 for apricot topping), if desired

Melt ¼ cup butter or margarine in heavy 8×8×2-inch baking pan. Brush melted fat over sides of pan so that they are well greased, but leave most of melted fat in bottom. Tilt pan back and forth several times so melted fat will spread evenly. Sprinkle sugar, also evenly, over fat in bottom of pan. Arrange fruit on sugar with rounded sides of peaches, pears, or apricots up. If desired, a cherry may be placed so that it will rest in the hollow of each piece of halved fruit or in the center of the pineapple ring, by arranging cherries on sugar and then covering with fruit halves or surrounding with pineapple rings. Spoon batter over fruit. Level top of batter with spoon and wipe away any splatterings on sides of pan. Bake in 350° F. oven 45 to 53 minutes until wire cake tester inserted in center of cake comes out clean. Remove from oven and quickly run a small knife around sides of pan. Turn cake out upside down on serving platter (fruit on top). Let pan remain over cake and on platter for 5 minutes to allow brown sugar mixture to run down sides of cake. Lift pan off cake. Serve warm or cold. *Serves 8.*

Serving Suggestion

Cut into 8 squares, place on individual serving dishes and top each portion with a scoop of ice cream.[2]

Gourmet Touch

If desired, before arranging fruit on sugar, brush drained fruit with rum, Cointreau, kirsch, or cognac, or brush peaches with peach brandy and apricots with apricot brandy. For a further Gourmet Touch, after pan is lifted off platter, spoon ¼ cup of same spirit that was used to brush fruit over cake.

II. 1–2–3–4 CAKES MADE WITH WHOLE EGGS BEING ADDED ONE AT A TIME

Pound Cakes—Line bottoms of 2 well-greased 9×5×3-inch loaf pans with brown or wax paper cut to fit and grease paper. Preheat oven for at least 10 minutes to 325° F. If desired, (and I hope you do) add 1 teaspoon mace to flour and baking powder.

When butter or margarine reaches consistency of stiff mayonnaise, gradually add sugar by tablespoons over a period of 7 minutes, continuing to beat on creaming speed of mixer or creaming with a spoon for the entire 7 minutes. After all of sugar has been added, beat 3 more minutes. Add eggs 1 at a time, beating 30 seconds after each addition. Blend in extract and then add flour mixture alternately with milk, starting and ending with flour, and stirring with spoon or folding with mixer after each

[2] See *Country Custard Ice Cream** or *Top of the Stove Custard—Frozen*.

addition only long enough to blend it completely with batter. Divide batter between 2 greased pans and place on center rack of oven. Place pans in opposite corners, but don't let them touch oven walls. Bake approximately 55 to 65 minutes until wire tester inserted in center of cake comes out clean. Remove from oven and let stand in draft-free spot 10 minutes. Turn cakes out on racks to cool.

Rum Pound Cakes—Prepare *1–2–3–4 Pound Cakes**. As soon as they are taken from oven, combine 1⅓ cups granulated white sugar and ⅔ cup water. Bring to a boil. Reduce to medium heat and cook 3 minutes. Add ⅓ cup rum. Turn cakes out of pans onto racks and immediately spoon syrup over tops and, using a small brush, "paint" sides with it. Let stand until cool.

Dobos Torte—Cut 1 of the cooled *1–2–3–4 Pound Cakes** lengthwise into 5 layers, or if you, like me, prefer the cake layers a little thicker, cut into 4 layers. As layers are cut, gently move all but the bottom layer and place the slices on a rack. Carefully transfer bottom layer to platter or aluminum covered cardboard. Prepare *Chocolate Butter Cream Frosting** or *Chocolate Double Boiler Mallow Frosting**. Spread frosting on top of bottom layer; cover with next layer and then spread frosting on top of second layer. Repeat until cake is reconstructed and then frost top and sides. Let cake stand at least 1 hour before cutting.

Fruit-flavored Mallow Frosted Pound Cake—Cut 1 of the cooled *1–2–3–4 Pound Cakes** lengthwise into 4 layers. As layers are cut, gently move all but the bottom layer and place the slices on a rack. Carefully transfer bottom layer to platter or aluminum covered cardboard. Prepare any one of *Fruit-flavored Double Boiler Mallow Frostings**. Spread frosting on top of bottom layer; cover with another layer and spread frosting on top of second layer. Repeat until cake is reconstructed and then frost top and sides. Let cake stand for 1 hour before cutting.

FRUIT CAKE

Starting with butter or margarine, ingredients are added in order listed.

1 cup butter or margarine
2 cups white granulated sugar
4 large eggs
3 cups sifted all purpose flour
2¼ teaspoons double acting baking powder
1 teaspoon cinnamon
1 teaspoon nutmeg
1 teaspoon cloves
½ teaspoon allspice
⅜ cup orange juice or Bourbon whisky
½ cup molasses
2½ cups pecans, broken in small pieces
15 ounces plumped seedless raisins or 8 ounces each *Plumped Raisins and Currants**
1¾ pounds (commercially) mixed cut candied fruit, or 1¾ pounds candied fruit of your choice, cut in pieces ¼ × ⅛ × ⅛ inch[3]
1 cup Bourbon whisky, brandy, rum, or sherry, if desired

Cut heavy brown paper to fit bottom of 10-inch tube pan. Grease pan well with vegetable shortening. Cover bottom of pan with brown paper and grease paper. Preheat oven to 300°F. Sift flour, measure, and put back in sifter. Add baking powder and spices.

Cream butter or margarine until it is the consistency of mayonnaise. Add sugar by heaping tablespoons, beating only long enough after each addition to blend fat and sugar. After all of sugar is added, cream for 1 minute more. Add whole eggs, 1 at a time, and beat 1 minute after each addition. If using mixer, all of foregoing should be done on creaming speed and the following should be done on lowest possible speed. Sift flour mixture and add by heaping kitchen tablespoons alternately, first with orange

---

[3] *A suggested assortment of candied fruit:* ½ pound each cherries and pineapple and ¼ pound each citron, orange peel, and lemon peel.

juice or whisky and then with molasses, using about ⅕ of total amount of liquid for each addition. Start and end with flour mixture. Stir nuts, raisins, and/or currants and candied fruit into batter alternately, a small quantity of each at a time, mixing after each addition so that nuts and fruit are well distributed throughout batter. Spoon into prepared pan. Place in middle of center oven rack and bake until cake tests "done"—from 2 hours and 40 minutes to 3 hours. Remove from oven and let stand in draft-free spot 10 minutes. Loosen cake from tube and sides of pan. Turn out on rack and quickly remove paper from bottom. If desired, while cake is still warm, spoon and brush with whisky, brandy, rum, or sherry. Let stand until cool. Wrap in aluminum foil and store in cake safe or securely covered box for at least 3 weeks. (If you wish, when cake is removed from cake safe or box, again brush with whisky, brandy, rum, or sherry.)

III. EGG WHITE CAKES

White Layer Cake[4]; White Oblong Cake[4]; White Cupcakes[4]— Omit yolks but use 6 whites of large eggs, beaten until stiff, but not dry. If an almond-flavored cake is preferred, use ¾ teaspoon vanilla and ¾ teaspoon almond extract as a substitute for the 1½ teaspoons vanilla, but this is a matter of choice.

After butter and sugar are creamed, blend in extract and then proceed exactly as directed in *Yellow Layer Cake**, *Yellow Oblong Cake**, and *Yellow Cupcakes**.

[4] These cakes are also known as *SILVER CAKES* or *BRIDE'S CAKES*.

VARIATIONS ON THE WHITE LAYER CAKE*, WHITE OBLONG CAKE* AND WHITE CUPCAKES*

Cocoa Egg White Layer Cake; Cocoa Egg White Oblong Cake; Cocoa Egg White Cupcakes—Substitute 2½ cups sifted cake flour and ½ cup cocoa, first measured and then sifted for the 3 cups of sifted cake flour.

Coconut White Layer Cake; Coconut White Oblong Cake; Coconut White Cupcakes—Just before egg whites are folded into batter, quickly stir in 1 cup grated canned coconut.

IV. EGG YOLK COOKIES

Starting with butter or margarine and vegetable shortening or animal fat shortening, the ingredients are listed in order in which they are added.

   ½ cup butter or margarine
   ½ cup vegetable shortening or mixture vegetable and animal
     fat shortening
   2 cups sugar
   4 egg yolks
   1½ teaspoons vanilla
   3 cups sifted all purpose flour
   ¾ teaspoon double acting baking powder
   ⅓ cup granulated white sugar
   ½ teaspoon cinnamon

Preheat oven to 400° F. Sift flour, measure, add baking powder and sift.

Combine butter or margarine and shortening in large bowl. Beat until light and fluffy—from 30 to 45 seconds. Add 2 cups of sugar by tablespoons, beating only long enough after each addition to blend sugar and fat. Add yolks and beat 2 minutes. If using mixer, foregoing is done on creaming speed and following is done on lowest possible speed. Add vanilla and beat only until blended with dough. Add flour and baking powder and mix only until all ingredients are blended. With lightly floured hands, roll 1¼-inch balls—may be slightly smaller or larger as you desire. Place balls 1½ to 2 inches apart on ungreased cooky trays. Dip tines of fork in sifted flour and flatten each ball by pressing tines across it (each of flattened cookies will be ridged). If desired, make ridges with the floured tines to crisscross those already on cookies. Combine ⅓ cup sugar and cinnamon. Sprinkle each cooky with sugar and cinnamon mixture. Place one tray on center oven rack and second tray on rack placed approximately 2 inches above center. Bake until cookies are a light golden brown . . . 11 to 13 minutes. Remove from oven and loosen cookies by running knife or spatula under them. *Yield: Approximately 60 1¼-inch cookies.*

17

The Frosting on the Cake

Quite often the words "the frosting on the cake" are employed to describe something which you can live without, but which, if you have it, does make life a lot nicer and more interesting. It is definitely a luxury. And certainly all of this is true of an icing: you don't have to have it, but if you do, it makes the cake much more handsome; it helps to keep the cake fresh a little longer and it does lend flavor that can be delicious and in some cases even exotic.

There are many different types of icing. This book will deal with only two, since they are the easiest to make, as well as the easiest to spread on a cake, and they come in just about every delightful flavor you can imagine.

Introduced in this book is a completely new fluffy icing—the *Fruit-flavored Double Boiler Mallow Frosting**. It's made with fruit-flavored gelatin dessert powders, either Jell-O or Royal, in 18 different flavors (at the time this is written, but by tomorrow the manufacturers may have 2 or 3 new ones on the market). Furthermore, as the frosting is a cross between a double boiler frosting and a marshmallow pudding, it is light enough to use with *Angel Food** or any other sponge without weighing down on the cell walls, but it is much firmer than the usual double boiler frosting so it doesn't melt as easily.

DOUBLE BOILER MALLOW FROSTING

This is a variation of the 7-minute frosting—a misnomer when a food mixer is used, since the frosting is then made in about 5 minutes.

FRUIT-FLAVORED DOUBLE BOILER MALLOW FROSTING

RASPBERRY — BLACK RASPBERRY — STRAWBERRY
STRAWBERRY-BANANA — ORANGE — ORANGE-PINEAPPLE
PINEAPPLE — LEMON — LIME — GRAPE
CHERRY — BLACK CHERRY — BLACKBERRY
SPICED PEAR — PEACH — PINK GRAPEFRUIT
MIXED FRUIT — TROPICAL FRUIT

2 whites of large eggs
1½ cups white granulated sugar
¼ teaspoon cream of tartar
⅛ teaspoon salt
⅓ cup tap water
3 tablespoons of any of the Royal or Jell-O fruit-flavored gelatin
    dessert powders[1] (flavors available at this time listed above)
⅔ cup confectioners' sugar, measured then sifted

Bring water in bottom of double boiler to a rapid boil. Combine egg whites, granulated sugar, cream of tartar, salt, water, and gelatin dessert powder in the top of the double boiler. Stir until well blended. Place top of double boiler over boiling water and beat frosting with a rotary egg beater for approximately 7 minutes or on creaming speed of mixer for 5 to 5½ minutes—until frosting will peak. (It is suggested that hands be protected with padded gloves). Do not overcook icing, but remove from over hot water as soon as it will peak. Add confectioners' sugar gradually on low speed of mixer or stir in with spoon. Then, using rotary egg beater or creaming speed of mixer, beat 45 seconds. Let stand about 4 minutes and spread on cool cake. Let cake stand for

[1] Waste not, want not: Either wrap remaining gelatin powder in aluminum foil or plastic wrap if another frosting is to be made soon or make salad or dessert by first adding 1 cup boiling water and stirring until powder is dissolved. Add ¼ cup cold water and, when blended, store in refrigerator until firm. Fresh or canned fruit, excepting fresh pineapple, may be added to gelatin when it thickens.

at least 1 hour after it is frosted—longer, if possible—before cutting.

Yield: Enough frosting for 10-inch cake baked in tube pan; frosting and filling for cake made up of 2 9-inch layers; frosting for tops and sides of 2 9×5×3-inch pound cakes[2] or one 13×9× 2-inch oblong cake; frosting and filling for 1 9×5×3-inch pound cake cut lengthwise into 4 or 5 layers (filling is, of course, spread just a little thinner for 5-layer cake).

VARIATIONS

Vanilla Double Boiler Mallow Frosting—Substitute 1 package Knox unflavored gelatine for the 3 tablespoons fruit-flavored gelatin dessert powder and just before stirring in confectioners' sugar, add 1 teaspoon vanilla.

Vanilla Double Boiler Mallow Frosting with Lady Baltimore Filling—Prepare *Vanilla Double Boiler Mallow Frosting**. Place approximately ⅓ of frosting in bowl and add 3 tablespoons chopped candied cherries, ¼ cup chopped dried figs, 3 tablespoons chopped raisins, ¼ cup chopped pecans or toasted slivered almonds, and 1 teaspoon grated lemon or orange rind. Spread fruit and nut (and frosting) filling on top of one 9-inch layer of cake,[3] top with second layer, and cover top of cake and sides with remaining frosting.

Butterscotch Double Boiler Mallow Frosting—Substitute 1½ cups firmly packed brown sugar for the white granulated sugar and 1 package Knox unflavored gelatine for the 3 tablespoons fruit-flavored gelatin dessert powder. Just before stirring in confectioners' sugar, add 1 teaspoon vanilla.

Chocolate Double Boiler Mallow Frosting—Substitute 1 package Knox unflavored gelatine for the 3 tablespoons fruit-flavored gelatin dessert powder and substitute ½ cup confectioners' sugar

[2] See *1–2–3–4 Pound Cakes**.
[3] See *1–2–3–4 Cakes**.

and ⅓ cup cocoa, both first measured and then sifted, for the ⅔ cup powdered sugar. Before adding sugar and cocoa mixture, add 1 teaspoon vanilla. Let frosting stand 6 to 7 minutes before putting on cake, stirring after it has stood about 4 minutes.

Mocha Double Boiler Mallow Frosting—Substitute 1 package Knox unflavored gelatine for the 3 tablespoons fruit-flavored gelatin dessert powder, ½ cup confectioners' sugar and ⅓ cup cocoa, both first measured and then sifted, for the ⅔ cup powdered sugar, and ⅓ cup strong black coffee for water. Just before stirring in confectioners' sugar, add 1 teaspoon vanilla. Let frosting stand 6 to 7 minutes before putting on cake, stirring after it has stood about 4 minutes.

Double Boiler Mallow Frosting with Fruit and/or Nut Filling— Prepare any desired *Double Boiler Mallow Frosting**; place approximately ⅓ of frosting in a bowl and stir in any one or any desired combination of the following: chopped nuts (if almonds are used, they should be toasted); chopped pitted dates; grated canned coconut; chopped candied cherries, and/or pineapple. Spread mixture on one 9-inch layer of cake[3], and cover with second layer. Use remainder of frosting to cover top and sides of cake.

BUTTER CREAM FROSTING

This is probably the most popular of all icings, both for bakery and homemade cakes, and in this case, the popularity is indeed deserved. The *Butter Cream Frosting** is easy to prepare, particularly when it's made with an electric mixer; it remains in excellent condition for a long time and for taste, it's tops.

VANILLA BUTTER CREAM FROSTING

½ cup butter, margarine, or vegetable shortening
5½ cups (approximate) sifted confectioners' sugar
⅓ cup (approximate) undiluted evaporated milk or
  breakfast cream or ¼ cup (approximate) fresh milk,
  if evaporated milk or cream is not available
1½ teaspoons vanilla

Let butter or margarine stand until room temperature (this is not necessary for the vegetable shortening, if it is used). Cream butter with wooden spoon or on creaming speed of food mixer until the consistency of mayonnaise. Beat in 2 cups of sugar. Add milk or cream and vanilla. Beat until smooth. Add remaining 3½ cups of sugar and beat until all ingredients are completely blended. If frosting is not stiff enough, beat in additional sifted confectioners' sugar very gradually and if frosting is too stiff, add, also gradually, additional liquid to make a frosting that can be easily spread.

Yield: Frosting for 2 9-inch cake layers; 1 cake baked in 10-inch tube pan; 25 to 30 small cupcakes (tops); 2 9×5×3-inch loaf cakes; 1 9×5×3-inch loaf cake cut in 4 or 5 layers (filling is, of course, spread just a little thinner for 5-layer cake); 1 9×13× 2-inch oblong cake.

VARIATIONS

Caramel Butter Cream Frosting—For the ⅓ cup evaporated milk or cream, substitute the following caramel mixture: 16 small (¼ pound) caramels; ¼ cup (approximate) undiluted evaporated milk.

Melt caramels over boiling water and when completely melted, stir in ¼ cup evaporated milk. Continue stirring until completely smooth and blended. If needed to make ⅓ cup of mixture, beat in additional evaporated milk. After all of sugar has been added to frosting, beat in 1 tablespoon evaporated milk, and, if necessary, add additional evaporated milk, by teaspoonfuls, until frosting can be easily spread. Should too much milk or cream be added and frosting as a result is not stiff enough, add additional sifted powdered sugar.

Chocolate Butter Cream Frosting—Substitute for the 5½ cups confectioners' sugar, 4½ cups of sifted sugar and 1 cup of cocoa that has first been measured and then sifted.

Coffee Butter Cream Frosting—Mix 1 tablespoon instant coffee with the ⅓ cup of evaporated milk or cream.

Mocha Butter Cream Frosting—Mix 1 tablespoon instant coffee with the ⅓ cup of evaporated milk or cream and substitute 4½ cups of sifted confectioners' sugar and 1 cup of cocoa that has first been measured and then sifted for the 5½ cups of sifted confectioners' sugar.

Orange Juice Butter Cream Frosting; Lemon Juice Butter Cream Frosting; Pineapple Juice Butter Cream Frosting—Substitute ⅓ cup (approximate) orange juice, lemon juice, or pineapple juice for milk or cream. Add 2 teaspoons grated orange rind with orange juice or 2 teaspoons grated lemon rind with lemon juice. Omit vanilla.

Spirit Butter Cream Frosting—Substitute ⅓ cup (approximate) rum, brandy, cordial, or dessert wine for the ⅓ cup evaporated milk or cream. Omit vanilla.

Strawberry Butter Cream Frosting—Substitute ⅔ cup (approximate) strawberry preserves for the ⅓ cup evaporated milk or cream or for the ¼ cup fresh milk. Omit vanilla. If after all of sugar is added, frosting is too stiff, add additional preserves gradually until frosting can be easily spread.

18

A Few Miscellaneous Recipes
to Round Out
Your Education

There are a few recipes referred to in the foregoing pages that just don't fit into any of the categories covered in this book, but I thought you would need them to round out your education.

BAKED OYSTERS ON HALF SHELLS

Place rock salt to a depth of 1 inch in pie pans. Allow 6 oysters for each serving. Thoroughly clean oyster shells and embed 6 in the salt in each pan. Let oysters stand until room temperature. Drain thoroughly and lightly sprinkle with salt and white pepper. Brush inside of each shell with ½ teaspoon melted butter. Place 1 oyster in each of the shells. Either top oysters with *Sauce Bienville** or other desired sauce or sprinkle with lemon juice and minced chives and dot with butter. Bake in 400° F. oven until edges curl (6 or 7 minutes).

CHOCOLATE SOUFFLÉ

The only tricky thing about a soufflé, despite the many rumors to the contrary, is getting it to the table and serving it without delay, since a soufflé left standing falls quickly.

Thick White Sauce* made without salt or pepper and with
1 cup milk or ½ cup milk and ½ cup breakfast cream as
liquid
2½ ounces melted unsweetened baking chocolate
1 cup sugar
6 egg yolks
⅛ teaspoon salt
6 egg whites
¼ teaspoon cream of tartar

Using a double boiler, prepare *Thick White Sauce**. Remove from
heat and stir in melted chocolate and then sugar. Set aside until
lukewarm (about 10 minutes). Meanwhile, preheat oven for 10
minutes to 350° F. As soon as oven is turned on, place a large pan
with a 2-inch rim in it. Fill pan to depth of 1¼ inches with very
hot water (pull oven rack out 2 or 3 inches to do this). Beat yolks
until thick and lemon-colored—approximately 5 minutes. Add
small amount of lukewarm sauce to yolks and stir until blended.
Then stir yolk mixture into remainder of chocolate mixture. Add
salt to egg whites; beat until foamy. Add cream of tartar and beat
until stiff. Put kitchen tablespoon of whites on top of yolk-choco-
late mixture and fold whites into mixture. Gradually add the
chocolate sauce, a couple of tablespoons at a time, to the whites,
folding the sauce into the whites after each addition. Spoon into a
2½-quart oval baking dish, which has been well greased with butter. Place dish in center of pan of water in oven and bake until
soufflé sets—approximately 48 to 58 minutes. And don't forget to
serve immediately! *Serves 6.*

CORNBREAD

1 cup all purpose sifted flour
1 cup yellow cornmeal
⅜ teaspoon salt
2 tablespoons sugar
3½ teaspoons baking powder
⅞ cup milk
1 large egg
¼ cup soft butter or margarine

Preheat oven for 10 minutes to 425° F.

Sift flour, meal, salt, sugar, and baking powder together. Add milk, egg, and butter or margarine. Beat with rotary egg beater or on ½ maximum food mixer speed for 1 minute (just until batter is smooth). Grease bottom and sides of 8×8×2-inch pan with vegetable shortening. Place in hot oven for a few minutes and when pan is hot, pour off excess melted grease. Spoon batter into pan and level top with back of spoon. Bake 20 to 25 minutes until cornbread starts to come away from sides of pan. If bread is not golden brown on top, place 4 inches under broiler unit. Watch closely as top should brown beautifully in 2 or 3 minutes. *Serves 8. Yield: Approximately 4 cups crumbs for stuffing.*

TO GLAZE ROAST CURED OR SMOKED PORK

Remove pork from oven at time specified for particular weight being cooked in the *CHECK THERMOMETER AFTER MEAT HAS COOKED* column of *The Internal Temperature and Time Chart for Roasting Various Cuts of Meat**. Remove rack and meat from pan. Pour drippings out of pan or use basting syringe to siphon them out. Remove thermometer from meat if one has been used. Cut rind from meat and then cut the exposed fat into diamonds or squares. If desired, insert stem of clove into center of each diamond or square. Place meat in roaster without rack or thermometer and cover with either of following glazes:

BROWN SUGAR GLAZE FOR ROAST HAM

Combine 1½ cups brown sugar, 1½ teaspoons dry mustard, and ¼ cup molasses, honey, vinegar, or Concord grape or port wine. Spread mixture over meat and place roaster in 325° F. oven. Cook 30 minutes, basting 2 or 3 times with apricot nectar, pineapple juice, orange juice or Concord grape or port wine. Use several kitchen tablespoons of the fruit juice or wine each time ham is basted, and also spoon some of the sugar mixture from roasting pan over meat.

MARMALADE GLAZE FOR ROAST HAM

Combine 1 cup orange marmalade with ⅞ cup dark corn syrup or ¾ cup dark corn syrup and 2 tablespoons rum or brandy. Spread mixture over meat and then place in 325° F. oven. Cook 30 minutes.

GRAHAM CRACKER CRUMB SHELL
VANILLA WAFER CRUMB SHELL

1½ cups graham cracker or vanilla wafer crumbs
½ cup melted butter or margarine
¼ cup granulated white sugar
For Graham Cracker Crumb Shell only:
   ½ teaspoon cinnamon and/or
   ½ teaspoon nutmeg

Combine ingredients. Set aside ¼ cup mixture to make *GRAHAM CRACKER CRUMB TOPPING* or *VANILLA WAFER CRUMB TOPPING*. Grease bottom and sides of 9-inch pie pan liberally with butter or margarine. Pat remaining crumb mixture onto bottom and sides of pan to make shell. Bake 10 minutes in 325° F. oven. Cool before using. *Yield: 1 9-inch pie shell and topping for 1 9-inch pie.*

HASH

DRY HASH

4½ pounds (approximate) beef shank, chuck, or brisket,
    which was used to prepare *Beef Broth**
    OR
Meat from 5- to 6-pound hen or veal or calf knuckle,
    which was used to prepare *Chicken or Veal Broth**
¾ cup cooked mashed white potatoes
2 tablespoons minced celery
2 teaspoons minced parsley
2 tablespoons minced onion
1 tablespoon Worcestershire sauce
1 well-beaten egg
Salt and pepper to taste

Remove bone and gristle from meat or chicken and remove skin
from chicken. Grind. Combine with remaining ingredients.
Spoon into greased baking dish and bake 20 minutes at 350° F.
Serves 8 to 10.

WET HASH

4½ pounds (approximate) beef shank, chuck or brisket,
    which was used to prepare *Beef Broth**
    OR
Meat from 5- to 6-pound hen or veal or calf knuckle,
    which was used to prepare *Chicken or Veal Broth**
*Onion Brown Sauce**
1 large peeled white potato, cut in very small chunks

Cut meat or chicken in pieces, removing bone and gristle and the
skin from chicken. Combine with sauce in which the potato has
been previously simmered until chunks were easily pierced with
a fork. Cook over low heat until meat is piping hot. *Serves 8.*

PLUMPED RAISINS AND/OR CURRANTS

Barely cover dried fruit with water or with equal parts water and sauterne. Bring to a boil. Reduce heat and allow fruit to simmer over very low heat just until raisins and/or currants plump.

19

Gilding the Lily

I trust that by the time you reach this point you will be one of the world's great cooks. Would you believe one of the great cooks on your block?

It won't matter one whit, however, how good you are if you don't know how or don't take the time to make the food you prepare look good. There can be no doubt that Cinderella was beautiful under the cinders and rags, but who knew it? It was quite a different story when, with the touch of a wand, the cinders disappeared and the rags turned into a magnificent ball gown.

The nice thing about garnishing food is that, except in those rare cases when you want to do something very special for an occasion, so much can be done with so little. If your education on this point has been neglected, make the acid test: let 2 whole, small, peeled potatoes simmer, and when they are done, drain; place each on a small plate; sprinkle one lightly with green dehydrated parsley flakes or fresh minced parsley leaves and then with paprika. Compare the garnished potato with the plain spud —an ugly sounding word whose use is most suitable for an unattractive dish.

Here then are suggestions for gilding the lily—both for everyday use and for special occasions.

GENERAL RULES FOR GARNISHING
FOOD AND DRINK

BEVERAGES

1. Use slices of orange and/or lemon with rind.
2. Use whole berries.
3. Use thin strips of citrus fruit peel.
4. Use maraschino or candied cherries.
5. Use sprigs of mint.
6. Use small scoops of sherbet, fruit ice, or ice cream.
7. Serve in *Sugared Glasses**.
8. Use ice cubes or large blocks of ice with candied or maraschino cherries, other candied or fresh fruit, and/or mint sprigs frozen into the ice.

APPETIZERS, HORS D'OEUVRES, SALADS

Fruit cups:

1. Top with whole berries or maraschino or candied cherries.
2. Decorate with sprigs or minced mint.
3. Top with small scoops sherbet or fruit ice, just before serving.

Vegetable juice or seafood cocktails:

1. Place cocktail containers in bowls—glass preferred—of shaved or finely crushed ice.
2. Use thin slice of lemon or lime, cut halfway through, so that it can be slipped on edge of glass and/or a sprig of mint. The stem of the mint may be slipped through the cut in the fruit slice before the slice is put on the rim of the glass.
3. Place any of *Vegetable Roses**, *Celery Garnishes**, and/or *Carrot Sticks** on plate holding cocktail glass.

Hors d'oeuvres and salads:

1. Use vegetables or other ingredients of contrasting colors and blending flavors.
2. Use lettuce, romaine, watercress, endive, parsley (sprigs or minced), and chopped chives. If desired, dust edges of leaves with paprika.
3. Sprinkle with paprika (color and flavor permitting).
4. Use plum or cherry tomatoes. If desired, stuff halved tomatoes with finely minced seafood, poultry, egg, or meat salad.
5. Press cream cheese (tinted with vegetable coloring and combined with just enough cream, sherry, or brandy to make a mixture that will pass through the decorating tube without trouble and yet is firm enough to hold its shape) through the tube around edges of canapés and halved hard-cooked eggs, to make borders.
6. Decorate aspics and molded salads with mayonnaise, either in its natural color or tinted a pale green with a few drops of vegetable color, by forcing salad dressing through a decorating tube. A leaf and stem design is particularly effective.
7. Decorate with caviar (black) or salmon roe (red).
8. Decorate fruit or cheese salads with dates, prunes, and figs, stuffed with seasoned cream cheese or nuts.
9. Use cream cheese balls, rolled, if desired, in chopped chives, parsley, or nuts.
10. Use thin strips pimiento, thin slices of pickle, stuffed olive slices, riced yolks and/or minced whites or slices, quarters or halves of hard-cooked eggs, whole small sweet pickles, anchovies.
11. Use Maraschino or candied cherries for fruit salads.
12. Use Maraschino or candied cherries, fresh or canned fruit and/or berries for cottage cheese salads.
13. For center of hors d'oeuvres platter, use *Flaming Apple**, *Flaming Grapefruit**, *Flaming Orange**, or *Grapefruit Porcupine**.
14. Use any of *Cucumber Garnishes**.
15. Use any of *Vegetable Roses**.

16. Use any of *Carrot Garnishes**.
17. Use any of *Celery Garnishes**.
18. Use *Cabbage Bowl** for salads, dips, or salad sauces.
19. Use *Simulated Mistletoe**, or *Simulated Strawberries**.
20. Use any of *Cheese Garnishes**.
21. Use *Salad Cake**.
22. Use *Salad Fish**.

SOUP

1. Serve with thin slices or quarters of lemon.
2. Just before serving cream soup, top each serving with a tablespoon of commercial sour cream or salted whipped cream.
3. Just before serving, sprinkle top with minced parsley, chives, or watercress.
4. Crumble crisp, fried bacon on top of cream soup.
5. Float slices of hard-cooked egg on turtle soup.

SLICED MEAT OR POULTRY

1. Arrange cold sliced meat or poultry around mound of potato, seafood, poultry, or meat salad. Decorate salad and sliced meat or poultry with paprika, olives, sliced, quartered, or halved hard-cooked eggs, parsley or watercress sprigs, sliced, quartered, or halved tomatoes, whole small pickles or sliced large ones, and/or lettuce, romaine, or endive.
2. Arrange cold sliced meat or poultry around *Cabbage Bowl** containing potato salad, and garnish meat with parsley sprigs or watercress.
3. Decorate with tomatoes, sliced or in wedges, or whole cherry tomatoes, watercress, sprigs of parsley, romaine, endive, lettuce, and/or whole unpeeled Italian pimientos, stuffed with slaw. Greens may be dusted with paprika.

4. Decorate with *Yellow Cheese Lilies**.
5. Decorate with any of *Cucumber Garnishes**.
6. Decorate with any of *Vegetable Roses**.
7. Decorate with *Carrot Curls** or *Carrot Daisies**.
8. Arrange meat around *Grapefruit Porcupine**.
9. Decorate with *Frosted Fruit**, or fresh, canned, cooked, brandied, or spiced fruit, or *Lemon Baskets** or *Orange Baskets**.
10. Use branches of kumquats or a combination of these branches and clusters of black, green, and/or purple grapes.
11. Use slices of unpeeled orange, topped with round slices of jelly of a contrasting color. The jelly slices should be slightly smaller in diameter than the orange slices.
12. Alternate rows of sliced meat or poultry with slices of avocado, which have been dipped in lemon juice. If desired, after meat and avocado slices are arranged, the avocado may be sprinkled with paprika.
13. Decorate platter with avocado halves or artichoke hearts stuffed with poultry, meat, or seafood salad.
14. Use *Simulated Mistletoe** or *Simulated Strawberries**.

BROILED OR FRIED FISH, MEAT, OR POULTRY

1. Use slices or wedges of lemon. If desired, sprinkle lemon with paprika and/or minced chives or parsley, or arrange sprigs of parsley or watercress around each lemon slice.
2. Use *Stuffed Baked Potato**, parsley potatoes, fried potatoes, or make a border of Duchess potatoes.
3. Use *Oven Broiled Tomatoes** or *Stuffed Tomatoes**.
4. Garnish *Oven Broiled Beefsteak** or *Oven Broiled Chicken** with *Oven Broiled Mushrooms**, cooked green beans, cooked carrots, and/or cooked green peas.
5. Use any of *Vegetable Roses**.
6. Use *Carrot Curls** or *Carrot Daisies**.

7. Use any of *Cucumber Garnishes**.
8. Use watercress sprigs, parsley sprigs, leaves of endive, romaine, or lettuce, lightly sprinkled, if desired, with paprika.
9. Decorate broiled meat or poultry with fresh, canned, cooked, brandied, or spiced fruit or *Frosted Fruit**.
10. Flambé hot *Oven Broiled Lamb Chops** or *Oven Broiled Veal Chops** by pouring heated rum, brandy, or gin over food on a hot platter and then igniting spirit (immediately).
11. Use *Simulated Mistletoe** or *Simulated Strawberries**.

WHOLE ROASTS OF MEAT AND POULTRY
(INCLUDING HAM)

1. Flambé by pouring heated rum, brandy, or gin over hot food, on a hot platter, and then igniting spirit (without delay).
2. Use *Stuffed Baked Potato**, parsley potatoes, or make border of *Creamed Potato**.
3. Use tomato, watercress, parsley, romaine, endive, lettuce, or whole unpeeled pimientos, stuffed with slaw. Greens may be dusted with paprika.
4. Decorate with fresh, canned, cooked, brandied, or spiced fruits or *Frosted Fruit**.
5. Top slices of orange with round slices of jelly of a contrasting, but blending, color. Jelly slices should be slightly smaller in diameter than orange slices.
6. Use *Orange Basket** or *Lemon Basket**. At least 2 of the *Orange Baskets** will be required for a large platter and at least 1 *Lemon Basket** should be provided for each person to be served.
7. Use kumquat sprays with plenty of leaves. If desired, small bunches of green, black, and/or purple grapes may be added.
8. Use *Oven Broiled Tomatoes**, *Stuffed Tomatoes**, or baked stuffed peppers.

9. Use any of *Vegetable Roses**, *Carrot Curls**, or *Carrot Daisies**.
10. Use *Simulated Mistletoe** or *Simulated Strawberries**.
11. Use *Brown Sugar Glaze for Roast Ham** or *Marmalade Glaze for Roast Ham**, and if desired, decorate with canned pineapple rings, apple rings, and/or cloves. Maraschino or candied cherries may be added, if you wish.

VEGETABLES

1. Flavor permitting, combine vegetables of contrasting colors.
2. Serve (separately) vegetables of contrasting colors in divided dish.
3. Decorate with whole or slivered toasted almonds or pecan pieces.
4. Flambé sweet potatoes.
5. Serve sweet potatoes or yellow squash pudding in orange cups, and if desired, top with marshmallows and brown in very hot oven.
6. Use sliced halves or quarters of hard-cooked eggs or the riced yolks or minced whites on spinach, broccoli, and asparagus.
7. Decorate with minced parsley or chives or sprigs of parsley, and if desired, sprinkle with paprika.

DESSERTS

Fruits

1. Top with spoonfuls of fruit gelatin.
2. Top with spoonfuls of whipped (sweetened, if desired) cream or commercial sour cream. If desired, sprinkle whipped cream with colored sugar crystals, chocolate trims, or *Shaved Chocolate**.
3. Garnish with sprigs of mint.

4. Garnish with whole berries.
5. Garnish with branches of kumquats.
6. Combine fruits of contrasting colors and blending flavors.
7. Flambé hot canned, brandied or spiced fruit with rum or brandy.

Puddings, custards, frozen desserts

1. Decorate with Maraschino or candied cherries or with glacéed fruits.
2. Use cubes or bits of bright-colored fruit, wine, or liqueur gelatin or jelly.
3. Use grapes, berries, or other fresh or canned fruit and/or kumquat sprays.
4. Dribble a sauce or 2 sauces of contrasting colors and blending flavors over top.
5. Dribble a sauce and a liqueur of contrasting colors and blending flavors, such as a chocolate sauce and green crème de menthe, over top.
6. Sprinkle with whole, chopped, or ground nuts. If almonds are used, they should be blanched and toasted.
7. Use whole or chopped marrons for topping.
8. Sprinkle with any of *Coconut Garnishes**.
9. Decorate with *Shaved Chocolate**.
10. Sprinkle with chocolate trims or with colored sugar crystals.
11. Flambé with rum, brandy, whisky, etc.
12. Decorate with whipped cream swirls, mounds, icing, or designs made by forcing the stiffly whipped cream through decorating tube. Cream may be sweetened if desired.

Cakes

1. Cover with frosting.
2. Place whole, halved, or quartered candied or drained Maraschino cherries on frosting.
3. Sprinkle frosting with whole, chopped, or ground nuts. If almonds are used, they should be blanched and toasted.

4. Sprinkle with colored sugar crystals or chocolate trims.
5. Decorate frosting with *Shaved Chocolate**.
6. Decorate fluffy frostings with *Allegretti Icing**.
7. Frost cake with white double boiler icing—*Vanilla Double Boiler Mallow Frosting** may be used—after setting aside ¼ cup of frosting. To the ¼ cup of frosting, add 2 to 3 drops of desired vegetable coloring. With point of small sharp knife, etch design with colored icing into the white frosting.
8. Decorate frosting with *Butter Cream Frosting** put through decorating tube. Icing used for decorating must be stiff enough to hold shape, but it should not be so stiff that it cannot be easily passed through the tube. If necessary, add a small amount of sifted confectioners' sugar to frosting to make it stiffer or if icing becomes too stiff, add a small amount of evaporated milk or cream. If desired, frosting may be tinted with vegetable coloring before it is placed in tube.
9. Use any of *Coconut Garnishes**.
10. Decorate sponge or spice cakes with *Sugar Topping for Cakes**.
11. Decorate with fresh flowers. This is particularly effective with cakes baked in tube pan.
12. Flambé fruit cake with whisky, brandy, rum, etc.
13. Decorate with sweetened whipped cream and with berries or sliced, fresh or canned fruit.

Pastry

1. Decorate pies with swirls or spoonfuls of stiffly whipped cream, sweetened, if desired.
2. Decorate pies with scoops of ice cream, and, if desired, with nuts.
3. Decorate fruit pies with slices of cheese, which may, if desired, be cut in fancy shapes.
4. Decorate *Pie Meringues** with *Shaved Chocolate**.
5. Before placing meringue-covered pie in oven, decorate meringue with grated coconut.

CABBAGE BOWL

Select large well-shaped red cabbage. This is one time when you should look for as many outer leaves as possible. Of course, they must be in good condition. Chill thoroughly. Wash and pat dry, being careful not to break off outer leaves. Place on round platter and then gently turn back the outer leaves. Slice off top of head so that it is flat and fill center of "bowl" with desired salad.

CARROT GARNISHES

Carrot curls

Using a vegetable parer, first pare and then cut a large, firm and well-shaped carrot into long thin strips. Roll each strip around tip of little finger and secure roll by running a toothpick through it. Place rolls on bed of chopped ice and store in refrigerator for an hour or two. Before serving, remove toothpicks.

Carrot daisies

Pare thick carrots with vegetable parer. Cut crosswise with parer into paper thin slices. Place slices in ice water and store in refrigerator. When ready to use, pat slices dry and arrange slices on the food to be decorated so that they form daisy petals, using 5 petals for each flower. Make centers with finely minced green pickle relish.

Carrot sticks

Scrape well-shaped carrots and cut into "sticks" about 2 inches long×⅜ inch wide×⅜ inch thick. Place sticks in ice water and store in refrigerator for at least 1 hour.

CELERY GARNISHES

Celery curls

Scrape strings from stalks of celery, using vegetable parer or small sharp knife. Cut celery into pieces from 3 to 3½ inches long. It is not necessary to cut off leaves. Make 3 or 4 lengthwise slashes in each piece from one end to within ⅔ of an inch of opposite end. Cover celery with ice water and store in refrigerator. When ready to use, pat stalks as dry as possible and, if you wish, either sprinkle paprika over about ½ inch of slashed ends or dip them into paprika to a depth of ½ inch.

Celery sticks

Scrape celery stalks and cut into "sticks" about ⅜ inch wide ✕⅜ inch thick✕2 inches long. Place sticks in ice water and store in refrigerator for several hours.

CHEESE GARNISHES

Yellow cheese lilies

Use approximately 1 teaspoon processed Cheddar loaf cheese for each "lily." Flatten this small piece of cheese with fingers and then shape it so that it resembles a tiny "horn of plenty," by curving the lower halves of 2 adjoining sides so that they will meet, thus forming a horn—one of the sides should just slightly overlap the other. Place "lily" on whatever it is to garnish. Cut a thin strip of sweet or dill pickle so that it is just a fraction of an inch shorter than the "lily" to form the stamen and anthers and insert one end of this strip into the center of the horn. If desired, sprinkle lily with paprika and use sprigs of watercress, parsley, or mint for stem and leaves.

Cream cheese orange blossoms

From processed cream cheese, shape with fingers, 5 thumb-nail-size petals. Immediately arrange petals on food that is to be garnished so that they form an "orange blossom." Use very small ball of processed yellow cheese to make center.

CHOCOLATE GARNISHES

Allegretti icing

1 square (1 ounce) unsweetened baking chocolate; ½ teaspoon butter or margarine.

Melt chocolate over hot but not boiling water, combine butter or margarine with chocolate. Dribble mixture—using a small amount at a time—from a small spoon over top and sides of cake iced with fluffy frosting.[1]

Shaved chocolate

Hold square of baking chocolate with wrapping in palm of hand until chocolate is slightly softened from the heat of the hand. With vegetable parer or thin, sharp knife, shave side of square.

COCONUT GARNISHES

Colored coconut #1

    1 cup water
    1 teaspoon food coloring
    1½ cups (approximate) grated canned coconut

Pour cool tap water into large jar. Add food coloring—1 teaspoon makes a rich dark shade, so if lighter shades are desired, use less coloring. Mix coloring and water thoroughly. Spoon coconut into jar, cover, and shake. Let stand about 3 minutes, shaking jar

[1] See *Double Boiler Mallow Frosting**.

from time to time. Drain coconut and pat as dry as possible with paper towels. Cover cooky sheet with paper towels and spread coconut on towels to complete drying. If in a hurry, after patting coconut as dry as possible, spread on cooky sheet and place in 300° F. oven for 5 to 6 minutes.

Colored coconut #2

  1½ cups (approximate) canned grated coconut
  3 tablespoons of fruit-flavored gelatin dessert powder
     (Royal or Jell-O)

Place coconut in container with cover. Add gelatin powder and cover container. Shake well.

Toasted coconut

Spread coconut on cooky tray. Place tray in 350° F. oven. Toast, stirring from time to time, until rich brown (10 to 15 minutes).

CUCUMBER GARNISHES

Scalloped cucumber slices

Select long, well-shaped cucumbers and insert tines of fork to depth of approximately ⅛ inch in one end of unpeeled cucumber. Pull tines down length of vegetable so as to make small ridges. Move the fork so that it is directly adjacent to ridged surface and again pull tines inserted to a depth of ⅛ inch down the length of the vegetable. Repeat until entire cucumber is scored. Cut crosswise into slices of desired thickness.

Cucumber slices filled with cheese

Cut cucumbers crosswise in ¾-inch slices. Scoop out centers about ½ way through the slices and fill the cup thus formed with Roquefort, bleu, or processed cream cheese softened with cream, sherry, or brandy. Processed Cheddar cheese spread seasoned to taste with sherry or brandy may also be used as the filling.

Stuffed cucumber dill pickles

With a small sharp knife, cut a thin slice from one end of a large well-shaped dill pickle. Using the knife or an apple corer, cut out center of pickle, leaving shell about ¼- to ⅓-inch thick. Stuff hollow with deviled ham or chicken or processed cream or pimiento cream cheese. If desired, cheese may be flavored to taste with sherry or brandy. Wrap pickle in plastic wrap or aluminum foil and store in refrigerator 5 to 6 hours. Cut crosswise into slices of desired thickness.

FRUIT GARNISHES

Flaming Apple; Flaming Grapefruit; Flaming Orange

Cut slice from stem end of fruit. Scoop out center of apple, leaving a shell thick enough not to break, or scoop pulp from grapefruit or orange and then let citrus fruit shell drain for a short time. Carefully line apple, grapefruit, or orange shell with aluminum foil. Place fruit in center of serving platter and pour a small amount of Flambé Fanfare into it. Since this is a pure alcohol concentrate, it does not have to be heated. Place in center of hors d'oeuvres platter (particularly effective with cocktail sausages, as guests can heat sausage in flame). Ignite Flambé Fanfare and serve.

Frosted Fruit

Wash and pat fruit dry with absorbent paper towels. Let fruit stand until completely dry. Combine 1 egg white with 2 tablespoons sifted confectioners' sugar and stir until blended. Coat each piece of fruit (or bunch of grapes) with egg white mixture and then sprinkle heavily with granulated sugar. Let stand on wax paper in a cool spot until dry. If desired, after frosted fruit is arranged on platter, sprinkle with green or red sugar crystals.

Grapefruit Porcupine

Completely cover grapefruit with toothpicks or cocktail picks. Place picks about ⅓ inch apart. Arrange rows of pickled onions, green olives, ripe olives, pimiento-stuffed olives, anchovy-stuffed olives, and tiny cucumber pickles on picks. Onions, olives, and pickles should be placed so close together that the "porcupine" has the appearance of a multicolored chrysanthemum.

Lemon Basket; Orange Basket

Cut oranges or lemons in halves. Scoop out pulp and drain baskets. Fill with jelly or preserves. The color of the jelly should contrast pleasingly with the color of the fruit. If desired, flavor preserves or cranberry jelly, if it is used, with Cointreau, kirsch, cognac, or sherry to taste. A small amount of crème de menthe added to mint jelly makes a delicious filling for the baskets.

SALAD CAKE

Tightly pack potato, poultry, or seafood salad into 1 8×8×2-inch cake pan and into a cereal bowl, approximately 2 inches high, 2½ to 3 inches in diameter at the base and 5 inches in diameter at top of bowl. Chill from 4 to 6 hours. Run a small thin knife between salad and pan and turn out onto center of serving platter. Run knife between salad and bowl and turn small salad "cake" out onto middle of first tier. If desired, frost entire "cake" with mayonnaise, which may be tinted a pale green with a few drops of vegetable color. Decorate with any of *Vegetable Roses**, *Carrot Curls** or *Carrot Daisies**, and/or *Scalloped Cucumber Slices**. Arrange sprigs of parsley and/or celery, romaine or endive leaves around "cake." Greens may be dusted with paprika.

NOTE: When entertaining for brides, small light plastic figures of a bride and groom may sometimes be obtained from your nearest Woolworth's at very reasonable prices and these figures can be placed on the center of the top tier of the salad cake.

SALAD FISH

Put potato, poultry, or seafood salad on an oval platter and with the hands shape salad into a "fish." Make ridge of minced parsley or green pepper down back. Fashion gills from thin strips of pimiento; make mouth of pimiento and make eyes of thin slices of pimiento-stuffed olives. Sprinkle body of "fish" with minced parsley and/or chives and/or paprika. Surround with cole slaw and/or other vegetable salads.

SIMULATED MISTLETOE

Arrange sprigs of parsley or watercress on plates or platters and place 2 or 3 tiny pickled onions at each of the points where leaves and stems meet.

SIMULATED STRAWBERRIES

Arrange sprigs of parsley or watercress on plates or platters and place *very* tiny canned beets along the stems. Arrange the leaves so that the "berries" (beets) are partially hidden.

SUGARED GLASSES

Fill saucer with white granulated sugar to a depth of ½ inch for a small glass and ¾ to 1 inch for a large glass or goblet. Fill second saucer to same depth as first with ice water or iced lemon juice, if the latter will blend with the flavor of drink that is to be served. Dip rim of each glass in cold water or juice and then immediately dip rim into sugar, giving glass several turns while rim is in sugar. Very carefully pour drink into glass so that sugar rim will not be disturbed.

SUGAR TOPPING FOR CAKES

Cut brown paper to same size as top of spice or sponge cake and then cut out small circles, squares, or whatever design you wish, to make a "lace pattern." If you prefer, you may use a lacy paper doily. Place pattern or doily on cake. Sift confectioners' sugar and then again sift the sugar, this time through the cut-outs onto the top of the cake. Carefully lift pattern or doily from cake so that the sugar design is not disturbed.

VEGETABLE ROSES

Beet Roses

Using a vegetable parer, cut a long spiral from a whole cooked, blanched or canned beet. Roll thin strip to form the flower. Watercress or parsley may be used for leaves of the "rose."

Radish Roses

Select well-shaped rounded radishes. Cut off all but 1 or 2 leaves of each radish. With a small and very sharp knife cut a small slice from the root end. Make 5 petals, by cutting, surrounding the white center, from root end to within about ⅜ inch from the stem end, the red skin with enough of the white center attached to each of the 5 pieces so that the petals will be thick enough not to break at the slightest touch. If desired, cut through white center of "rose," being careful not to cut deeply enough to sever a section or break off a petal. Make second cut through center diagonally across first cut, again being careful not to cut too deep. Place in ice water and store in refrigerator for an hour or two.

Tomato Roses

Using a vegetable parer, cut peel from a tomato in a long spiral. Roll the thin strip so that it forms a "rose." Watercress or parsley may be used to form the leaves of the flower.

INDEX